Unfolding
the Moon

Unfolding the Moon

Enacting Women's *Kastom* in Vanuatu

LISSANT BOLTON

UNIVERSITY OF HAWAI'I PRESS
HONOLULU

© 2003 University of Hawai'i Press
Printed in the United States of America
08 07 06 05 04 03   6 5 4 3 2 1

Library of Congress Cataloging-in-Publication Data
Bolton, Lissant.
    Unfolding the moon : enacting women's kastom in Vanuatu /
Lissant Bolton
      p. cm.
Includes bibliographical references and index.
    ISBN 0-8248-2535-7 (hardcover : alk. paper)
1. Women—Vanuatu—Social conditions. 2. Textile fabrics—Vanuatu.
3. Women in development—Vanuatu. 4. Vanuatu—Social conditions.
I. Title
    HQ1867.5.B65 2003
    305.42'099595—dc21

                        2002009059

University of Hawai'i Press books are printed
on acid-free paper and meet the guidelines for
permanence and durability of the Council
on Library Resources.

Designed by Josie Herr

Printed by The Maple-Vail Book Manufacturing Group

for
Rosemary Dobson Bolton
and
Alec Bolton

with gratitude

Contents

Acknowledgments IX

Introduction XIII

1 🔁 History/*Kastom* 1

2 🔁 *Kastom* in the National Arena 26

3 🔁 Women without *Kastom* 51

4 🔁 *Ples* 67

5 🔁 Ambae: On Being a Person of the Place 78

6 🔁 Plaiting: "The Reason That Women Came into
the World" 106

7 🔁 Dyeing: Designs, Power, Status 130

8 🔁 Making Textiles into *Kastom* 152

🔁 Conclusion: Women with *Kastom* 183

Epilogue 193

Notes 197

Glossary 205

Bibliography 209

Index 223

Acknowledgments

This book has been written over a long period, and it owes a great deal to many people and institutions.

My initial fieldwork in 1991–1992 was funded by the Wenner-Gren Foundation for Anthropological Research and the Emslie Horniman Scholarship Fund administered by the Royal Anthropological Institute of Great Britain and Ireland. Subsequent research has been funded, variously, by the Australian Museum, the Australian Research Council, and the Australian National University. I have also been supported in implementing programs at the Vanuatu Cultural Centre by the Australian National Commission for UNESCO, the Australian Government's South Pacific Fund, and AusAID (1992–2001). Manchester University provided a stimulating context in which I first attempted to write about this material, but this book was largely written in the generous environment of the Centre for Cross-Cultural Research (CCR) at the Australian National University. The final revisions were completed while working for the British Museum. I am grateful to all these organizations and their staff, most especially to the CCR: many thanks to Jenny Newell for invaluable editorial assistance. The form and style of the Women's Culture Project was influenced by the approach to cross-cultural collaboration developed in the Division of Anthropology at the Australian Museum: I thank Jim Specht in particular for the standards he set and the opportunities he provided.

My debts within Vanuatu are literally innumerable. Many, many people have helped me there—with information, advice, rebukes, and insights and with practical assistance of many different kinds. Several of these people appear regularly in this book, and their contribution can be judged from the text, but I would like to thank here especially James Gwero, Grace Molisa, Chief Willie Bongmatur Maldo, Jack Ketadi,

Leah Ture Leo, Selwyn Aru, Sam Chanel, and David Boe. Other people have provided support and insight over the decade since the project this book describes. I would like to thank the Ambae women fieldworkers, especially Roselyn Garae and Jennifer Mwera, for improving my understanding of matters Ambaean, and the staff of the Vanuatu Cultural Centre and all the fieldworkers for continuing my education about *kastom*. I thank Ralph Regenvanu, VCC director since 1995, for consistent assistance and in particular for his example of respect and commitment to cultural issues in Vanuatu. I thank both Annie Walter and Reece Discombe for their generous hospitality and for practical and intellectual help with my research, and Sue Antoniou and David Luders for many conversations.

Kirk Huffman "opened the road" for me to go to Vanuatu and has sponsored and supported my involvement there ever since. His interest in and contribution to this project have been great, and I owe him an especial debt for his help in enlarging my understanding of *kastom*. Darrell Tryon has consistently supported both my research and the development of the women fieldworkers group, which was founded in 1994. I am grateful for many valuable conversations and for his sustained encouragement and practical assistance over many years. Jacob Sam Kapere was a sterling colleague and friend during the Ambae project and has continued to advise, encourage, and assist both me and the Women's Culture Project ever since.

This book has been discussed with and read (mostly in sections) by many people. I thank in particular Jean Mitchell, James Leach, Margaret Rodman, Annie Walter, Jimmy Weiner, Tim Curtis, Ian Coates, Bill Rodman, Michael O'Hanlon, Penny Harvey, and Nicholas Thomas. Catriona Hyslop very helpfully advised on and corrected all my North-East Ambaean language terms. Klaus Neumann provided valuably trenchant editorial and intellectual criticism. Marilyn Strathern supervised my Ph.D. and has continued to stretch my anthropological understanding ever since: by giving me confidence in my ideas she has enabled me to go far further in my thinking than I could ever have gone alone.

My debt to Jean Tarisesei is enormous. She supported the Ambae project before she joined it as trainee coordinator, Women's Culture Project, and in joining the project she gave it her wholehearted support. In years of conversation and friendship she has given me much information about Ambae, many ethnographic insights, and a great deal of extremely sensible advice, about life as well as work. In 1995, the women of Lovonda said that we should reassign my Ambaean adoption—that the reality of Jean's and my association as colleagues and friends should be made straight as a family one. We became sisters, and through that I have learned how classificatory kinship can, over time, become real.

I have applied that lesson about kinship elsewhere in my life. At a personal level I would like to thank my other "classificatory-but-real" kin, Carol and Andrew Mason, for support at many levels and for their practical concern for the Vanuatu Cultural Centre. My greatest thanks go to Rosemary and Alec Bolton, to whom this book is dedicated, for their faith in me and their enduring interest in this project.

* * *

All field photographs were taken by me, unless otherwise indicated.

Introduction

When women exchange textiles on the island of Ambae in north Vanuatu, they move onto the exchange plaza carrying the textiles in great
baskets on their heads. When they reach its center they drop the baskets
and take out the textiles, unfolding them and laying them out in piles
upon the ground. There is a proper and important order to this. The
women first remove and lay out the most valuable textiles, the *maraha,*
according to their kinds, and then on top of them less valuable textiles,
the *qana,* according to their kinds. There is a specified sequence in
which each kind of *maraha,* and each kind of *qana* is laid out so that
either the *qana* called *qana vivi* or the clothing textile *sakole* graces the
top of each pile. In east Ambae the most common design decorating
both of these textile types is *vule* (the moon). The presentation represents a moment at which the women's immense labor in making the
textiles, and their commitment to the social relationships in which they
are enmeshed, takes visible form. In unfolding and presenting these
textiles, the women are not only making a gift in exchange, but demonstrating their knowledge, skill, and labor.

In Vanuatu, in 1992, a program initiated by an organization called
the Vanuatu Cultural Centre (VCC) made an alteration to national
ideology. It extended the practical application of the term *"kastom"* to
include women's knowledge and practice, making the claim that
"women have *kastom* too." *Kastom* is the word that people in Vanuatu
use to characterize their own knowledge and practice in distinction to
everything they identify as having come from outside their place. Until
the early 1990s, *kastom* in Vanuatu had, for all practical purposes, been
treated as referring only to things that men do and know, to men's
dances, stories, rituals, and preoccupations. The cultural centre's
women's *kastom* program focused on Ambae, and specifically on

Ambaean women's skills and understanding related to plaited pandanus textiles; but, in asserting the idea of women's *kastom,* the program had a national effect. This book is about the idea of *kastom* in Vanuatu —about how and why the idea of *kastom* initially excluded women— and about women's production and use of textiles on Ambae and how Ambaeans responded to the suggestion that these things now be recognized as *kastom.* The acknowledgment that "women have *kastom* too" represented a new and significant alteration in the status of women in the national context.

The introduction of the idea that women have *kastom* too was driven by the VCC in collaboration with a number of other organizations in Vanuatu: the Ambae/Maewo Local Government Council, the Vanuatu National Council of Women, the Australian High Commission in Port Vila, and Radio Vanuatu. In 1991, the VCC initiated a program called the Women's Culture Project (WCP), recruiting an Australian volunteer to train a woman to be WCP coordinator. I was this training officer. Thus although much of this book describes the situa-

Fig. 1 Women laying out textiles in an exchange at Boeboe hamlet, Lovonda, east Ambae. The textiles are being presented by a man's kinswomen to his bride's family at marriage. May 22, 1992.

tion that led to the Women's Culture Project, and that the WCP then altered, in describing that alteration itself, I am describing something in which I took an active part.

Anthropology generally involves what is known as participant observation. The anthropologist participates in, observes, and subsequently describes the life of a community or group, but avoids making any changes to it. I, on the other hand, participated in community life in Vanuatu generally, and especially in Ambae, with the express objective of making changes. By agreement with the VCC board, I documented my participation as my doctoral fieldwork, which I subsequently described in a thesis (Bolton 1993). My role might thus be better described as participant engagement. In working for the VCC and collaborating with the other organizations involved I sought to enact their objectives and to reflect their preoccupations, but nevertheless, it was I who developed the Women's Culture Project, trained its coordinator, and implemented its first program, which was the Ambae Project.

The difficulty that participant engagement poses to the writing of ethnography is the difficulty of acknowledging the effect of one's own involvement in the events described and yet of not overrating it. In the end, one individual can have little influence on a community unless his or her actions are endorsed and supported by community members. As WCP training officer I built upon the work of or collaborated with a number of people in the Vanuatu Cultural Centre and the other organizations involved. Each of these people also influenced the formulation of *kastom* in Vanuatu or specifically contributed to its extension to include women's knowledge and practice. My contribution was to various degrees dependent on what these other people had done or were doing, and in following on from and imitating them I was operating in an established mode within the cultural sector in Vanuatu. My engagement in this project was also an engagement in Vanuatu at that particular period. The various collaborations that led to the Women's Culture Project were very much a product of their time. To describe them is to describe a specific moment in Vanuatu history: the beginning of the 1990s, a decade after the country achieved independence, when the population was still only about 150,000, and when the achievement of independence, and the ideals that went along with that, were still very much in people's minds. Things change very fast in Vanuatu; an ethnography of the early 1990s is already history.

This book is thus an ethnographic description of a historical process that culminated in events in which I myself took an active part. I
describe it as an "ethnographic description" intentionally. This is
description in the sense used by Marilyn Strathern: "description presupposes analysis, and analysis presupposes theory, and they all pre-
suppose imagination" (1999:xi). Description is the end point, not the
beginning, of anthropological analysis: all description is, in one way or
another, theoretically informed. This book does not concentrate on
my role, but rather describes the contexts against which the Women's
Culture Project developed—on local understandings of *kastom* and
women's knowledge and practice with respect to textiles on Ambae—
and on the transformations that the WCP effected to both (in which I
was involved). The role of the VCC as a museum with links to the academic disciplines of anthropology, linguistics, and archaeology was
important to this historical process: the theoretical understandings that
people involved brought to the work of the Cultural Centre have been
significant to the constitution of *kastom*. Equally, my preoccupations,
derived from my own museum experience and my anthropological
understanding, influenced the form the WCP took. This introduction
provides some background to my participation and to this broader
museum/academic setting. It also introduces some of the people and
the institutions that were active in the initiative to assert that "women
have *kastom* too."

Beginnings

The Vanuatu Cultural Centre is an umbrella organization that in the
early 1990s incorporated a museum, library, and archives. Founded in
1956, it appointed its first salaried museum curator in 1976, and from
this time onward, the museum became the leading Cultural Centre
department. Housed in a purpose-built structure on the main street of
the small national capital, Port Vila, the VCC was a dominant public
institution both through the last years of the colonial era and during
the decades after independence.

The first curator was Kirk Huffman, an English anthropology student. Huffman, who took up his appointment in 1977, had been working in the archipelago since 1973, doing research on Malakula for postgraduate studies in ethnology at Cambridge University. The lineage of
his interest in the region went back to the anthropologist John Layard
(1942), whose work had drawn him to Malakula. Like Layard before

him, Huffman became deeply involved in the practice of the community in which he was based. Coming to the VCC from extended fieldwork in central Malakula, he brought this involvement, rather than a commitment to anthropology, to his curatorship. He also brought his very considerable linguistic skills and a phenomenal memory, enabling him to operate very much in an oral tradition. Having some resources of independent income, and significant skills in making and using networks with people all over the world, Huffman acted with a degree of autonomy in his work as curator, helping out both the museum and the fledgling nation in diverse ways. He became deeply involved in the independence movement during the 1970s and was, in his advocacy of the importance of *kastom*, influential at national and local levels through the country.

In 1976, just before joining the Cultural Centre, Huffman spent six months as acting Pacific curator at the Australian Museum, Sydney. A strong connection between the two institutions was forged during that period, and the Australian Museum has offered the Cultural Centre training and assistance of various kinds over the ensuing decades. Huffman himself was never preoccupied by the conventional work of a museum—by the care of objects—but focused his attention instead on the creation of a network of local men recruited to work as volunteers in their own islands and districts, documenting and reviving *kastom*. These men were and are known as fieldworkers. Huffman's enthusiasm and commitment to *kastom* was the driving force behind the establishment of the fieldworker program.

In 1985, five years after achieving independence, the Vanuatu government imposed a moratorium on all social sciences field research in Vanuatu. Although there were a few exceptions to this ruling, in general no expatriate field research was permitted for the following nine years. Instead, a distinctive kind of research developed locally through the Cultural Centre. Huffman recruited a New Zealander, Darrell Tryon, a linguist based at the Australian National University, to direct annual two-week training workshops for the fieldworkers, providing them with basic training in linguistic and anthropological recording techniques. The workshops provided opportunities for fieldworkers to discuss *kastom* in considerable comparative depth and to debate ways in which local knowledge and practice could be maintained and developed in a climate of ongoing social and economic change. Tryon, who had completed a survey of the 113 languages of Vanuatu during the 1960s

(1972, 1976), has returned to Vanuatu every year since 1981 to direct the training workshops and has himself substantially contributed to the fieldworkers' understanding of the nature of *kastom*. His consistent commitment to the fieldworker program has been of inestimable value to the formulation of *kastom* in Vanuatu as fieldworkers have transmitted workshop outcomes throughout the country. Under his and Huffman's care, the fieldworker group grew steadily during the 1980s; by 1991 there were about forty-five men fieldworkers (see Huffman 1996a; Tryon 1999).

Although Huffman added to the museum's object collections over the period of his curatorship, these remained uncatalogued and were rather haphazardly displayed and stored in the Cultural Centre building on the waterfront in Port Vila. When family circumstances forced his resignation in 1989, Huffman set in motion a project to catalogue the collections. He invited the Division of Anthropology at the Australian Museum to set up a collection cataloguing system and train Cultural Centre staff in its operation. As Pacific collection manager at the Australian Museum, I was among those who went to Vila to undertake this task. In 1990, after Huffman had resigned, Darrell Tryon arranged Australian funding for me to return and continue the cataloguing and training process.

MUSEUMS AND MATERIAL CULTURE

I had by this time been working with the Pacific collections at the Australian Museum for more than a decade. Working at the Australian Museum during the 1980s introduced me to three significant debates about museum collections of ethnographic objects: the question of the relationship between object and meaning; the idea of "art"; and, using what were then newly introduced terms, the relationship between indigenous people as traditional owners and their cultural property— the objects in museums. All these debates affected the way in which I subsequently set up the first WCP program, the Ambae project.

The Australian Museum Pacific collection contains one of the great collections of Melanesian material internationally, and I was always entranced by the objects I looked after. But to work with such material is to become conscious of the artifice of museum collections, of the way in which they have been constituted by considerations such as the portability and durability of individual objects. It is objects that could survive the rigors of international transportation that became part of museum ethnography collections. Objects whose size defied transportation, such as dancing grounds, and those whose fragility defeated it, such as leaf and flower decorations, were usually not included.

As has often been observed, in the very beginnings of the discipline of anthropology, objects were seen as a crucial source of information about other places. In 1895, W. H. Flower, president of the British Association for the Advancement of Science, observed, "One of the most potent means of registering facts, and making them available for future study and reference, is to be found in actual collections of tangible objects" (Flower 1895:764).[1] This importance of collections to early anthropological research has left a theoretical legacy, which is the idea of material culture—objects—as a distinct subject within the discipline. Museums have thus been instrumental in creating a category of theoretical analysis, material culture, on the basis of largely practical discriminations about what could and could not be collected and displayed. Anthropology collections (often described as "ethnographic collections") were generally built up during the last century of European colonialism: anthropology, and ethnographic collections, mostly relate to the indigenous inhabitants of European colonies and of settler/colonial states such as Australia.

The development of fieldwork methodologies for anthropological research at the beginning of the twentieth century demonstrated the limits to what could be learned from objects, as Malinowski observed in 1922:

> A canoe is an item of material culture, and as such it can be described, photographed and even bodily transported into a museum. But . . . the ethnographic reality of the canoe would not be brought much nearer to a student at home, even by placing a perfect specimen right before him. . . . For a craft . . . lives in the life of its sailors, and it is more to a sailor than a mere bit of shaped matter. To the native . . . a craft is surrounded by an atmosphere of romance, built up of tradition and of personal experience. It is an object of cult and admiration, a living thing, possessing its own individuality. (Malinowski 1922:105)

As fieldwork became increasingly important to the discipline, most anthropologists turned aside from an interest in objects. For most of the twentieth century, research focused, so to speak, not on the canoe, but on "the life of the sailors" of which the canoe was just a part. Anthropology and museology diverged (see Strathern 1990:38). While anthropologists focused on field research, museum curators, the canoe in their storerooms, remained attentive to objects and developed questions posed by their materiality, questions about technology, form, style, distribution, and provenance. These questions did lead to fieldwork, but fieldwork of a particularly focused kind. During the 1980s, for example, the Australian Museum implemented two field-documentation projects. Photographs of objects in the collections were taken back to their place of origin in search of further documentation about the manufacture, use, and significance of the objects. I was the junior partner to one of these projects, documenting collections from the Lower Sepik, Papua New Guinea (Barlow, Lipset, and Bolton 1988; Barlow 1990).

The experience of taking photographs of objects back to their places of origin was very instructive. In the storeroom, there is a sense in which all objects are equal. Some may be better documented and some may be aesthetically more striking or historically important, but all require the same care and the same documentary attention. All have the potential to be revealed as significant—by a research project of one kind or another. Returned to their place of origin as photographs, objects fall into a different set of relations with each other. Things that people still make (grass skirts, cooking pots) may not interest them, and things that people have forgotten their ancestors made may be regarded similarly as irrelevant. On the other hand, photographs of objects that embody ritual or social power—clan symbols or religious paraphernalia—may be of great interest and emotional significance to a community (see Barlow 1990:18).

Collection-based research is an honorable tradition, one that is now being given new impetus by the theoretically sophisticated initiatives of authors such as Nicholas Thomas (1999) and Michael O'Hanlon (1999), who both interpret objects found in museum collections in the light of historical and anthropological texts and images to offer new perspectives on their meaning and purpose. However, my experience of field documentation made Malinowski's comment about the canoe real to me, demonstrating the widely made observation that meanings are invested in objects by people, so that a different human context may allocate an object an entirely different meaning. I became interested in the possibility of field research that focused on objects in context—on the significance of the canoe to the life of the sailor.

Museums made another contribution to the constitution of the category material culture through the development of the art gallery as a specific museum type. Western society in the twentieth century has invested considerable value in the idea of art and in the art museums that display it and has established a system by which objects deemed suitable to be displayed in art galleries are granted an especially high status.[2] It is thus not just that material culture has been created as a category, but that this category exists within a system of relative value. Objects displayed in art galleries are counted as having a higher value (both financially and in terms of cultural capital) than objects in other kinds of museums. Generally it is objects from the Western art tradition that are displayed in art galleries, so that ethnographic collections labor under the linked disadvantage of being from outside the Western art tradition and being displayed in ethnographic museums. In response to this, curators have often sought to draw attention to the aesthetic power of objects from their artifact collections, asserting their suitability to be displayed as art (see Stocking 1985:6).

This move to define ethnographic objects as art was echoed in recent decades by a concomitant move, on the part of some indigenous artifact producers, to be represented in art galleries rather than in ethnographic museums. This has been the case for many Aboriginal Australian makers of objects, for example. The politics of this is easily understood: it is a claim to a high-status position in the dominant cultural milieu. Indeed, as Fred Myers pointed out, Aboriginal people produce some objects—such as acrylic paintings—specifically to sell them into the art world, both for the high prices they afford and as a way of "representing culture"—representing aspects of their knowledge and practice to the wider community (Myers 1995:56–57). Howard Morphy made this role further apparent in his discussion of Aboriginal art. He commented, "The recent history of Aboriginal art has been a dialogue with colonial history, in which what came before— . . . with its emphasis on affective social and spiritual relationships to the land—is continually asserting itself over what exists in the present" (Morphy 1998:4).

Questions about what is and is not art are constantly debated within the frame of the Western tradition. Because the category is essentially a category that assigns value, its flexibility is crucial to its operation, and its parameters are consequently hard to identify. One frequently proposed account of art has reflected this in proposing an institutional definition: art is what is displayed in art galleries and acknowledged as such by the art world (collectors, dealers, critics) (Danto 1964). Alfred Gell very neatly explained the currency of this perspective, observing that it "has arisen precisely to accommodate the historic fact that western artworks no longer have an aesthetic 'signature' and can consist of entirely arbitrary objects, like dead sharks in tanks of formaldehyde" (1999:210). The pertinence of these debates here lies in the fact that textiles have, in the Western system, generally not been defined as art but rather as craft. And although art galleries may be willing to display the works of artists such as Damien Hurst (who put the dead shark in the formaldehyde), they are still often resistant to the display of textiles, and especially of textiles such as the plaited pandanus textiles from Ambae. Despite the fact that most ethnographic objects circle uneasily in the system of relative value established between museums, some objects are even less successful there than others. Often damned with the classification "craft," textiles, and especially non-loom-woven textiles, are among the least well regarded.

There is nothing inherently wrong about the Western system of assigning value to objects as art: it is as much a local cultural practice as any other. However, with the partisanship that most collections staff develop for some apparently underrecognized part of their collection, I began to take exception to an art-based approach that focused on sculptural and painted materials and overlooked textiles and other kinds of objects made by or associated with women. At the end of the 1980s, as I began to plan my doctoral research, I was determined to work with a group of women and to focus on the significance to them of a group of objects they both made and used.

The 1980s was a decade of upheaval for anthropology museums in Australia. In 1978 UNESCO organized a regional seminar in Adelaide that brought together indigenous Australians and anthropology curators (Edwards and Stewart 1980). Indigenous delegates argued forcefully for the right of Aboriginal people to influence the curatorship of collections of Aboriginal material. They advocated the employment of Aboriginal staff to manage Aboriginal collections and greater indigenous involvement in the development of exhibition and education programs. They also raised concerns about the management of secret/sacred or restricted objects and the management and reburial of collections of Aboriginal human remains. This seminar was enormously influential, and over the following decades most Australian museums accepted and implemented most of the seminar recommendations. The Australian Museum Division of Anthropology, under the direction of Jim Specht, responded quickly to the seminar, employing Aboriginal staff and seeking the advice of Aboriginal communities about the management of collections. As Pacific curator, Specht had already initiated collaborative programs with museums in Melanesia and continued to do so during the same decade (Specht and MacLulich 1996).

To work at the Australian Museum in the 1980s was to be continually drawn into interaction with traditional owners of collections and to learn and come to terms with their specific and not necessarily curatorial priorities for their cultural property. It was an opportunity to learn how to work, as a colleague, with people whose priorities for that work were not the same and whose emotional investment in objects was often quite different from those of academically trained curators. As I have discussed elsewhere, there were significant differences between the response of indigenous Australians to collections and those of Melanesians, differences that relate in part to issues of colonial history and political autonomy (Bolton 2001b). I developed some sense of Pacific Islander perspectives through training Pacific museum staff over a number of years, both in programs offered at the Australian Museum and through the Australian National Council for UNESCO. By the time I first worked in the Vanuatu Cultural Centre, cataloguing the collections, I had learned to assume that my ideas about the importance of objects were quite unlikely to be shared by the people with whom I was working.

THE INCEPTION OF THE WOMEN'S CULTURE PROJECT

When I returned to Vanuatu in 1990 for the second cataloguing and training program, Kirk Huffman had left the Cultural Centre. The new curator was Huffman's former deputy, a ni-Vanuatu from the island of Aneityum called Jack Keitadi. (The indigenous citizens of Vanuatu are known as ni-Vanuatu, rather than as Vanuatuan, or any other such construction.) Keitadi had received some training in museum work and anthropology in both Papua New Guinea and Sydney, but Huffman was an extremely hard act for anyone to follow. The Cultural Centre museum had a slightly disconsolate air, and there was in fact not really anyone in the museum for me to train. Keitadi was assisted by Jacob Sam Kapere, a young ni-Vanuatu from the island of Tanna.[3] Kapere had trained as a filmmaker in Melbourne and had been brought into the Cultural Centre by Huffman in about 1988, to look after the substantial audiovisual archives. A skilled cameraman, Kapere was also deeply committed to the VCC project to document and revive *kastom* and was a strong supporter of the fieldworker group, providing assistance to them as he was able.

During my visit there was a staffing crisis. The first female professional staff member (as opposed to secretarial and cleaning staff), Nadia Kanegai, whose return from tertiary education in Australia to take up a position as education officer had been long awaited, started work but resigned two days later, citing the absence of an education program budget as a reason. Although Kanegai's position was as an education officer, the fact that a woman was to take it up had become increasingly significant as the Cultural Centre waited for Kanegai to return from her studies. As I will set out in more detail in chapter 3, the male bias at the Cultural Centre had been more and more criticized within Vanuatu, and the appointment of a woman had therefore become more and more important.

My experience in training Pacific-region museum staff had convinced me that in-country training is far more useful than anything that can be offered overseas. Overseas training, based on the expectation of significant funding and infrastructural support—such as Kanegai had received in Australia—does not equip staff to work in contexts where salaries are low, equipment inadequate, and operational budgets dependent on external aid. Moreover, overseas training in museum work is often based on nonindigenous priorities and sets professional standards devised in Western institutional and academic contexts. In 1990 I was planning a doctorate in anthropology, based on fieldwork in Melanesia on women's material culture. Until the turn of events in Vanuatu that year, I had anticipated doing research in Papua New Guinea, knowing that Vanuatu's research moratorium would prevent my working there. However, in discussing Kanegai's resignation, and the importance of in-country training with Cultural Centre staff and some members of the management board, I eventually suggested that I come to Vanuatu for a year, to work without salary as a training officer for Kanegai's replacement. In return, I asked to be granted an exemption from the research moratorium and allowed to undertake a project, with the appointee, about which I could subsequently write my doctoral thesis.

It is here that both Huffman's and Tryon's roles in the Cultural Centre become relevant. As expatriates deeply committed to ni-Vanuatu notions about *kastom,* they had established a precedent that made my proposed role as training officer both comprehensible and appealing to VCC board members. My status as an Australian Museum staff member—and the fact that I had been introduced to the country by Huffman and brought back by Tryon—enhanced my credentials, as did my familiarity with the Pacific region and the fact that by then I already spoke the lingua franca, Bislama. I proposed that I implement the training program through a research project, negotiating the details with management board members. I declared my interest in women's material culture; the board accepted this focus but themselves decided on the subject of the project. The choice of an area—the island of Ambae—and the specific focus of the project—textiles—were both decided by the Cultural Centre management board. In making their decision they were influenced both by Kirk Huffman, who retained a considerable influence (albeit from Spain, where by then he lived), and by a very influential board member, Grace Molisa, then personal private secretary to the prime minister. Molisa herself was from Ambae and wanted to see research undertaken into the importance of Ambae textiles in the regional trade that had once characterized the north of the archipelago. The starting salary for Kanegai's position had been provided by the Australian High Commission, which accepted with good grace a further delay to the appointment of a woman staff member, until such time as I was able to return to begin work as training officer.

When I returned to Vanuatu as training officer in August 1991, Jack Keitadi arranged the appointment of a trainee women's culture project coordinator. Kirk Huffman, who was visiting Vanuatu at the time, contributed to the selection process. They chose Leah Ture Leo, a young Ambaean who had previously worked as Cultural Centre secretary. Ture Leo had left Ambae about eight years previously, at the age of approximately fifteen. By 1991 she had married a man from the island of Pentecost who worked in the Vanuatu Mobile Force, and they had a small child. A capable secretary, charming and slightly frivolous, Ture Leo did not find the Ambae project congenial. She was nervous about sorcery in villages other than her own and was worried by and about her husband and son, left behind in Port Vila. Eventually, in January 1992, she resigned from the project.

In advocating Ambae as a focus for the first WCP project, the VCC board member, Grace Molisa, had originally recommended that a woman called Jean Tarisesei be appointed as trainee. When Ture Leo and I started visiting villages in east Ambae, looking for a place to base our project, we quickly met Tarisesei, who was the leader of the women in the coastal wards of the Ambaean district of Longana. When Ture Leo's discomfit in the Ambae project became evident, the Ambae/Maewo Local Government Council and villagers in Longana all urged me to replace her with Tarisesei. When Ture Leo resigned, I learned that Tarisesei was one of the privileged few who had attended the British Secondary School in Port Vila, as had Jack Keitadi. She was thus well known to him, and he was very happy to support her appointment as the new WCP trainee.

Fig. 2 Jean Tarisesei. 1998.

Jean Tarisesei was ideally suited for the position of Women's Culture Project coordinator, a position that, in 2001, she still holds. In 1991 she was a widow in her early forties with five children, the youngest of whom was then about six years old. She had married an east Ambaean, Lawrence Tarisesei, soon after completing her English O-level exams at the British Secondary School, at the age of about twenty-one. Her husband worked for the Vanuatu Education Department, and they lived for most of their married life in Port Vila. In 1986 he had died suddenly, possibly as a result of poisoning related to a land dispute on Ambae, and Jean had returned, with her children, to live with her parents in Longana, east Ambae. Raised in Longana, she was well versed in Ambaean knowledge and practice; educated to secondary level, she understood the documentary concerns of the Cultural Centre. She was used to town life, but also to living in a rural area, and she was well able to understand the problems and concerns that rural ni-Vanuatu women have. Partly because of her keen interest in the Ambae project, Ture Leo and I had selected Lovonda as our base on Ambae, so that when Tarisesei was appointed to the project, she and I were already living in adjacent hamlets. I was, and am, extremely privileged to work with her.

The Cultural Centre goals for the Ambae project were documentation and revival—both to record information about women's production and use of textiles and to encourage them to retrieve knowledge and skills that were being lost and to pass them on to the next generation. In implementing the project Tarisesei and I took different responsibilities. While Tarisesei did learn new information about textiles during the project, for her this was revival rather than documentation: she did not need to write it down. It was I who was forever making notes and then attempting to make sense of what I was learning. The documentation for which Tarisesei took special responsibility was audiotaping stories, songs, and other information for use on the VCC radio program and for storage in the audiovisual archives. She also made a major contribution to several filming projects for which Kapere came to Ambae. As I will discuss later, these aspects of the project were also very much focused on revival. This division of labor continued through the decade after the Ambae project, as both of us maintained our commitment to the Women's Culture Project. Tarisesei is continuing to produce radio programs, to make films, to run workshops. While I have had an ongoing involvement in the development of a women field-worker program, I have devoted considerable energy into transforming all those notes into documentation of various kinds, and notably into this book.

PREVIOUS RESEARCH

In setting out to study women's production and use of textiles on Ambae, I joined a research group that had been largely stalled by the research moratorium. Academic study moves forward by a process of interaction and stimulation, through the influence that information and analysis in one project has upon the next. Without the stimulus of new data and new theoretical perspectives arising from new fieldwork, Vanuatu studies had slowed. Research in the archipelago has had a somewhat checkered history, so that the moratorium was in this sense only the next occasion on which a developing dialogue halted.

Michael Allen commented in 1981 in his introduction to the first collection of essays on the region, "Anthropological research in Vanuatu has, thus far, been afflicted with a curious tendency towards non-publication" (Allen 1981a:xiii). In fact, the area was the subject of some of the earliest published ethnographic surveys in Melanesia, notably those by Codrington (1891 [1981]), Speiser (1913), and Rivers (1914). Several of Rivers' Cambridge students followed him to the archipelago. Of these John Layard (1942) and Bernard Deacon (1934) made the only two extensive focused field studies during the first half of the century, both on the island of Malakula. Both Deacon and Layard were particularly interested in what they described as graded societies, ritual cycles that dominated life in both the areas in which they worked and for which north Vanuatu is (ethnographically speaking) famous. Neither Deacon nor Layard was able to continue making substantial contributions to anthropology. Deacon died shortly before completing his fieldwork (his notes were edited for publication by Camilla Wedgwood), while Layard suffered an extended period of ill health on return to England, which much delayed the publication of his research. Others of Rivers' students, such as T. T. Barnard, never published the results of their fieldwork.

From the 1950s several French researchers, notably the anthropologist Jean Guiart and the cultural geographer Joel Bonnemaison, began working in the archipelago, generally under the auspices of the French

Government research organization ORSTOM. At the end of the same decade, Michael Allen worked on Ambae (then known as Aoba) for a doctorate at the Australian National University (1964). Although Allen has never published a monograph on the region, it is as a result of his efforts that some further research took place, for not only did he direct a series of students to Vanuatu from Sydney University, but he drew together their work and that of a number of other then-new anthropologists in his edited collection (Allen 1981c). The majority of papers in this volume address political process and leadership, through graded societies, hereditary chieftainship, or colonial processes. Only a few of the anthropologists who worked in the archipelago in the 1970s and early 1980s have published substantial ethnographies.[4] Peter Lovell, William Rodman, and Margaret Rodman all worked in east Ambae in this period: while both Rodmans have published many articles, only Margaret Rodman has published a monograph about Ambae (1987a). Communication between French and English-speaking researchers has never been extensive.

The moratorium brought the impetus from Allen's collection to a halt, and there was little ongoing dialogue among anthropologists who had worked in the country. Only a few of the major theoretical debates in Melanesian anthropology have engaged with ethnographic data from the archipelago. The notable exceptions to that have been the literature about the "invention of tradition"—*kastom*—which has been a consistent focus of publications since the early 1980s, and literature about leadership and hierarchy. Both Margaret Jolly and Lamont Lindstrom, in particular, have brought information about north Vanuatu "graded societies" and south and central Vanuatu chiefly systems into the latter debates (Jolly 1991b, 1994b; Lindstrom 1997; see also Guiart et al. 1973). Jolly has also addressed debates in gender studies at a number of levels (1989, 1991a, 1991c).

During and despite the moratorium, a second collection of essays about Vanuatu was brought together, this time by a consortium of Anglo-French editors, in association with the touring exhibition *Arts of Vanuatu*, which was organized by the Museum für Völkerkunde, Basel, and the Musée Nationale des Arts d'Afrique et d'Océanie, Paris (Bonnemaison et al. 1996). These mostly short essays focus on various aspects of the material culture of the archipelago, broadly interpreted, and draw on library and archival research, earlier field research, and some projects undertaken under the auspices of the Cultural Centre during the moratorium. The collection includes an essay by Annie Walter, a French anthropologist and ethnobotanist, who worked for many years on the island of Pentecost (which lies adjacent to Ambae in the archipelago). Walter studied women's knowledge systems, focusing in part on the production and use of Pentecost mats. Her work is immediately relevant to the Ambae project but had in 2001 not yet been published in any depth.

Since the lifting of the moratorium in 1994 a new generation of doctoral students has begun projects in Vanuatu. Among these Susanna Kelly completed research on the central island of Tongoa, writing her doctorate about the pandanus mats women make and use there (1999). A small collection of articles describing new research in anthropology, archaeology, and linguistics was produced in 1999. This latter publication, which I edited, emphasized the impact the moratorium has had on research agenda, demonstrating the influence of the Cultural Centre, and especially the fieldworkers on the development of new research projects (Bolton 1999).

A Word on Terminology and Construction

In building upon the existing literature about Vanuatu, this book takes two terminological departures from established conventions. Both these innovations are descriptive strategies: they are designed to provoke new ways of thinking about the material I am discussing. The first of these is that I have chosen to describe what Ambae women make as textiles rather than as mats. "Mat" is the word used for these objects when English is spoken in Vanuatu, and they have been described in the literature as such by a number of authors, myself included (Bolton 1996). "*Mat*" is also the Bislama term for them. Moreover the term "mat" is used to describe plaited pandanus fabrics made in various parts of the Pacific, notably in Samoa and Tonga, where it is particularly associated with what are known as "fine mats"—high-status valuables, which often have personal names and histories and which are kept for many generations (see Herda 1999; Kaeppler 1999; Schoeffel 1999).

My decision to break with this established precedent has a number of motivations. First, the English term "mat" refers to a coarse textile used as a protective surface of some kind, as a floor covering or as a surface on which to sleep or sit. Ambae textiles are by no means accurately described as mats in this sense, since they are used for a variety of purposes and are by no means all coarsely made. In fact, as I will argue in more depth, these objects are not, on Ambae, classified into a single category at all. They are not all the same kind of thing. It is useful to describe them as textiles precisely because the term "textile" implies no single set of uses: it depicts a material form without suggesting how it is used or classified. Moreover "mat" quite misleadingly allocates these objects an extremely low status in the system of relative value established by museums in the Western popular imagination. The parallel with mats and fine mats in Polynesia is also unhelpful. It implies an equation between the two systems where no such equation can be made. There are many crucial differences between the two. My intention in altering the terminology and writing about these objects with the more neutral term "textiles" is to dislodge some of the many assumptions that attend the word "mat" and to introduce some new perspectives.

There is some disagreement among textile specialists about the terms used to describe different fabric construction techniques. Several authors describing "mats" have chosen to use "weave" to describe how they are made (Buck 1926; Ewins 1982). However, the verb "to weave" refers strictly speaking to fabrics produced on a loom of some kind; another term should be used for textiles produced without a loom. Irene Emery, in her survey of textile techniques, describes the construction technique for Ambae textiles as "oblique interlacing" (1980:62), while in her survey Annemarie Seiler-Baldinger terms it "diagonal or oblique plaiting" (1994:38). My compromise, in deference to these debates, is to use "plaiting."

My second terminological innovation relates to what are commonly known in the Vanuatu literature as graded societies. "Graded societies" are systems of ranked status grades through which men (and sometimes women) climb, commonly achieving each specified status position through rituals in which they kill or exchange pigs. These systems have been described throughout north Vanuatu (see Blackwood 1981; Bonnemaison 1996). There are also many references to similar systems, commonly described as "secret societies," that usually exist in tandem with a central public male graded society, and that offer other avenues for status enhancement through the performance of prescribed rituals

(Allen 1981a; Vienne 1996). What is less well described in the literature is the widespread existence of equivalent systems by which women achieve status: such women's systems do occur throughout the whole of north Vanuatu, and are often very important. Some women's systems, such as the *lengwasa* practiced in central Maewo, are explicitly paired with a male ritual system that in the literature would be described as a secret society; *lengwasa* is paired with the Maewo men's ritual complex known as *kwatu*. In other places, such as east Ambae, the women's ritual *(huhuru)* is explicitly linked to the male public graded society *(huqe)*. While some women's systems involve accession to a series of higher and higher ranks, in other cases they do not, and while some might accord with the criteria for defining "secret societies" this is not always the case.

In fact, the existence of these women's rituals throws into question the terminology generally used for men's systems. What is common to all these rituals is the achievement of status, but this status is not always a matter of an explicit movement upward through a series of named grades. Sometimes there is no specific sequence in which the individual rituals must be performed, and an individual's negotiation of them is a matter of opportunity and ambition. Classification of men's systems as either graded societies or secret societies seems to constrain understanding of how they may in fact operate. More specifically, this terminology does not allow for the variety of forms that women's sys-

Fig. 3 *Qana vivi* (strictly a *qana mwaho*) with a stencilled *vule* (moon) pattern. The lengthwise central seam divides the textile into two "sides"; the imposition of the stencil completes the textile. Drawing © Rebecca Jewell. L: 158 cm; W: 46 cm. Photo: British Museum.

tems take. For this reason I prefer to use "status-alteration systems" as an umbrella term that includes all the various forms these rituals take. I use this term throughout this book.

When women make textiles on Ambae they make a long starting edge by joining pandanus threads side by side and plait outward from this edge, creating one panel or side of the textile. Then they join new pandanus to the starting edge and plait outward in the other direction to create the second panel, or side. The starting edge remains visible as a longitudinal central seam through the length of the textile and is a positively valued feature of it. After the textile is plaited it is still considered as unfinished until it has been dyed, either with a single block of color or with a stencilled pattern imposed onto it. Plaited and dyed it is completed, and can be used. The structure of this book replicates this process: the structure of my argument follows the structure of the textile. One "side" of my book, chapers 1 through 3, addresses one "side" of my topic; that is, in these chapters I consider ideas about *kastom* in Vanuatu. I then join to this the second "side" of my argument, an ethnographic account of Ambae textiles, in chapters 5 to 7. The two sides are linked by chapter 4, which discusses the ideas about place that are integral to the arguments in both. In chapter 8 I describe the progress and effect of the Ambae project, and in 9 I draw together a conclusion, in both chapters imposing on the two sides of my discussion an account that joins them and makes them complete through an analysis of the redefinition of textiles as *kastom*.

UNFOLDING THE MOON

In calling this book *Unfolding the Moon,* I am making a shift similar to this parallel between constructing a texile and constructing my text. The phrase "unfolding the moon" refers to the way in which east Ambaean women unfold a *qana vivi* with the *vule* (moon) design, to lay it on the top of the piles of textiles they are presenting in exchange. Although the title is thus descriptively correct, it is not an Ambaean phrase. To me the title invokes many of the issues the book discusses. But both Jean Tarisesei (who helped me to find the title) and I have discussed it with women in east Ambae and have been met only with bemusement. They argued that it does not make sense linguistically—that one cannot speak of unfolding the moon but rather only of its rising. Translated into English the title works metaphorically: it describes the movement in which women unfolded an aspect of their knowledge and practice and laid it out in the national arena, asserting and defining it for the first time as *kastom*.

There was a specific moment at which this movement could be said to have happened. At the end of the Ambae project, in June 1992, Tarisesei and I organized a workshop, held at the local government headquarters at Saratamata, east Ambae, to which we invited women from all the different Ambae districts. The workshop, which lasted five days, was an opportunity for women to share with each other the knowledge and skills they had in relation to textiles. The fifth day was devoted to a day of public festival. Not only was this the first time in more than sixty years that women had danced on Ambae wearing their traditional costume, plaited pandanus textiles: it was the first time a public occasion in Vanuatu had been marked by the performance of women's *kastom*. Chief Simon Garae, a new VCC fieldworker, who was based in Atavoa, a nearby village, attended the public occasions of the Saratamata workshop. A month later he attended the men fieldworkers annual workshop at the Cultural Centre in Port Vila. At that workshop Jacob Sam Kapere screened a video about Ambae textile production that he, Jean Tarisesei, and I had just completed editing (Sam, Bolton, and Tarisesei 1992). After it was screened, Chief Simon made a speech to the other fieldworkers.

Chief Simon described the effect of the WCP Ambae project on Ambaean men. He recalled that at the time of the tenth anniversary of independence celebrations in 1990, when the Vanuatu government had called for people in every area to perform *kastom* dances, he had tried to find men who knew about *kastom* dances and to persuade both men and women to dress in textiles and to learn the dances and their meanings. He had failed, he said, to find ten young men who knew about such *kastom*. When Tarisesei and I came to run the textile workshop at Saratamata, he reported that there were men who said that we had come to steal *kastom* and to make money from it. But Chief Simon himself and several others, along with the local government council, had tried to clear away this talk. When the workshop opened with a public ceremony at the local government headquarters, men from Chief Simon's village—Atavoa (although he was probably also referring to the adjacent settlements of Navonda and Lovatmemea)—attended the opening as if it were some kind of celebration. Minister Sethy Regenvanu, the deputy prime minister, came to close the workshop (also a public occasion), and there were dances. Every man smiled and was glad. That night we showed some of the video (footage Kapere had recorded earlier in the year and that he had edited roughly). The next morning, Chief Simon reported, the men said that the WCP was a good thing and that they must try hard to help women with their *kastom.*[5]

Although, in this account, Chief Simon makes some comments on *kastom* in general, what he makes clear is that the WCP, and specifically the Ambae project, made a difference to how people defined women's knowledge and practice. It altered the contexts in which that knowledge and practice could be presented, and it did so in a national context, before the deputy prime minister. By dancing in their textiles that day, Ambae women brought forward their knowledge and practice as *kastom.* This book describes *kastom,* and describes Ambae textiles, in order to then decribe how this happened—how, in my metaphor, Ambae women unfolded the moon.

◎ ◎ ◎ *1*

History/*Kastom*

The beginning of the story about how it came to be said that "women have *kastom* too" is about the idea of *kastom* itself, how the term appeared in the ni-Vanuatu lexicon, and what it was understood to mean. "*Kastom*" is a term with a history. First used in the early colonial era, it was invested with new meaning and importance during the movement for independence and, after 1980, through the ongoing creation of Vanuatu as a nation-state. In Vanuatu, in the early 1990s, I encountered talk about *kastom* at every turn. I found ni-Vanuatu to be interested in ideas about *kastom,* affirming in conversation a strong positive appreciation of it. As I discussed it with my colleagues in the Vanuatu Cultural Centre, with the people with whom I lived and worked on Ambae, with government officials at all levels, with chance acquaintances at airstrips and at markets, I found very few people who were not interested to say at least something about the importance of *kastom.*[1] Jennifer Mwera, a woman I met in a remote village in north Ambae in 1991, encapsulated many of these conversations when she remarked "*Kastom* is the life of the people—as the government is always saying on the radio." In this chapter I trace the history of the concept of *kastom* until 1980, a history closely linked to that of the archipelago as a whole.

The nation of Vanuatu is constituted over an archipelago of about eighty widely dispersed islands that lie roughly on a north-south orientation over a distance of 850 kilometers, in a formation resembling the letter Y (see fig. 4). The archipelago lies east of northern Australia

1

and is the westernmost part of the great sweep of islands that starts in the Bismarck Archipelago in northern Papua New Guinea and continues through the Solomons. Most of the islands of Vanuatu are small, and many are surrounded by open sea. They are almost all "high islands," volcanic in origin, mountainous and rugged in landscape. Several of them have active volcanoes, and the archipelago is subject to frequent earth tremors. The archipelago regularly experiences wild

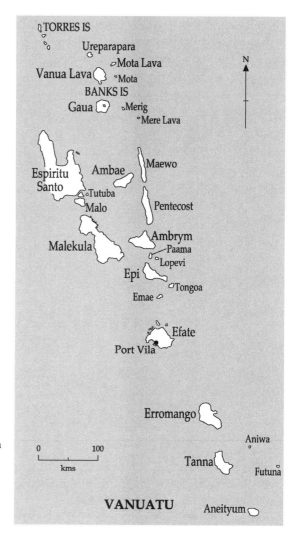

Fig. 4 Map of Vanuatu. (Cartography Unit, Research School of Pacific & Asian Studies, the Australian National University)

weather and cyclones. As one former resident recalls, "Tropical depressions moved in and out like trains, pulling their high precipitation, Force 8 winds and immoderate sea states behind them" (Frater 1991:2).

Between them, ni-Vanuatu speak 113 languages (Tryon 1996:171), all but three of which are Austronesian. Since independence Vanuatu has had three national languages: French, English, and the neo-Melanesian pidgin, Bislama. Archaeological research suggests that people came to the archipelago in a series of population movements, arriving mainly from the islands to the northwest, and settling first some three thousand years ago (Bedford et al. 1998:189). There was also some immigration from the western Polynesian islands to the east. The prehistory and history of the region indicate considerable trade and exchange, warfare and settlement between the inhabitants of the archipelago and the islands that surround them—the southeastern Solomons, New Caledonia, and western Polynesian island groups such as Fiji and Samoa (see Spriggs 1997:221; Wilson 1999:89). Indigenous histories of central and southern Vanuatu report considerable disruption to islander lives through invasions and warfare from neighboring regions.

The linguistic diversity is matched by a great diversity of knowledge and practice throughout the archipelago, although a very broad distinction can be made between the north, central, and southern areas. North Vanuatu was characterized above all by the prevalence of status-alteration systems—ritual cycles by means of which individuals achieved higher and higher spiritual, economic, and political status. Commonly, these rituals were and are based on the exchange and killing of pigs but there are also several women's status-alteration systems based on the production and exchange of textiles. Status-alteration systems, generally described as either graded societies or secret societies, are the subject of much of the anthropological research that has been undertaken in north Vanuatu (such as Deacon 1934; Layard 1942; Vienne 1984; and Jolly 1994b).

A concern with rank and status is a feature of local practice throughout the archipelago, taking other forms in other areas. Central Vanuatu is characterized by systems of hereditary chieftainship (Guiart et al. 1973), while in the south of the group, on the island of Tanna, men achieve status through the "control, production and transmission of knowledge" (Lindstrom 1984:293). The preoccupation with rank and status is allied today with a widespread concern with the idea of respect

(Bislama: *rispek*)—the showing of honor and respect to others. This is a firmly indigenous concept; there is at least one word meaning "respect" in every language spoken in the archipelago. Ni-Vanuatu often identify the "way of respect" as a defining characteristic of *kastom*. Ideas of rank and status have been to some extent transferred to the national level, post independence, through the formalization of local leaders as chiefs, who are represented in Malvatumauri, the Vanuatu National Council of Chiefs, an advisory body to the Vanuatu government.

A 1989 census recorded the population of Vanuatu as 143,000, with a growth rate of 2.4 percent (Statistics Office 1991a). By 2001, the population had grown to nearly 200,000, of whom 50 percent were under eighteen years old. The effects of this population growth were implicit in 1991–1992, the period on which this book focuses, but the old did not yet feel overwhelmed by the young. The 1990s also saw a significant alteration in the balance of the population between island and town, so that by the turn of the century there was a growing population of young people living in town who had never been to their "home" island and for whom both indigenous practice and the colonial era had little immediate significance.[2] In the early 1990s, however, most adults had experience of their home island and some sense of participation in local practice; the nation was characterized by island preoccupations and lifestyles. Most people lived in villages on their own land, practicing subsistence agriculture, growing crops such as taro, yams, and plantain bananas, and raising pigs. Supplementary rural income was obtained through small-scale cash cropping.

In this period Vanuatu's main cash crop was copra, with cocoa cultivation and a developing beef industry gaining in importance (Whyte 1990:142). The country depended also on revenue from a financial and banking industry stimulated by the country's status as a tax haven and on foreign aid. Tourism was also a major source of revenue. After independence fairly strict controls were initially maintained over the small but successful tourist industry, tourists mostly staying at resorts in the capital, Port Vila, on Efate Island. Although guide books mentioned the attractions of other islands, policy discouraged tourists from travelling extensively within the country, encouraging them to enjoy instead the tropical ambience, the French influence, the scuba diving, and the duty-free shopping in Port Vila. From the mid-1990s this policy changed, and small tourism developments in the islands were encouraged.

Radio Vanuatu, the most important channel of communication in the nation, uses both English and French but broadcasts primarily in Bislama, which is the most widely used language in the country. Transmitting on short and medium wave to the whole archipelago, Radio Vanuatu was the main medium of communication at all levels for the first two decades after independence. Short information messages, known as service messages, were submitted by government departments and organizations, and by individuals, and were broadcast twice daily. Through them, for example, shipping agents notified people in rural areas when to expect the delivery of orders of corrugated iron, local government councils announced meetings to their constituents, and families sent "dead messages" to announce the death of individuals to kin working in other parts of the country. Many organizations had their own programs, including both the Vanuatu National Council of Women (VNCW) and the Vanuatu Cultural Centre.

After the creation of the Vanuatu Television and Broadcasting Corporation in 1994, government departments and other organizations were charged for airtime, and the amount of information-based programming dropped sharply. As a result, Radio Vanuatu broadcast increasing amounts of music. Rural listeners, however, were not prepared to use up radio batteries listening to music, and listening overall declined. But until these programming changes, ni-Vanuatu listened attentively to the radio. My closest neighbor in the Ambae village in which I was based had his radio tuned to Radio Vanuatu from morning to evening, and I overheard the service message broadcast in many remote parts of the island. People listened to the news, to service messages, to cyclone warnings, to shipping movements. Our Ambae project was the subject of numerous items on the VNCW program and, as news, on a current affairs program produced by Studio Five North, which is based on Santo, as well as being the basis for many of the Vanuatu Cultural Centre's own programs. I frequently met people who had already heard about me, and knew about my movements, from the radio.

Ni-Vanuatu also use both radio telephones and telephones to communicate between the islands. In 1991–1992 in east Ambae people walked considerable distances to one of the few public telephones to call, or wait to be called by, family working in Santo or Vila. By the end of the decade the growing telephone network supplanted service messages as the principal means of individual-to-individual communication, although people still used the radio for messages to larger numbers of people, as for example in announcing deaths. In the 1990s people travelled between the islands by ship and, very often, by small plane. Small and often rather rusty cargo vessels, known as copra boats, plied their trade between the islands, taking stores to and copra from rural areas from bases in Santo or Vila. People also travelled on these boats. Vanair operated a busy schedule of flights throughout the region, and in general it was ni-Vanuatu, rather than expatriates, who travelled on these planes. A considerable amount of airfreight, mostly food, was sent around the country. People in the towns sent bread and other luxuries to the islands; people in the islands sent garden produce to the towns.

THE EUROPEAN INCURSION

"*Kastom*" is a cognate term for culture in Bislama, Vanuatu's lingua franca. It is used to refer to the knowledge and practice that ni-Vanuatu understand to be authentically their own, deriving from their pre-colonial past and from their place. This widely used term seems to have been introduced from English at the beginning of the century, but it gained significantly in prominence and importance during the movement for independence in the 1970s. It is a term that derives from contact with outsiders and yet describes what belongs to the people of the place.

In Bislama in the early 1990s, the word "*kastom*" had a number of specific usages. It was used as a noun, standing alone, to mean a ceremony—*wan smol kastom* (a small ceremony). It could be used to qualify an activity, for example *kastom danis* (traditional dance) as opposed to *danis disko* (disco dancing). The term was not used to refer to an entire way of life but rather to such distinctive features seen to derive from local precolonial practice. It was, however, used to encompass all such features retained in a particular area of the country, in which case *kastom* was nearly always presented as belonging to an individual or set of individuals—*kastom blong yu* (your *kastom*), *kastom blong olgeta man Maewo* (the *kastom* of the Maewo islanders). This use of the term always implied a contrast: *hemia hemi no kastom blong yumi ol man*

Ambae, olgeta man Malakula ol i mekim (this isn't our *kastom* on Ambae, it's what they do on Malakula). The term *"ful kastom"* (whole, complete *kastom*) described a way of living that draws as much as possible on these distinctive features, as in *ol i liv long ful kastom* (they live predominantly according to *kastom*). These meanings and uses can be seen to have developed over the period since Europeans first visited Vanuatu.

The presence of Europeans in the archipelago was fitful for many centuries after their first appearance in 1606. In that year the explorer Fernandez de Quiros led a Spanish expedition to the shores of a northern island that he named Australia del Espiritu Santo. There the expedition unsuccessfully attempted to establish a settlement, New Jerusalem. De Quiros set a pattern from which later European visitors hardly deviated. Captain Cook passed through the islands in 1774, mapping many of them, and naming the archipelago the New Hebrides. From the 1820s the islands were subject to the successive depredations of explorers, whalers, sandalwood traders, missionaries, labor traders, and planters, but they were never declared the colonial possession of any nation. In 1887 they became the subject of a Joint Naval Agreement, under the terms of which the British navy operating from Fiji and French warships based in New Caledonia patrolled the archipelago to protect the interests of their respective nationals. In 1906 this rather haphazard arrangement gave way to a most eccentric form of colonial government, the Anglo-French Condominium Government of the New Hebrides.

As Margaret Rodman reports, "The Condominium was created largely to provide the legal machinery for processing the claims of those who alienated land from customary owners" (1987a:2) and paid little attention to the administration of the islanders. It left a legacy of two new languages and a population further divided between those who had had access to British resources and those who had had access to the French administration. Under the terms of the condominium many institutions of colonial management were duplicated: a British hospital and a French hospital, a British prison and a French prison, two police forces, two resident commissioners. A Joint Court was created to bring the two administrations together. The first president of the court was Spanish; familiar with neither English nor French, he was in addition somewhat hard of hearing (Douglas and Douglas 1990:43).

No provision was made for an education system—except such schools
as were set up by various missions—until in the 1960s each administration took on the school systems operated by missionaries, Protestant
and Catholic respectively. Although there were planters and traders in
most islands, there was no large-scale appropriation of land until the
1960s, when the developing cattle industry prompted settlers to bring
larger areas of land under their control.

It has often been argued that the encounter with Europeans was an
encounter with difference so substantial that it required a conceptual
acknowledgment and a linguistic label (see Jolly and Thomas 1992a;
Keesing 1982; Lindstrom 1982). However, it has also been suggested
that the shock and amazement with which Europeans expected themselves to be greeted, and which they therefore discovered in Melanesian responses to them, was not necessarily the reaction of the Melanesians themselves (see Strathern 1990). The ideas of cultural variability,
and of the arrival and departure of visitors from elsewhere, were intrin-
sic to the extensive trade networks that islanders already operated: at
first contact the difference between the two groups may not have
appeared as significant to islanders as it felt to Europeans. Thus the
advent of Europeans may not have created an intellectual trauma sufficient to invoke a new self-consciousness of difference. The ongoing
effect of Europeans in the archipelago was traumatic, but wars and loss
of life and land to invaders were the experience of many islanders prior
to European arrival. Thus it was not the arrival of the Europeans but
rather their subsequent assumption of the right to direct islanders'
lives and practices that was significant. It was when Europeans began
to direct what islanders could and could not do that differences in
knowledge and practice became important.

Of all the Europeans interacting with ni-Vanuatu, labor traders and
missionaries had the greatest effect on the lives of individual islanders.
Between the 1860s and the early 1900s more than forty thousand laborers were taken to work in the Queensland sugarcane fields (Douglas
and Douglas 1990:37). Laborers were also taken to work in New Caledonia and Fiji. From 1882 on, laborers were also recruited to work on
the plantations that began to develop in coastal areas throughout the
archipelago. Local labor recruitment on a contract basis continued until
independence. Significant antagonism toward Europeans arose as a
result of the labor trade because of the cavalier and inhuman practices
of many labor traders and of conditions on plantations. It was, for

example, an aggrieved returning laborer, Ala Memea, who murdered an Anglican missionary on Ambae, Charles Godden, in 1906. At the same time, by offering contract-based labor elsewhere, the labor trade enabled islanders to have some measure of control over their engagement with Europeans and to maintain some autonomy in their own places (see Jolly 1981:288).

Presbyterian and Anglican missionaries began working in the archipelago in the 1840s, struggling against strong opposition to white presence in many islands (six missionaries met their deaths on the island of Erromango, for example). Catholic missionaries joined the fray in the 1880s, the Church of Christ and the Seventh-Day Adventists in the 1920s. The Presbyterians have always been the dominant denomination in the archipelago: Tom Harrisson observed of them in the 1930s that "practically nothing of the old culture was tolerated by the missionary" (1937:168). The Anglicans and Catholics were generally more accommodating. Early missionaries made considerable use of Polynesian "teachers," converts from established missions in Samoa, the Cook Islands, and elsewhere, as the first representatives of the Gospel in the New Hebrides. About fifty of these teachers were among the martyred, murdered or dying of unfamiliar illnesses such as malaria (Jolly 1991c:29).

The condominium government itself placed very little pressure on islanders to change their practices. In 1913, after spending a couple of years travelling in the archipelago, Felix Speiser wrote, "The Government has so far had practically no influence on the lives of the people . . . for nine-tenths of the people Government does not exist" (cited in Jacomb 1914:30–31). In many ways this remained true until the 1960s, although expatriate influences did almost entirely curtail the extensive indigenous trade networks (see Huffman 1996c). Significantly, the government made no attempt to formalize or objectify local practice, something that did happen in other places, such as Fiji. In the New Hebrides however, as Jean-Marc Philibert points out,

> no administrative codification of customs took place, not even the codification of native laws as called for in the 1914 Protocol. The unworkable nature of the Anglo-French Condominium acted as a brake on any attempt to systematize native culture. . . . So the "traditional" culture is not the result, as it is in other colonial situations, of Europeans interpreting "traditions" to natives and natives in turn

manipulating such models to fit (as profitably as could be managed) the colonial order. (Philibert 1986:11)

The Second World War had a brief but substantial effect on islanders (Lindstrom and Gwero 1998; Moon and Moon 1998). The United States Army had a major base at Luganville on Espiritu Santo where more than a hundred thousand soldiers were based (this at a time when the entire population of the archipelago was no more than fifty thousand). The military demand for labor was so great that in 1942 the resident commissioners permitted compulsory conscription of men on three-month contracts to work with the armed forces—ten thousand men were temporarily recruited. When the Americans departed, they bulldozed a very considerable proportion of their equipment into the sea at a site now known as Million Dollar Point. Today, rusting Quonset huts and the wide streets of Luganville are the principal legacy of a base that at its height boasted forty-three cinemas. Despite its brevity, the U.S. presence influenced a number of community and political movements in the archipelago—notably the John Frum movement on Tanna, and Nagriamel, an organization based near Luganville—which played a major role in the events leading to independence.

Thus in Vanuatu it was not the specific colonial experience that was crucial to the development of the formal category *kastom* but rather missionization, the attempt to alter local ways of life by imposing another knowledge and practice. Although the degree to which local practices were opposed by missionaries depended on their denomination, conversion to Christianity requires not merely the recognition of difference but the rejection of one set of beliefs, and some associated practices, for another set of beliefs. For a conversion from one to the other to be effected, they must first be established as two distinct categories. It is in the context of evangelism that the term "*kastom*" took hold, as a way of indicating the local practice that should give way to the new faith. And in fact, in Bislama, the term "*kastom*" was for many years opposed to the term "*skul,*" a word that refers to the whole missionary project of education.

It is not clear when these terms first entered Bislama. Significantly, unlike *rispek* (respect), *kastom* does not have direct cognates in the indigenous languages spoken in the archipelago. The linguist Darrell Tryon suggests that although the term "*kastom*" was introduced into

Bislama in the 1920s, it was not widely used until the 1960s (pers. comm. 1999). It is not recorded in the early short lexicons of Bislama, such as Colomb (1913) and Schmidt (1956–1957), and appears for the first time in Camden's 1977 descriptive dictionary. Bislama itself was widely used in the archipelago only after the early 1960s. However, the English word "custom" was part of the missionary discourse from the beginning. The Vila-based lawyer Edward Jacomb, writing in 1914 about the experiment of the condominium, urged missionaries to document the customs they were replacing. His remarks emphasize both the use of the word and the oppositional context in which it was used: "The instant branding of all native customs as bad merely repels the native. . . . If we wish to replace them by other and better customs, we must treat him sympathetically. . . . How can one convince him of the superiority of our customs unless one's knowledge is sufficient to enable one to contrast the two?" (Jacomb 1914:192)

Jacomb's comments draw attention to the significance of the English word "custom" as the basis for the Bislama *kastom.* The English word refers to specific practices, rather than to the whole interlocking network of knowledge and practice denoted by "culture." In Bislama *kastom* has always had this implicit reference to specific practices, or a group of specific practices, rather than to the whole of life.

The experience of conversion differed greatly from area to area, as did its effect on people's lives. Missionary attitudes differed. For most denominations, *kastom* was negatively valued, associated with the "time of darkness" into which the light of the Gospel had now shone. By the 1960s, *kastom* and *skul* were widely perceived as being two different roads that people could choose to follow. Margaret Jolly reports that in the early 1970s, the traditionalist villagers of south Pentecost saw *kastom* and *skul* as "antagonistic and opposed"; she quotes a leader of a *kastom* village in the area as saying "the ways of *skul* exist, and its laws follow behind it; the ways of *kastom* exist, and its laws follow behind" (Jolly 1982:339). Jolly comments: "*Kastom,* from the viewpoint of the traditionalists of south Pentecost, is resolutely anticolonial, antichristian, anticapitalist, and antigovernment. In opposing the ways of *skul,* they are opposing not just 'schooling' in the sense of education, but rather the reconstruction of their religious, economic and political life to conform to European models" (Jolly 1982:341).

"*Kastom*" has always been a term loaded with a moral weight. However, the question of whether *kastom* is a good or a bad thing has always been debated. Kirk Huffman recalls that in the early 1970s, people on Malakula perceived themselves as belonging to two groups, *man blong kastom, man blong skul* (*kastom* people, *skul* people). Coastal people, who belonged to the latter group, used *man blong kastom* as a derogatory term for the inland groups, but for the *kastom* people, the term was a matter of pride (Huffman pers. comm. 1993). Until the independence movement in the mid-1970s, then, *kastom* was mostly discussed in contrast to *skul*. The contrast is significant; it suggests not simply the existence two different categories, but that each existed largely in the frame formed by opposition to the other. The development of *kastom* as a category was, I suggest, principally the effect of missionary endeavor, the reification of islander ways of living as a category that could then be opposed to European practices conveyed in a package with Christian beliefs.

POLITICS

In the late 1960s and the early 1970s, New Hebrideans began to form political movements calling for independence. The first of these developed as a response to increasing land alienation on the island of Espiritu Santo. In 1962 Jimmy Stephens, a man with Banks Islands, European, and Tongan antecedents, became associated with a Santo chief named Buluk in a protest against land alienation by French settlers. By 1965–1966 this protest had developed into the movement known as Nagriamel, and in 1967 Stephens became the Nagriamel leader, joining Buluk and his followers in Vanafo, a settlement on the disputed land, which became the movement's headquarters. Part community, part political movement, Nagriamel grew through the next few years, drawing followers from many parts of the country who were trying to regain alienated land (Van Trease 1987:139). Nagriamel explicitly opposed European ways, synthesizing various local practices and espousing them as *kastom*.[3]

The other major political development was the founding of the New Hebrides Cultural Association in 1971 by a number of young educated New Hebrideans, who met, as one of them recalls, at a "crowded cocktail party held at the British Paddock in Santo" (Lini 1980:24). The aims of the association were concerned with the self-conscious acknowledgment of local "culture," made explicit in the organization's very name. Their aims were "to promote, to preserve, to revive and to encourage New Hebridean culture. To seek the advancement of the New Hebrides socially, educationally, economically and politically in relation with New Hebridean culture and western civilization" (quoted in Kele-Kele et al. 1977:24).

In a brief autobiographical sketch published in 1980, the National Party cofounder and leader Walter Lini explained that his experience of education overseas, at St. John's Theological College in New Zealand, had made him aware of his identity as a Melanesian.

> In 1967, my second year at St John's, I began to realise that most of the teaching materials in books on philosophy and theology were all foreign. They were either European or American ideas. . . . I began to grow uneasy about the way New Zealanders and Pacific Islanders were forced to learn theology, ethical principles, philosophies, and ideas which were completely foreign to us. . . . By the end of that year I had become even more frustrated. Everything was being taught without any reference to my traditional thinking, to Melanesian culture and the Pacific viewpoint. (Lini 1980:15)

Such an identity does not, of course, in any sense pertain to precontact practice. Before contact, islanders had no notion of belonging to the category Melanesian, nor did they imagine themselves as Pacific Islanders in distinction to Americans and Europeans. It was in response to another way of thinking that he was being *taught to adopt* that Lini obtained a sense of his own "traditional thinking"; at the same time the form in which that sense developed was a product of that other way of thinking itself. *Kastom* refers to non-Western ideas grouped together by Western concepts.

After a brief three months the Cultural Association was re-formed as the New Hebrides National Party. As with Nagriamel, the issue that transformed the Cultural Association into a political party was land. A circular explaining the aims of the new party read:

> Our aims in forming a National Party are to preserve the New Hebridean people; their culture and their ways of life are in immediate danger of large scale settlement by Europeans. Already large areas of land [have] been bought . . . on Santo. . . . These pieces have been subdi-

vided and resold. This means that a lot of Europeans will be coming to
settle on them. . . . We must bring pressure on the Governments to
stop this settlement before it is too late. (cited in Van Trease 1987:207)

The National Party grew rapidly from these beginnings. Largely
anglophone in membership, the party was mostly made up of Anglicans
and Presbyterians, and it turned to the British Residency for informal
advice and support. This development precipitated other political align-
ments in the country: it prompted the founding of several francophone
parties, composed both of French nationals and of some French-speak-
ing New Hebrideans.[4]

National Party leaders initially hoped to harness Nagriamel to their
cause. However, Jimmy Stephens was suspicious of the educated young
leaders of the National Party, perceiving their strong church affiliations
as inconsistent with the defense of *kastom*. National Party leaders, by
contrast, considered Stephens' mixed-race background to be inconsistent with his claims to high *kastom* rank (Henningham 1992:32). Thus,
instead of unifying under the banner of a *kastom*-based indigenous
identity and a mutual preoccupation with land issues, Nagriamel and
the National Party drew apart. An unlikely rapprochement between the
French and Nagriamel followed, brought about by the French perception of the National Party as a threat to their interests. By 1972 Nagriamel had begun to undergo a significant change in orientation, moving
from a position of hostility toward land alienation to a close affiliation
with a number of land alienators, both French and American. The condominium replicated itself: indigenous political parties divided along
anglophone/francophone lines, the National Party opposing a constantly shifting alliance of Nagriamel and several francophone parties.

With these developments the stage was set for the conflicts that
characterized the lead-up to independence. The years before the
achievement of independence on July 30, 1980, were distinguished by
demonstrations, secessionist declarations, debate, intrigues, overseas
interference, and changes in condominium policy, all of which contributed to an evolving political consciousness in the country and all of
which revolved around a number of key issues. The division between
the National Party and its francophone opponents was, in significant
part, phrased in terms of a debate about which group more authentically represented *kastom* and hence which could more legitimately represent the islanders.

The Nagriamel espousal of *kastom* was manifest in practice, and especially in the practice of Jimmy Stephens himself, who made his way through the ranks of a status-alteration society under the sponsorship of Chief Buluk and exchanged pigs (and married many wives) to create alliances with groups in other islands. The key to the National Party espousal of *kastom* was identity, and the connection between *kastom* and national identity was a continuing theme of their political platform. The party was concerned to establish a sense of identity for islanders that united them and distinguished them from both colonial powers. In articulating *kastom* as a foundation for a new national identity, Lini and other National Party leaders were constituting *kastom* in a new way. No longer a label that characterized local practice in opposition to *skul, kastom* became, by means of political discourse, constituted as a defining characteristic that united people throughout the archipelago. As Tonkinson points out, *kastom* also provided legitimation for a number of items on the National Party's political agenda: "*Kastom* . . . had its political use in the party's criticism of the manner and extent of land alienation in Vanuatu, and of the relevance of alien legal systems in a Melanesian cultural milieu" (Tonkinson 1982:309).

The debates about *kastom* and political affiliation were conveyed to islanders throughout the archipelago by representatives of the political parties who toured the islands, holding meetings to discuss their views. Although the condominium government censored political news, radio also gave people the opportunity to stay in touch with the broad political developments taking place in the country. The significance of radio to the political debate is evident in the establishment of an illegal transmitter by Nagriamel in 1976. Radio Vanafo broadcast Nagriamel's position to the nation until events overtook the organization.

The effect of the political discourse about *kastom* on islanders was reported by a number of anthropologists then working in the country. Changes in the characterization of *kastom* had a number of effects, one of which was to cause confusion. People in rural areas often interpreted the ideological commitment to *kastom* made by politicians literally. Bob Tonkinson remarks that islanders

> worried about a return to grass skirts and penis wrappers, spears and bows and arrows, and wondered whether they would have to destroy non-*kastom* things such as hunting rifles, aluminium dinghies, outboards and so on. If they were to return to the rule of *kastom* law, and

revive the graded society or male initiation, who among them still
remembered enough to make such things feasible? (Tonkinson
1982:310)

On Tanna, however, people did not have this problem of recalling their
practices. On hearing the message that both *kastom* and Christianity
are valuable, the Tannese began reinterpreting and reviving traditional
events and objects, with increasing frequency. A *nokwiari,* an exchange
of pigs and dances between two local groups, was held in southeast
Tanna in September 1978—the first *nokwiari* to take place there in over
half a century (Lindstrom 1980:26). In his history of Tanna, Joel Bonnemaison described *"kastom"* as being a "quasi-magical word" meaning
"our traditional way of life" (1994:xvi) and as being central to the Tannese history of resistance to outsiders in all guises. Bonnemaison did
not describe *kastom* as the product of anticolonial struggle but as prior
to it. He suggested that "the cultural strength of Tannese society derives
from [the] vital connection between space and humans" and linked *"le
sentiment géographique"*—"a form of emotional and spiritual attach-
ment to a landscape" (Bonnemaison 1994:326)—to the maintenance
of *kastom.* In his analysis, *kastom* was always present in Tanna.

In most islands, changes in attitude to *kastom* could not have been
achieved without the support of the churches, which retained the most
significant influence on islanders. Most of the Protestant churches
were self-governing and locally led from the 1960s, and the National
Party's pressure for independence received strong support from them.
In an article tracing the changing relationship between church and *kastom* in southeast Ambrym, Tonkinson observes that it was the fact that
several of the most forceful party leaders were also Protestant clergy
that helped swing the churches from a neutral position into active support for the independence movement (Tonkinson 1981). By 1973 the
General Assembly of the Presbyterian Church of the New Hebrides,
representing more than half the country's population, was calling for
the cooperation of the colonial administrations in achieving self-gov-
ernment without delay (Tonkinson 1982:308).

The support of the churches for independence required a reevaluation of their approach to *kastom,* in that the separate identity of islanders that legitimized the call for independence was made evident by *kastom.* The change in the relationship between church and *kastom* is the

most significant alteration in the characterization of *kastom* during the 1970s. This change involved a moral reevaluation by means of which some *kastom* could be identified as good and worthy of revival within Christianity. The author of an article in the National Party newspaper, *New Hebridean Viewpoints,* spells out this process.

> Christianity is still a foreign and external thing, which still tends to destroy our way of life; good customs should be kept as our heritage and be baptised into Christianity. Then our faith will be a reality, constructed in our inmost being and not something imposed on us externally. A strong culture gives to people a strong physical and mental character. Our culture will indicate our existence as a people with a history and destiny. (Kalkoa cited in MacClancy 1983:102)

Discussions contrasting Christianity and *kastom* developed in a number of contexts. It was, for example, the subject of specific debate between Nagriamel and the National Party. In an article originally published in *Pacific Islands Monthly,* Jimmy Stephens claimed that

> the National Party pays only lip service to [tribal] customs, while the Nagriamel has made respect for them a basic part of its party's philosophy. The reason for this conflict is that the [National Party] is dominated by, and is indeed a creation of European missionaries. These missionaries hope to use the National Party as a tool in building these islands into a kind of theocracy, or religious dictatorship which would have little respect for the customs of the people. (Stephens 1977:40–41)

There were similar debates in related contexts. The John Frum movement, which is often characterized as a cargo cult, was founded in 1940 and became affiliated with Nagriamel during the 1970s. Lamont Lindstrom reports a debate on Tanna in which "John Frum movement members accuse Christians of not knowing true *kastom.* Christians, in return, pointedly argue the non-traditionalness of John Frum and the fact that his cargoistic proclamations are not *kastom*" (Lindstrom 1982:327). Tonkinson reports that in 1974 the new Presbyterian pastor in southeast Ambrym began to question whether church and *kastom* are antithetical. His call to retrieve "the traditions and crafts of before" was a response "to a widespread realisation among educated Melanesians that too much of their traditional cultures had already been irrev-ocably lost" (Tonkinson 1981:261). The pastor sought to end his own ignorance of his people's indigenous practice and to restore to respectability aspects of that practice, some of which had originally been opposed by the church (Tonkinson 1981:262).

Robert Rubinstein also offers an interesting sidelight on the way in which the debate about *kastom* was understood at the local level. Dis-cussing his fieldwork on Malo in 1975–1976, he reports on the recent development of "highly articulate political factions" in the area:

> the conflict between missionised and non- or recently missionised people on Malo is pronounced. This revolves around the highly charged word "custom" (*kastom* in Bislama). . . . The rise of political factions on Malo relates to orientations away from or towards custom. One orientation, supported in name by the Nagriamel cult, believes that "custom" is an important part of life and must be salvaged or pre-served. The other faction, supported in name by the National Party, believes that while "custom" governs some situations, times have changed and new situations must be met with new techniques. (Rubinstein 1978:31)

Kirk Huffman, who was himself active in these debates, suggests that during the 1970s many expatriates perceived Nagriamel as being more authentic. However, his own perspective is that the National party had better connections with *kastom* people (as opposed to *skul* people) than did the opposition parties. Huffman said that whereas in the early 1970s New Hebrideans talked in terms of the opposition between *kas-tom* and *skul,* by about 1977 people said that church and *kastom* must come to an accord and achieve a mutually dependent balance like that of a canoe and outrigger. He observed that a lot of the New Hebridean church officials of the era were men who did have a good knowledge of their own practices, of *kastom,* so that an accommodation between church and *kastom* was implicit and needed in such cases only to be formalized (pers. comm. 1993).

ACTING ON *KASTOM* NATIONALLY

From the mid-1970s, however, the importance of *kastom* to the politi-cal debate began to be reflected in action at the national level as well as at local levels. In 1974, in response to increasing pressure for independence, the condominium government agreed to set up a representative assembly, the majority of whose members were to be elected by universal suffrage. The assembly also included a number of seats allocated to represent economic interests—the Chamber of Commerce elected six members, the indigenous cooperatives three. Keith Woodward, then the political adviser to the British Residency, reports that subsequently a number of "leading New Hebrideans" suggested that chiefs be elected to the representative assembly as a special category "to represent custom" (n.d. [1978]:5). The difficulty with this proposal was identifying men eligible to stand for election for this category, since "chief" was a category devised by the condominium administration, one that did not directly correspond to any of the diverse systems of leadership that existed throughout the region. Indeed, the introduction of chiefs into the representative assembly was a significant first step toward the development and elaboration of the category *kastom jif* (traditional community leader) in independent Vanuatu (see Bolton 1998).

The problem of the election of chiefs to the assembly became a highly politicized matter. Eventually, a meeting of the representative assembly decided that "a Council of Chiefs should be set up to advise the Representative Assembly on all matters concerning Custom" (Woodward n.d. [1978]:18). The National Council of Chiefs, later renamed Malvatumauri, which met first in 1977, had twenty full members, with the four chiefly members of the representative assembly also attending the council as full members. The Vanuatu constitution subsequently allocated to Malvatumauri the same advisory role to government that it had before independence. The creation of the National Council of Chiefs was a significant development: it had the effect of formalizing chiefs as a group, a distinct category, within the archipelago. Even more significantly, it gave them an importance beyond the local level. Chiefs became part of the new nation. It was thus in the process of achieving independence that the first attempts were made to codify local practice at the national level.

Chief Willie Bongmatur of north Ambrym, a strong supporter of the National Party, was elected as the first chairman of the National Council of Chiefs, holding the position until 1993. A biographical sketch published at independence described Chief Willie as having little formal education but as being regarded as "an extremely wise man and a dynamic speaker who claims public respect and recognition" (Aaron et al. 1981:95). Chief Willie was a most influential figure in the development of Malvatumauri and more generally in the development of the nation of Vanuatu, both before and during the decade after independence. Although his work often took him away from his island, and from a daily engagement with local practice, Chief Willie was always notable for his respect for and practice of *kastom*. He frequently used the symbolic modesty of *tok haed* (hidden speech, or hidden meaning) in public speaking,[5] and one of his greatest skills was his use of locally derived symbols and symbolic action in the new contexts of the nation.

Malvatumauri was not universally welcomed. In October 1977 some men from Erakor village near Port Vila uprooted a *namele* (a cycas palm) that had been planted in front of the condominium offices as a symbol commemorating the renaming of the Council of Chiefs as Malvatumauri, at Chief Willie's initiative. This uprooting caused deep offense to the chiefs. In a radio interview the leader of the Erakor group, Maxime Carlot, explained the action as a response to what was perceived as the overly political actions of Malvatumauri (Woodward n.d. [1978]:55). The action can also be interpreted as a protest against the incorporation of *kastom* into political development, an incorporation particularly offensive to Erakor, which had embraced Christianity and dispensed with all non-Christian practices after a dysentery epidemic earlier in the century (Huffman pers. comm. 1993).

The First National Arts Festival took place in December 1979 in Port Vila. The festival was strongly promoted by the National Party (now renamed the Vanuaaku Pati) and was organized by Godwin Ligo (a Vanuaaku Pati supporter who worked for the radio) with assistance from the VCC and others. Performance groups from all over the archipelago presented to each other songs, dances, magical skills, carving, and more in a festival in the true sense of the word—an occasion of extraordinary vibrancy and enthusiasm. Writing about the festival a year later, Ligo makes explicit the connection between *kastom*, identity, and independence that the Vanuaaku Pati and the independence movement had brought about. The festival, he says,

> has brought about an awareness amongst Ni-Vanuatu of the importance and the vividness of our own culture. There is also a realisation of the importance of preserving and developing culture, custom and traditions as a means of reinforcing national identity. The first Cultural Festival came at a vital moment in the history of Vanuatu, and showed

to the world at large their identity, which was their passport through the gate of independence as "Ni-Vanuatu." (Ligo 1980:65)

These associations were again offensive to some. Once again the francophone Erakor villagers protested. Philibert reports:

A villager from . . . Erakor sent a recorded message to Radio Vanuatu explaining that the reason they had so few traditions left was because they sacrificed them in order to bring about the new social order. Other islanders, he went on to say, now benefit from this new social order by coming in droves to Port Vila to seek employment. (Philibert 1986:11)

For most New Hebrideans, however, the festival provided an opportunity to affirm and celebrate the new positive evaluation of *kastom*. More significantly, it also established a new role for local practice—that of performance to others within the nation but outside the local community. While the idea of *kastom* as performance may have been established to some extent in greeting and honoring ceremonies made for expatriate visitors to communities, the festival established the idea that *kastom* could be performed by one local group for another.

The British, willingly, and the French, reluctantly, parted with their joint authority over the New Hebrides on July 30, 1980. A secession attempt led by Nagriamel was defeated by the new government with the help of Papua New Guinean troops. About seven hundred members of the French settler community in Santo who had supported the secession were expelled from the country. The new constitution restored all land to "indigenous *kastom* owners and their descendants" (chapter 12, article 71). Expatriate freehold titles ceased to exist: land was restored to the traditional owners or reacquired from the traditional owners as leasehold. By the early 1990s there were few expatriates living in Vanuatu outside of Vila and the diminished township of Luganville. Both as a result of the rebellion and in response to the new provisions for *kastom* ownership of land, the expatriate population of the archipelago was significantly reduced.

After independence the Vanuaaku Pati government continued to assert the importance of *kastom* in public speech and in actions. *Kastom* was promoted in the conscious creation of a series of national symbols (the flag, the national anthem, the coat of arms) all of which visually or verbally refer to *kastom*. It was also used as a justification for the introduction of kava as a recreational drink in urban contexts. Kava, a drink prepared from the roots of a pepper plant *(Piper methysticum)* that has a soothing, euphoric effect on the drinker, was formerly restricted to predominantly male ritual contexts of island life, but it now became a *kastom* practice of urban ni-Vanuatu. By such means *kastom* was not only written into the political structures of the new nation, but also symbolically affirmed in everyday life.

Kastom, Culture, and Anthropology

The last decades of the twentieth century saw the almost global acceptance of a number of concepts, even while aspects of their local meanings varied. "Culture" is one of the most potent of these. It is a word that is often applied loosely, but it is widely used to distinguish a group of people on the basis of the knowledge and practice that they hold in common. Before about 1980 the word was mostly used within the discipline of anthropology, so much so that Wagner was able to suggest that it would be possible to "define an anthropologist as someone who uses the word 'culture' habitually" (1981:1). By 1993, however, Marilyn Strathern (n.d.) remarked upon "a world busy rendering some of anthropology's central concepts rather difficult to think clearly with" by overusing them: "[e]verywhere witness the proliferation of cultures, conscious of themselves as such." Culture is often explicitly linked to another very loosely defined term, identity. Identity has been astutely defined as "a mobile, often unstable relation of difference" (Gupta and Ferguson 1997a:13); ironically, the term is often used to assert fixity and permanence. The claim to cultural identity is often made to justify political autonomy, and many analyses understand the phenomenon of "culturalism" as a primarily political development (see, e.g., Sahlins 1994:378–379).

Since the early 1980s the use and significance of *kastom* (and its counterparts in other areas of Melanesia[6]) have been discussed in numerous anthropological studies of the region (Keesing and Tonkinson 1982; Linnekin and Poyer 1990; Jolly and Thomas 1992b; White and Lindstrom 1993). These discussions have linked to wider anthropological debates addressing identity and nationhood (Anderson 1983; Hobsbawm and Ranger 1983; Otto and Thomas 1997), and accounts of *kastom* have long characterized it as a product of and weapon in the anticolonial struggle. Robert Tonkinson notes in his introduction to a 1982 volume about *kastom* that at "both local and national levels *kastom* is inextricably linked with political process" (1982:302). Margaret Jolly, comparing Fiji and Vanuatu, demonstrates how divergent histories of colonization and decolonization have affected local formulations of tradition (1992).

Kastom invokes a particular set of issues for anthropologists because of the equation of the term with "culture." The complexities and uncertainties of anthropological understandings of culture are introduced by this equation into the discussion of *kastom*. Roger Keesing asked about *kastom*, "What is the relationship between a culture as lived and a culture as abstract symbol?" (1982:298). Margaret Jolly and Nicholas Thomas (translating *kastom* as "tradition"), queried, "How satisfactory is the idea of tradition itself? What is the relation between the concept in English, its uses in anthropological discourse and the congeries of terms in Pacific languages which we have translated by it . . . ?" (Jolly and Thomas 1992a:241).

Jolly and Thomas considered self-consciousness to be crucial to distinctions between *kastom* and culture: identifying *kastom* as refering to practices from the past, in distinction to "unconscious cultural inheritance" (1992a:241). If, as is inevitable, one can perceive another culture only through the lens of one's own, what happens if the culture one is observing is actually one's own, self-consciously objectified as *kastom?* Moreover, how does such self-observation come about? The answer most often given for Melanesia is it came about through the encounter with Western ways of living. Keesing argued, "Perhaps it is only the circumstances of colonial invasion, where peoples have had to come to terms with their own powerlessness and peripherality, that allow such externalisation of culture as symbol" (1982:300).

The idea that the self-conscious objectification of culture as *kastom* is a product of the colonial encounter led many commentators to a further conclusion—that this process of reification involves what Keesing and Tonkinson called "invention" (1982), what Jocelyn Linnekin called "cultural construction" (1992:249). This is not "invention" in Wagner's sense—"the use of meanings known [to a person] in constructing an understandable representation of his subject matter" (1981:9) whereby "invention . . . *is* culture" (1981:35). Rather, invention was understood by these commentators to be the creation of something new that nevertheless claims to be a true representation of what already is or was. Early analyses tended to doubt the validity of this representation, so that Keesing, for example, talked in terms of "spurious *kastom*" (1982:300). Jean-Marc Philibert made a very strong statement of this position in reference to *kastom* in Vanuatu: he declared that "tradition, and more so the invented kind, then, is conscious custom, dead custom, empty practice" (1986:2).

Jocelyn Linnekin used a different model in her own overview of the topic. She put a case for *kastom* as cultural construction, invoking post-modernist paradigms of the symbolic production of culture (1992:251). Although Linnekin identified Keesing as having a primarily objectivist perspective on *kastom* (1992:255), and distinguished her own perspective from his, in fact the difference between their views was principally moral. Whereas Keesing deplored "spurious pasts and false histories" (1989:20), Linnekin allowed "cultural meanings and representations" (1992:259). Linnekin's work reflected developments within anthropology at large during the 1980s that, as Lindstrom and White observed, asserted "that culture is not given but is rather actively and continuously constructed within networks and systems of power" (1993:469). Lindstrom and White summed up the understanding of *kastom* in 1993: "constructions of tradition are, at some level, always (1) about the present, (2) historically contingent, and (3) oppositional . . . separating the indigenous and the Western" (1993:470).

If there are diverse academic perspectives on the nature of *kastom,* the argument that underpins most of them is that *kastom* is a "polysemic and contested concept" (Jolly 1992:340), "an apt and powerful symbol precisely because it can mean (almost) all things to all people" (Keesing 1982:297; see also Keesing 1993:590). Analyses of *kastom* have had something of the same multiplicity of versions and interpretation. The developing popular appropriation of "culture," internationally, and the consequent refiguring of anthropological understandings of the term can be seen to be reflected on a smaller scale in analyses of *kastom.* Not only does *kastom* have a history, but so do the arguments that have been presented about it.

The analysis of *kastom* also reflected the complexity of the debate about *kastom* in Vanuatu during the 1970s and early 1980s and the changes and developments in the concept that occurred over that period. Before the independence movements of the 1970s, *kastom* was primarily a way of talking about, of classifying, certain practices and beliefs. At that time, *kastom* was negatively valued in local discourse. The independence movement overturned this negative evaluation. This change in the evaluation of *kastom* was not, however, simply an alteration from one moral evaluation to another. The identification of *kastom* as the characteristic that made local people different from expatriates in turn acted upon the way in which *kastom* itself was understood. It came to signify that very difference. However, there was no examination or codification of the kinds of knowledge and practice that could be identified as *kastom*. Rather, *kastom* came to indicate the practices and characteristics that distinguish ni-Vanuatu from other people. While the legitimation for *kastom* is that it represents an identity that has historical continuity, *kastom* does not prejudge where the best exemplars of that identity lie, in the past or in the present. *Kastom* in Vanuatu developed as an indigenous concept quite distinct from anthropological notions of culture or tradition. It became a marker of difference, a means of making distinctions.

◎ ◎ ◎ *2*

Kastom in the National Arena

Port Vila, the capital of Vanuatu, climbs the hills that
surround a harbor on the south coast of the central Vanuatu island of
Efate. The seat of the condominium government, during the colonial
era it was inhabited primarily by expatriates. New Hebrideans lived in a
number of villages nearby and were employed on adjacent plantations,
but it was not itself a village site. It was constituted primarily as white
space: the movement of local people was restricted between 9 P.M. and
5 A.M. (M. Rodman 2001:33–35). After independence ni-Vanuatu began
to move there for employment and entertainment, and by 1989 it had
a population of 19,300, of whom more than 16,000 were ni-Vanuatu
(Statistics Office 1991a). In the early 1990s quite a few of these people
lived in sometimes crowded settlements on vacant land in and around
the town, but the impression given by the main street was of a pros-
perous and significantly European environment. It was a very pleasant
place to visit and catered very well to tourists and other visitors, with
cafes, restaurants, hotels, banks, rental car services, taxis, and other
such other amenities of modern life. The Cultural Centre building, on
the main street between the taxi rank and the Hotel Rossi, was at this
period a little scruffy in appearance—an advantage in not intimidating
ni-Vanuatu who wished to visit. The new Radio Vanuatu premises, built
in 1984, stood on a hill nearby, overlooking the harbor.

These two institutions were key to the development of the discourse
of *kastom* after independence. Although politicians continued through
the 1980s to affirm the importance of *kastom* to the new nation, grad-

ually the source of the discourse about *kastom* moved from the party-political arena to the Cultural Centre, and in the same period the Cultural Centre began to dominate the view of *kastom* broadcast by Radio Vanuatu. The VCC approach to *kastom,* the developing discourse about what *kastom* is, and how it can continue to be practiced, was communicated to ni-Vanuatu via the Cultural Centre's own radio program and through the work of the fieldworkers. [1]

RADIO

From its earliest transmissions in 1966, Radio Vila (as it then was) included "items of local culture" in its broadcasts (Page 1993:172). When transmission hours extended, so did the broadcast of local knowledge and practice. In 1971, after Australia donated a 2-kilowatt transmitter dedicated to broadcasting, Godwin Ligo started to make a program called *Taem nao, taem bifo* (The present, the past). Ligo had been recruited in 1969 by the British Information Office, which produced the British component of radio broadcasts. *Taem nao, taem bifo* was broadcast on Tuesday evenings and repeated on Thursday evenings, possibly not with great regularity. Ligo's responsibilities at the British Information Office also included touring Efate and other islands, showing films. Wherever he went he took a reel-to-reel tape recorder with which he recorded songs and stories for the program. Recordings were made principally in Bislama. Later Ligo found his

Fig. 5 Port Vila, capital of Vanuatu, in 1994.

way to various islands specifically to record stories and songs for the program. He sent messages on the radio to announce his arrival, telling people to prepare stories and songs to record, and then went to record them.

Until 1974–1975 there was little local interest in the news, either global or local. People's principal interest in the news was to hear when officials of the two governments were to visit their village, so that they could prepare a welcome, and then to hear about the event afterward on the radio. People were interested in hearing record requests and indigenous stories and songs. From the beginning, they responded to this material with correspondence, and Ligo's program generated a form of competitiveness. People would hear a story from another island, or another village on their island, or even from another clan in their own area, which was similar to one they themselves told, and would write to the radio requesting that their own version be broadcast. Sometimes, Ligo says, they wrote to say that the version first broadcast had been stolen from them. Or they wrote that they had the same story in their own island, but that it went further than the story that had been broadcast. Ligo responded by broadcasting all versions "so that people could hear the difference." The interest the program generated is striking in that at this time the word *"kastom"* still had a pejorative ring to it; *kastom* was still the negative opposite to Christianization and development. The response to the program demonstrates deep interest in the substance of the local knowledge that Ligo was broadcasting.

In 1975, as the independence movement became an increasingly significant force, the French resident commissioner Robert Gauger invited a French teacher, Paul Gardissat, to take up a position as chief of the Bislama Section, French Residency Information Service.[2] The commissioner's idea was that Gardissat, who spoke Bislama, had worked in radio in Algeria, and had spent the previous thirteen years teaching in the archipelago, could provide a kind of liaison service for the French government with the islanders. Principal among Gardissat's responsibilities in this position was the making of radio programs for Radio Vila. From the beginning he made Bislama programs about *kastom*, recording and broadcasting ceremonies, songs, and stories. For some time, Ligo and Gardissat both made programs about indigenous knowledge and practice for their respective information offices. But once Ligo began working as a political reporter in 1976, the bulk of *kastom* programming was undertaken by Gardissat.

Gardissat's various programs were extremely popular, generating a large correspondence with people in the islands. He remembers receiving more than fifty letters a day, some of which he still holds in his private archives. People often sent stories for him to broadcast. A letter dated May 3, 1976, and written in English, from Taes Thomson from Hokua village, northwest Santo, begins, "It is my own pleasure to write you this Custom Story. I'm very interested of listen to the Custom Stories from all the islands in the group. So I would like to tell one story. It's a really true story" (Gardissat archives).

Gardissat also sometimes received tapes. Gaetan Bule from Narovorovo village, Maewo, for example, sent a cassette with a letter dated December 5, 1975, explaining that it contained a recording of a dance called *nalenga,* which had been performed three days earlier at a marriage. In 1977 Gardissat introduced a system called "walkabout cassettes," sending a tape recorder and tapes to the islands, on request, for people to record stories to be broadcast. He also travelled himself and was invited to attend particular ceremonies and to record and subsequently broadcast them. Gardissat called his *kastom* program *Kastom, Kalja mo Tredisin* (Custom, culture and tradition), thereby introducing the terms *"kalja"* and *"tredisin"* into the Bislama vocabulary. People were, he says, glad to have their stories broadcast because the performance on the radio gave them importance, status, like the medals Napoleon gave to his soldiers.

Gardissat's interest in and support of *kastom* on the radio were important. Given that most expatriates had condemned local practice as a bad thing, a European on the radio arguing that people should be proud of their *kastom* made a significant impact. However, if some ni-Vanuatu responded positively to Gardissat's program, others opposed it. In 1975, he says, people often said *"Kastom hemi dakness"* (*Kastom* belongs to the time of darkness), reflecting the missionary discourse of darkness and light. Some educated islanders, he says, saw *kastom* as something for the uneducated rural population (*samting blong ol man bus).* He was also much criticized for his Bislama. Expatriates chided him for speaking it at all, and islanders for speaking it badly.

Gardissat's radio production skills developed, and his ni-Vanuatu colleagues at the radio taught him to speak Bislama properly. His own interest in *kastom* increased as he worked on the program, and the political discourse about *kastom* continued to alter attitudes to it. Gradually, all these factors combined to make Gardissat's program more and more important and influential. After some time, he also began producing a French-language program about *kastom: Contes et légendes des Nouvelles Hébrides*. His approach to the broadcast of traditional material often involved both dramatization and interpretation. He scripted stories and used sound effects and other devices to enliven the account. Gardissat attributed the success of his programs at least partly to his attempt to provide some contextualization for the stories, so that people not familiar with the region from which the story came had access to information that enabled them to understand how the story fitted in.

Gardissat saw the importance of his programs as linked to the speed of political development between 1975 and 1980. His programs substantiated political rhetoric about the importance of *kastom* at a national level by presenting the *kastom* of the whole archipelago to its people—demonstrating the depth and content of local practices throughout the region. As time passed and the country came closer to achieving independence, there was more and more interest in *kastom*. Gardissat saw this interest as reaching its high point in the First National Arts Festival, observing "Everyone came to Vila, men and women, from the north, the south, the central regions, they came and showed their *kastom*." Radio played a major role, not just in that Radio Vila helped to organize the festival, but also in that it had generated this groundswell of interest in *kastom* and had, by presenting the *kastom* of different islands over the airwaves, developed a new role for *kastom* as performance (see Bolton 1999a). Godwin Ligo, in convening the arts festival, named it after his *kastom* radio program: *Taem nao, taem bifo*. The festival, Gardissat comments, was the first time that the country comprehended itself as a country, and (literally) saw itself.[3]

The name Gardissat chose for his Bislama program—*Kastom, Kalja mo Tredisin*—is important. For Gardissat, each of these three terms had a distinct meaning, and he often explained the distinction he made between these terms in the program. He used *"kastom"* to denote indigenous knowledge and practice, *"tredisin"* to denote introduced practices that had been incorporated into people's lives, such as the singing of New Year *(Bonne Année)* songs (a speciality of Erakor village on Efate), and *"kalja"* to refer to all contemporary practice, whatever its source. He made programs devoted to each of these three terms and attempted to reinforce the distinction between them in a number of different ways.

In this introduction of the English terms "culture" and "tradition" into Bislama, Gardissat extended the ongoing exchange of ideas between Western concepts of culture and local formulations. The phrase *"kastom, kalja mo tredisin"* was partially taken up in 1991–1992. It was used by educated ni-Vanuatu such as government officials or people involved in one way or another in the Vanuatu Cultural Centre. The phrase did not have wider currency. Crowley's 1990 Bislama dictionary listed neither *tredisin* nor *kalja* and translated both "tradition" and "culture" as *kastom,* listing as an alternative rendering of "culture" *fasin blong laef* (way of life). His 1995 edition listed *kalja* and translated it as "culture," suggesting that the term gained in usage during the early 1990s. However, the 1995 edition did not list *tredisin,* translating "tradition" as *kastom.* Throughout the decade most people only used *kastom.*

Here then is an important point concerning the nature of the influence of radio. While Gardissat's three terms were quickly adopted by politicians and other urban ni-Vanuatu, the distinction between them was never successfully introduced. I had a number of extensive discussions with people in Vanuatu about *kastom, kalja,* and *tredisin,* and, with the exception of Grace Molisa, found no one who made a distinction between the three. People who used the expression *"kastom, kalja mo tredisin"* seemed to do so to reinforce their emphasis on *kastom* and not to distinguish between the terms. Radio was thus successful in introducing new concepts and ideas where there was already an openness to those concepts within the audience. People welcomed the broadcast of *kastom* by the government, and the implicit assurance that it was a positive phenomenon, because they themselves were willing to adopt that positive perspective. A distinction between various forms of local practice did not meet with an already receptive audience and was never established, although the phrase *"kastom, kalja mo tredisin"* was gradually adopted as a way of speaking with emphasis about *kastom.*

Paul Gardissat gradually extended the range of his program, interviewing anthropologists, archaeologists, and other researchers working in the archipelago and reading and broadcasting material drawn from the anthropology of the region. He also made programs about the

European discovery of the New Hebrides—about Captain Cook, for example. As well as welcoming visiting researchers onto his program, he also welcomed the staff and fieldworkers of the Cultural Centre. The involvement of the Cultural Centre increased until in the early 1980s it took over the *kastom* program—the presentation of local people telling their own stories—and Gardissat devoted himself to the production of programs about history and research.

THE DEVELOPMENT OF THE CULTURAL CENTRE

In 1956 the Condominium Government of the New Hebrides marked its fiftieth anniversary by laying the foundation stone for a cultural centre. The Jubilee Planning Committee had suggested that a museum be founded to mark the anniversary; the British Residency had advised that while British Development Funds could not be used to build a museum, money could be provided if the institution were to be called a Cultural Centre (Woodward n.d. [1978]). A building was erected in the main street of Port Vila against the harbor wall, next to the infamous Hotel Rossi. It was completed in 1959 but initially stood empty, being used for various condominium purposes like a July 14 ball and, more important, for meetings of the Advisory Council, which were held there

Fig. 6 The Vanuatu Cultural Centre museum entrance in 1989.

until the early 1970s. In 1961 a library was installed in the eastern side of the building and a librarian appointed.[4]

The institution, which was originally known as the Vila Cultural Centre, was established by a New Hebrides Condominium Joint Standing Order (No. 2 of 1960), which provided for its management. As an institution it comprised both museum and library and, during the 1980s and early 1990s, the national archives.[5] Official responsibility for the whole institution rested with a Board of Management, initially comprising two French residents, two British, two New Hebrideans, and, ex officio, the two district agents from the Central District (which covered Port Vila). The museum was for many years cared for by Keith Woodward, a British Residency staff member, who was asked by the British resident commissioner to take an interest in the VCC in his spare time. Woodward oversaw the library, but was primarily concerned with the museum. He also acted as secretary of the Board of Management.

During the 1960s and early 1970s the VCC was primarily a Western institution in its scope and preoccupations. The standing order cites as the objectives of the institution the providing of facilities for "the exhibition of objects which illustrate the history, literature and natural resources of the New Hebrides; [and] scientific, artistic and literary activities of general interest" (Joint Standing Order [No. 2 of 1960]). A Joint Regulation (No. 11 of 1965) provided for "the preservation of sites and objects of historical ethnological or artistic interest," giving the resident commissioners, in consultation with the VCC Board of Management, the right to classify such sites. The VCC board became the body within the condominium government to which issues relating to the ethnology and history of the archipelago could be referred.

Woodward looked after the museum as a volunteer until 1976. He obtained artifacts for the collections through the limited means available to him and organized the displays, educating himself as much as possible about professional collection-management practice. Anthropologists and archaeologists working in the country provided objects for the collection and gave lectures in the meeting room. The French anthropologist Jean Guiart, in particular, greatly encouraged Woodward in the early days of the museum and provided some objects for its collection. A German naturalist, Heinrich Bregulla, collected and mounted a number of birds, which were put on display, and contributed a collection of shells. A number of expatriates involved in the collecting or trading of artifacts in the New Hebrides were interested in the institution and at times attempted unsuccessfully to exert considerable influence over it. Several such people served on the VCC board.

Woodward (pers. comm. 1993) recalls that there was little interest in the VCC on the part of local people during the 1960s. There was a very small Melanesian population resident in Vila at that time, but Woodward considers this an insufficient explanation, suspecting rather that the expatriate librarian may have discouraged any shabbily dressed islanders from entering the building. From the 1970s, however, a local woman looked after visitors to the museum, and a lot of local people visited it. Woodward found it difficult to interest New Hebrideans in joining the Cultural Centre board. One who did in 1962 was Maxime Carlot from Erakor village, who, as I mentioned in chapter 1, later protested against the use of *kastom* as a means of establishing indigenous identity. During the 1960s islanders do not appear to have seen the VCC as having any relevance for them. This may have been because the museum, which displayed objects in glass cases, seemed as far from the realities of indigenous practice as other expatriate activities rather than because it was explicitly connected with the still negatively valued *kastom*.

This lack of interest among islanders in the Cultural Centre museum reflects problems that have dogged many Pacific region museums. Such problems have been discussed in a number of different contexts (such as in Eoe and Swadling 1991; Lindstrom and White 1994). Charles Hunt, writing about the Fiji Museum, commented that "The problem is that . . . the Fijians do not want (need) to look at their society objectively. Culture, custom, traditions are for experiencing and acting out rather than for peeping into" (Hunt 1978:72, cited in West 1981:13).

Similarly, Soroi Marepo Eoe, director of the Papua New Guinea National Museum and Art Gallery, commented that for the great majority of indigenous Pacific Islanders museum collections are often "the unimportant relics of almost forgotten cultures" (1991:1). He argued that Western intellectual categories and Western professional objectives for museums have no relevance in the Pacific. This irrelevance sits squarely upon the concept of culture, upon what Roy Wagner has described as "the paradox created by imagining a culture for people who do not imagine it for themselves" (1981:27). Ethnographic museums imagine cultures by selecting artifacts to be "strategic relics"

(Wagner 1981:28), a process entirely to do with Western preoccupations with reification. But for Melanesians, who have no preoccupation with reification through objects, the whole project of museums is of no importance.

In several cases indigenous Pacific museum ethnographers grappling with a sense of the irrelevance of museums have attempted to legitimize them by implicitly redefining them through analogy with local practice. Using analogies with indigenous systems for keeping precious objects (for example in dedicated space in men's houses), they have suggested that museums serve a similar function, not of presenting whole "cultures," but rather of preserving valued objects. As an assistant director of the Cook Islands Museum commented:

> Our societies had museums prior to the coming of the whiteman. It was not called a museum then because it had various traditional names. . . . The staff who manned these institutions were called Taunga or experts in their own right. They displayed our objects of mana [power] and dressed and fed them on the marae or sacred grounds. The house where these things were kept was tapu [forbidden] to the public just as our storerooms are today. (Tutai 1991:201)

The problem with this approach is that the objective of preserving valued objects can be met without invoking the whole machinery of Western museums. Margaret West of the Northern Territory Museum, for example, has discussed the traditional storage of secret/sacred material by Aboriginal men in northwestern and central Australia. She described the development of both museums and "keeping places" in the region and argued that the "peculiarly Aboriginal" reasons for storing secret/sacred material are on the whole met by small buildings used purely as stores or "keeping places" for the objects, but are not met in the museums, which remove the objects from their context of use (West 1981).

The question is not only one of relevance. As Emmanuel Kasaherou, then director of the New Caledonia Museum commented: "We often explain why there should be a museum in New Caledonia, but there is some conflict with traditional attitudes. Some of the objects exhibited are very strong and sacred. In traditional society it is a mark of disrespect to show sacred objects to everyone" (Kasaherou 1991:165). Kasaherou explained further that Kanaks are reluctant to visit the museum out of fear of entering a place where artifacts of the past are displayed: visitors "feel as if they were entering a cemetery where devils live" (1991:165–166). Pacific museums have consistently faced the issue of spiritual powers embodied in or associated with objects. Curators are wary of the danger that unrecognized spiritual power could and does cause them in their own museums and elsewhere.

Pacific Islanders working in their national museums struggle to reconcile these contradictions, trying to find ways to become meaningful to the people they represent without totally letting go of the framework of Western museum practice. As a secretary of the Tongan National Commission for UNESCO, 'Eseta Fusitu'a, observed, "We must move away immediately from the narrower confines of museum concepts and museum thinking. . . . I am not suggesting that the traditional roles of museums be bypassed. What I am saying is that we need to broaden our concept of museums so that our people find museums meaningful to them" (1991:198–199). The striking characteristic of the Vanuatu Cultural Centre is that from 1977, under the curatorship of Kirk Huffman, it developed both programs and attitudes that anticipated Fusitu'a's call to action. In doing so it moved away from Western museum practice to a very considerable extent.

THE ORAL TRADITIONS PROJECT

In 1972 or 1973, Jean Guiart gave a talk at the VCC in which he suggested that the Board of Management initiate an oral traditions recording program. The board discussed the idea for some time, starting to plan seriously for such a program in 1974. This development was in line with thinking within the Pacific region, as sponsored by organizations such as UNESCO (which, for example, sponsored an oral traditions training course for Pacific Islanders in Auckland in May 1974). It also echoed conversations between the two expatriates who subsequently became involved in the project, Kirk Huffman and Peter Crowe. Huffman was then, as I described in the introduction, working on Malakula toward postgraduate studies in ethnology. Crowe, an ethnomusicologist, was at that time doing research on several islands in the north of the country. Huffman recalls that he and Crowe had several long conversations in 1973, trying to think of ways "to get the Melanesians interested in the documentation and revival of their traditional cultures" (pers. comm. 1991).

In 1976 money from the South Pacific Commission was made available to initiate an oral traditions project in the archipelago. The Australian government also contributed funds through the newly formed South Pacific Cultures Fund. The grants were used to get the Oral Traditions Project off the ground and to employ the first curator for the VCC. Although appointed to this position, Huffman was unable to take it up in 1976. A French linguist, Jean-Michel Charpentier, was appointed as museum curator temporarily. Charpentier worked in the museum (where, for example, he initiated the first collection catalogue), and both he and Crowe, acting more or less independently of each other, developed the Oral Traditions Project.[6]

Charpentier approached the project by training ten students from the teachers' college in Port Vila in oral tradition recording techniques. These students were then sent to other islands for short periods. Late in 1976 seven of these teacher trainees attended a three-week UNESCO training course in Honiara, Solomon Islands. Crowe took a different approach. He ran a two-week training course at the Anglican Church's Torgil Centre on Ambae for four men from north Vanuatu. These were all older men who were knowledgeable about practices in their own communities. Charpentier's trainees subsequently lost interest in the project. Two of Crowe's trainees, James Gwero of west Ambae, and Jeffrey Uliboe of central Maewo, have continued recording oral traditions and in 2001 were still actively involved in the project. In 1977 Charpentier's period as curator concluded, and Kirk Huffman took up the position, which he held until 1989. Crowe did not continue to be involved in the Oral Traditions Project.

The UNESCO focus on the recording of oral traditions reflects an essentially museological concern with preservation through collection. By recording oral traditions on audiotape, it is possible to reconstruct them as objects that can be treated more or less in the same way as headdresses or bowls—labelled, documented, stored, displayed. The project as it was originally conceived was a natural extension of the Western museological concerns that were then the motivation for the VCC museum. Both Crowe's and Charpentier's projects produced a considerable volume of material. A 1978 report lists the following project objectives: "to publish books and pamphlets, issue recordings, make films and video and radio broadcasts" (VCC files n.d. [1978]). There were then, however, neither adequate studio facilities nor sufficient funding resources in Vila to achieve these objectives.

If the original objectives for oral traditions recording were museological in emphasis, Crowe and Huffman introduced something
entirely different when they strove to "get Melanesians interested"
(Huffman pers. comm. 1991). Their focus was, and Huffman's focus
continued to be, on the effect of the project on the islanders, rather than
on the recorded material it produced for the museum. As Crowe commented in a report to the VCC board, "The aim of our project is to
record all forms of unwritten knowledge, aural and visual, by hand, on
tape, video, cine or any available way. . . . But it is not entirely for
preservation as if we were making another kind of museum. We also
want to stimulate the revival and continuance of traditional ways, where
the people feel it appropriate" (Crowe n.d. [1977]:6).

Huffman's emphasis was always more on the ideas and practices of
the ni-Vanuatu in their own communities than on anything that was
kept in the museum—a stance for which the VCC was often criticized
by expatriates (see Kaeppler 1994:40). Such criticisms draw attention
to the gap between the work that became the focus of the Cultural Cen-

Fig. 7 Kirk Huffman, outside the Vanuatu Cultural Centre building in 1994.

tre and conventional museum anthropology. The VCC did continue to resemble a conventional museum at some levels, acquiring objects and displaying some of them alongside material Woodward had set out in the exhibition cases. Objects not on display were stored in heaps in lofts under the roof, subject to wildly fluctuating temperature, and insect and rodent damage.

Crowe wrote a number of significant characteristics into the project when he established criteria for the selection of his oral traditions trainees. First, he decided that the project be implemented among Bislama speakers; he did not require that trainees be fluent in either French or English. He thereby moved the project away from the educated elite into the rural community, a move reinforced by his decision to hold his training course on an island in the north of the group rather than in the capital. Second, he selected men who had some considerable knowledge of their own local practices, rather than young students who had been educated outside the village context. In a report on the project to the VCC board, he explains that he chose middle-aged men who, he felt, would have "sufficient [power] to penetrate the heart of their traditions," rather than younger people who would "find difficulty in obtaining anything but the most well-known and public material" (Crowe n.d. [1977]:4). Third, and most importantly, he selected his trainees on the basis of local advice within north Vanuatu, asking community leaders to suggest potential trainees.

James Gwero subsequently wrote a report on his participation in the project that includes a description of Crowe's training course (Gwero n.d. [1981]). Written in 1981, the language of the report shows the influence of training Gwero later received; its sentiments, however, reflect the response of Crowe's trainees to his initiative:

> Peter Crowe held this course to help men who are interested in the culture and tradition of the country of Vanuatu. I went on the course because I was very interested in work like taping *kastom* stories and taking photos of people. . . . I went to school in Ugi in the Solomon Islands for three years but I never came across a subject like this. . . . [Crowe] is a great person because he is concerned that our *kastom* stories should not be lost — that's why he ran the course. He had a lot of respect for our *kastom*. (Gwero n.d. [1981]:1; translated from Bislama)

Crowe's course also initiated a strong connection between the record-ing of oral traditions and the radio. On the first day of the course his trainees made a radio program that was broadcast by Radio Vila a week later, while the course was still running. Crowe also established a num-ber of other practices for the Oral Traditions Project, sending away the trainees with their own recorders, batteries, and tapes. Gwero reports that he started making recordings as soon as he returned home to his village (Gwero n.d. [1981]:2).

Huffman and Crowe, and Woodward, Guiart, and Charpentier, were "imagining a culture for people who do not imagine it for them-selves" (Wagner 1981:27) and introducing that imagined culture into local conceptualizations of *kastom.* They were working with ideas of culture and tradition derived from Western models, which allocate these terms a descriptive rather than an analytical status. Thus Crowe comments on his training course that "all the men proved to be thor-ough members of a living oral culture" (n.d. [1977]:5). Culture in this sense is an interlocking and bounded combination of practices and beliefs that constitute an entire way of living but that can be "invaded" by extraneous practices belonging to another way of living, another cul-ture. Traditions represent component parts of cultures that in a situa-tion of "cultural invasion" obtain authenticity from the fact that they are remnant parts of a past whole. This formulation of tradition intro-duces ideas of continuance, of salvage, and hence of revival. Huffman's summary of the discussions he and Crowe had in 1973 also illustrates this kind of thinking—"getting Melanesians interested in the . . . revival of their traditional cultures" (Huffman pers. comm. 1991).

The emphasis on revival resonated with rural experience. As I have shown in the preceding chapter, during the 1970s it became possible for islanders to reconsider practices and beliefs that had fallen into dis-use under the influence of missions and other aspects of contact, and to choose to revive them. While the legitimation for *kastom* is that it represents an identity that has historical continuity, *kastom* does not prejudge where the best exemplars of that identity lie, in the past or in the present. Nevertheless, and crucially, it *is* the past that provides this legitimation, in that it is the source of many practices now labelled *kas-tom.* The distinction between expatriate views of *kastom* as culture and tradition, and local identification of *kastom* as expressing an autono-mous identity, belonging to the place, is obscured by the match between the effect of these two perspectives. The outcome of both, a concern with revival and continuance, is the same.

As several examples in the last chapter illustrated, local attitudes to the revival of *kastom* varied from area to area in Vanuatu. While the Tannese eagerly reintroduced the *nokwiari* (Lindstrom 1980:26), in other areas people were less sure of how and what to reintroduce (Tonkinson 1982:310). Commonly, the reintroduction of practices and beliefs in new circumstances altered their constitution and their purpose. Ceremonies began to be practised or revived both for the value and meaning they had to their practitioners in and of themselves and also as an assertion of local and national identity. The presentation of *kastom* on the radio and at the arts festival demonstrated this second purpose in particular. At the same time the fact that the changing discourse about *kastom* stimulated by the independence movement was reflected in actions at local and national levels substantiated the rhetorical assertion of the importance of *kastom*. VCC programs were designed to encourage the practice and revival of *kastom* for both local and national purposes.

Huffman's objective as curator was to interest the ni-Vanuatu in their traditions, to instill pride in them, and to discuss ways in which they could accommodate the changing circumstances of national development. He developed the Oral Traditions Project, expanding it beyond a central emphasis on recording and documentation to a concern with maintenance and revival. He spent a lot of time visiting various islands (tending to concentrate on those areas that he perceived as less tainted by missions), talking to people about *kastom* and its importance. This message was reinforced in radio programs. The VCC program (inherited from Gardissat), which was broadcast every Saturday evening, drew on recordings made in the Oral Traditions Project. The program emphasized the importance of *kastom,* extending the discourse about it. In particular, Huffman built up the group of Oral Traditions Project trainees, whom he dubbed "fieldworkers," with the ultimate objective of appointing a fieldworker in each language group. When he heard of a man who was interested in *kastom,* Huffman would either visit him in his village or bring him to Vila, spending several weeks with him, teaching him how to use recording equipment (provided with mostly Australian aid) and talking to him about the work of fieldworkers.

Shortly after Huffman started work, Jack Keitadi was appointed as trainee curator. Over the next few years the number of ni-Vanuatu on both the staff and the board of the VCC increased, and the character of the institution changed. The VCC became a place for ni-Vanuatu, specifically for ni-Vanuatu men. As Huffman and other VCC staff became known throughout the archipelago, the museum became a center for rural people visiting the capital. Of all the museums in the Pacific region, the VCC was the only one where you were likely to find substantially more local people than tourists leaning on the cases. The slightly dilapidated appearance that weather and circumstance gave the building, and its location on the main street, made it both attractive and accessible for local visitors. The intimacy of radio, which made Cultural Centre staff into familiar voices in the islands, also drew people to visit. Throughout this era, the Cultural Centre was seen as the place to go to find out what was happening in Vanuatu.

Although Huffman's role was crucial, he was by no means the only person involved in developing VCC programs. Several members of the VCC board made a strong contribution to this development of the Cultural Centre, chief among them Godwin Ligo, who had been recruited to the board by Keith Woodward before Huffman's appointment. Ligo was involved in the fieldworker program and recruited many men to be fieldworkers. Huffman's role was, as Keith Woodward put it, that of an animateur, stimulating and encouraging the interest and involvement of others (pers. comm. 1993).

Although the Vanuaaku Pati was concerned with the revival of *kastom*, party members did not initially perceive the VCC as an appropriate agent for the representation and promotion of *kastom* within the emerging nation of Vanuatu. Grace Molisa, as a senior member of the Vanuaaku Pati and sometime member of the VCC board observed that it was hard to get politicians to understand how the VCC could be used in their aspirations for the preservation and revival of *kastom*. She said that it was hard to get the politicians to understand that politicians merely talk, they don't act, but that the VCC was a venue in which actions could be taken with respect to *kastom* (Molisa pers. comm. 1992). It was Malvatumauri (the National Council of Chiefs) that was seen by politicians of all parties as the main locus of *kastom* in the new political and administrative arrangements for the country. The chiefs in Malvatumauri, men regarded as by definition knowledgeable about *kastom,* were to provide informed advice to the new government in the making of policies. In a debate in the Vanuatu Parliament on November 20, 1985, in which the minister of home affairs proposed a bill concerned with the constitution of the VCC and in particular of the VCC board, two speakers proposed that he consult with Malvatumauri before giving direction to the VCC board. One speaker, Vincent Bulekone, said,

> We made the National Council of Chiefs, which is now part of the Constitution, to be a body which represents *kastom,* and which can give advice and direction to Parliament. So I think it is appropriate that [such an] executive body can and should have consultation with [the Minister] always, before [the Minister] gives any directions about our *kastom,* culture and tradition. . . . [The VCC board] is all right . . . but we shouldn't forget the national body we have created as the body which is responsible for *kastom.* (National Audiovisual Collections, tape 41/246; translated from Bislama)

The Malvatumauri role as the representative of *kastom* in the new nation was one that the Cultural Centre had to negotiate carefully. Huffman says that he always described the relationship as being between older and younger brothers: Malvatumauri the older brother giving leadership and direction, the Cultural Centre fieldworker group the younger brother enacting those directions. In fact, however, Malvatumauri's chosen task of codifying *kastom* posed many problems that absorbed the organization's energies to a considerable extent in early years. In 1983 Malvatumauri published their policy on *kastom;* its forty articles cover issues including land, movement of people between places, language, ceremonies, sorcery, illegitimate children, and adultery (Malvatumauri 1983). The very term "chief" caused considerable difficulties. Early Malvatumauri meetings spent considerable time attempting to define what a chief is. In the compromise solution that was eventually reached, the definition depends largely on *kastom*—a chief has to be recognized and installed according to *kastom* (article 7A)—and hence embodies uncertainty at a different location.

At the conference "Developing Cultural Policy in Melanesia" in Honiara, Solomon Islands, in 1992, Chief Willie Bongmatur, who was at that time both president of Malvatumauri and chairman of the VCC board, presented Malvatumauri as the preeminent locus of *kastom* within Vanuatu. It is the chiefs, Chief Bongmatur said, who deal with conflict over land, marriage problems, and disputes and who are involved in the development of cultural policy. It is true that chiefs, both at local and at national level, deal with disputes. Village courts, for example on Ambae, were presided over by local chiefs, and Chief Bongmatur himself, while president of Malvatumauri, regularly arbitrated interpersonal disputes among ni-Vanuatu brought to him in Port Vila. Overall, the Malvatumauri policy has not had much relevance in everyday life in Vanuatu, but Malvatumauri has consistently introduced issues of *kastom* into the national political arena.

This is, in fact, the crucial distinction between Malvatumauri and the VCC. Malvatumauri represents *kastom* at the national political level. The VCC through various programs, but in particular through the fieldworkers, has acted on *kastom* at the rural level. Larcom, writing in 1982 about the effect of the political reevaluation of *kastom* during the 1970s, commented that "[t]he success of *kastom* as a rubric for national unity will . . . depend on its concrete local resonances" (1982:333). Through the fieldworkers and through Radio Vanuatu, the VCC has located *kastom* in the discussions and the actions of islanders, creating just such local resonances. Assertions of the importance of *kastom* made by the Lini government throughout the 1980s resonated with local projects to practice and revive *kastom*. VCC programs have given substance to political rhetoric.

THE FIELDWORKERS

The number of oral traditions trainees, soon known as fieldworkers, grew steadily throughout the 1980s, so that by the early 1990s there were about forty-five of them. As well as those whom Huffman and other VCC staff members recruited, some men approached the VCC themselves asking if they could become fieldworkers. In many cases they volunteered because they had listened to the VCC radio program. Some joined the group as a result of their participation in the arts festival in 1979. As the fieldworker group became established, the leaders in a particular area (identified in ordinary parlance as chiefs) sometimes approached the VCC and asked to have a fieldworker to represent them. The VCC accepts the advice of local chiefs in appointing a fieldworker. The degree to which fieldworkers have become a recognized group within Vanuatu is reflected in Crowley's Bislama dictionary, which has an entry for *filwoka*. The entry reads "fieldworker (the Vanuatu Cultural Centre has an extensive network of local people who gather historical and cultural information that is stored in Vila)" (1990:78). Not all men appointed as fieldworkers have continued as such. The work is voluntary, and some men are not interested in continuing under such circumstances. Some fieldworkers have died and have been succeeded, sometimes by their own sons. Others have been deposed in political moves within their own communities. Some have moved on to other things: when he formed his government in 1992, Maxime Carlot (by then known as Maxime Carlot Korman) appointed Roman Batik, a former fieldworker, as minister of education. In 2002 the fieldworker program is continuing to develop; the following account describes the situation as it was in 1992.

In nearly all cases, the fieldworkers lived in their own communities, supporting themselves by means of subsistence agriculture, supplemented with a little cash cropping. They were not all community leaders. Some were quite young. Huffman was as interested in recruiting young men who wanted to learn about *kastom* as he was in recruiting older, more knowledgeable men. In some cases men became fieldworkers because of the advantages that accrued to them from doing so. The position carried some cachet; it linked a man into a network that gave him connections in other islands, and it occasionally provided opportunities to travel for training purposes, to Vila and sometimes farther afield. It also provided access to the radio. Some fieldworkers produced radio programs in the islands; they sent these to the VCC to be broadcast in the VCC Saturday night slot. Others sent recordings to be edited and used. Fieldworkers could thus offer members of their own communities access to the radio.

In 1981 Huffman instituted annual training workshops for the fieldworkers. Recognizing the importance of language to the maintenance of local knowledge and practice, he recruited the linguist Darrell Tryon to teach the fieldworkers about language and to direct the workshops, which were funded with Australian aid. Early workshops concentrated on language studies and on *kastom* stories. The 1984 workshop, for example, produced a volume of *kastom* stories, one from each of the twenty-four fieldworkers who attended, each story told in the fieldworker's own language and in Bislama and illustrated by an artist from

Malakula then working for the VCC (VCC 1984). Later workshops took a particular topic, such as pigs or birds; fieldworkers exchanged non-restricted information on these topics and recorded related vocabulary. A volume of the proceedings of the workshop on pigs, held in 1990, was produced in Bislama in 1992 (Tryon 1992).

The fieldworker workshops also involved training in various linguistic and anthropological techniques. Tryon had an ongoing objective to help the fieldworkers produce dictionaries of their own languages, and a large part of each workshop was dedicated to dictionary work. He also taught fieldworkers how to draw up genealogies and imparted some skills in reading and writing, greatly increasing the literacy of the group over a number of years. Tryon and Huffman both contributed to the fieldworkers' discourse about *kastom*. Tryon, for example, always emphasized the nonparty-political nature of *kastom*, representing it as a unifying force in the country. Huffman was always concerned with issues of preservation, with the importance of recording and passing on knowledge while it is still available. The objective of the fieldworker program, reinforced in workshop discussions, was the preservation, promotion, and development of *kastom*.

In workshop discussions Tryon used the term *"kalja"* frequently, and fieldworkers themselves used it, both in the workshops and outside it. Thus James Gwero, speaking to women on Ambae, said that the work of a fieldworker is to "preserve, promote and develop the cultures of each island in our country, Vanuatu" (Gwero n.d. [1992]). While in general it seems that the words *"kalja"* and *"tredisin"* were mostly used by speakers educated in English or French, who tended to draw on those languages when speaking in Bislama, in the case of the fieldworkers the usage reflected the influence on them of the fieldworkers' workshops. For them, *"kalja"* invoked the more extensive discourse about *kastom* in which they participated. It referred to the developed concept of *kastom* with which they operated. Fieldworkers were also concerned with the connotations of the term *"kastom"* in some rural areas. Longdal Nobel Maasingyau, from the Nahai-speaking area of south Malakula, proposed that some other term be found. In his own area, where conversion to Christianity took place only quite recently, *"man blong kastom"* continued to indicate someone who had not joined the church.

Several important figures in the Vanuatu government always

attended the opening and closing of the workshops and spoke about *kastom,* affirming its importance and legitimating it by their presence. At the 1992 workshop, for example, Sethy Regenvanu, the deputy prime minister and minister for justice, culture, and women, opened the proceedings, while Rebecca Wieser, a representative of the Australian High Commission, Roman Batik, the minister for education, and Chief Willie Bongmatur, the President of Malvatumauri, all spoke at the closing ceremony. The head of the Media Services section also came to speak to the fieldworkers during that workshop about the effect of the newly introduced television service. The fieldworkers saw themselves as a group representing and advocating *kastom* within Vanuatu, a group of the same order as the Vanuatu Christian Council, which represents all the mainstream denominations within the country. They had their own executive committee and held their own annual general meeting during each workshop, making recommendations to the government on issues that concerned them.

Each year the workshops began with a session in which every fieldworker reported on the work he had done in the preceding year. The kinds of work in which fieldworkers were involved reflected both their own interests and the extent to which, as a group, they were involved in all VCC programs in one way and another. A sample of reports from the 1992 workshop will give an idea of the variety of fieldworker activity. Titus Joel from the Torres Islands reported that the local chiefs had asked him to write down the family trees of all the people in the Torres Islands; he at that point had completed records for three of the four islands in the group. Jerry Taki of Erromango reported that he had been trying to revive some of the languages on Erromango. He had made an application for funding to the Australian High Commission's South Pacific Cultures Fund. Phillip Tephahae of Aneityum mentioned that he now had a dictionary of 3,250 words of his local language. Many other fieldworkers reported undertaking a small amount of work on their dictionary projects. James Gwero and Simon Garae reported on their involvement in the Women's Culture Project on Ambae.

Several fieldworkers, notably Richard Leona from north Pentecost, had been helping with a project that was set up under the aegis of the VCC in 1990, the Vanuatu Historical and Cultural Sites Survey. This project, funded by the European Community, employed a French and a British archaeologist and several ni-Vanuatu and was designed to

produce a register of historical and cultural sites throughout the country for use in the planning of development projects of various kinds.
Project staff worked through the fieldworkers both in obtaining access
to communities and in carrying out the actual registration of sites
(Yorigmal et al. 1992).

   Involvement in projects of this kind reflects on the extent to which
fieldworkers had become the *kastom* representative for their areas. The
ORSTOM ethnobotanical survey, which recorded fruit and nut trees
in the archipelago for the Agriculture Department over several years in
the 1990s, for example, worked through fieldworkers when entering
new areas. Film crews wanting to shoot footage on outer islands were
usually directed to fieldworkers. In my own project it was James Gwero
who introduced me to the Ambae/Maewo Local Government Council
and set up contacts for me in west Ambae, his own area. Fieldworkers
monitored and sometimes controlled the access of visitors to their
areas, ringing the VCC to check on the credentials of unheralded visitors who expressed interest in *kastom*.

Fig. 8 A group of men fieldworkers at the July 1991 fieldworkers workshop.
From left: Alben Rueben (Malakula), Kolambas Totali (Pentecost), James Gwero
(Ambae), Jeffrey Uliboe (Maewo), and Philip Talei (Malakula).

Some fieldworkers were involved more directly in the practice of *kastom.* Selwyn Liu, from Pentecost, reported at the 1992 workshop on his own pig-killing ceremony, undertaken during the year. Aviu Koli, one of the nation's most feared and respected sorcerers, practiced his skills on behalf of the VCC until his death in 1994. For example, before I and other Australian Museum staff were seconded to the VCC in 1989 to catalogue the collection, Koli undertook measures to prevent the power of the objects in the collection from harming us: we were understood to be vulnerable because we were women. Similarly, when Huffman became seriously and inexplicably ill in 1984, Koli identified the cause as a sorcery object Huffman had recently acquired for the collections that had not had its potency neutralized. Koli counteracted the malevolent effect, and Huffman (who was hospitalized at the time) recovered immediately.

Although itself operated through the medium of Bislama, the fieldworker program always emphasized the importance of local languages. In their own areas fieldworkers worked in local languages, making recordings in them. It is VCC policy to recognize that some recorded material may be restricted information. Fieldworkers marked cassettes of such material with the names of the individuals and "families" who had the right to hear this material, and the VCC undertook to ensure that only those people ever had access to the tapes. Fieldworkers also recorded in Bislama; it is the Bislama material that was used on Radio Vanuatu.

At the 1992 workshop some fieldworkers complained that their cassette recorders did not work or that they were lacking batteries and tapes. While in some cases this represented a legitimate frustration, in others it appeared to be in the nature of an excuse. Some fieldworkers worked very little, both because of personal disinclination and, in some cases, community politics. There were also political undercurrents in the fieldworker group itself—jealousies between islands, for example. As fieldworkers developed skills and understanding about *kastom,* the VCC selected some to send on training courses and projects of various kinds, both inside and outside the country. James Gwero travelled to Hawai'i to work on a project on the impact of the Second World War on the islands.[7] Richard Leona travelled to Australia to work on a language project at the Australian National University. VCC staff attempted to distribute these opportunities among the different regions of the country to minimize jealousy within the fieldworker group. At the same time, Huffman always made explicit use of jealousy in promoting *kastom*. He used news of programs (such as regional arts festivals) in one area to stimulate groups in other areas to similar achievements.

The fieldworker program was successful because islanders were concerned about *kastom*. The VCC provided both training and moral support to the fieldworkers, creating a context in which the discourse about *kastom* could be extended and developed. At the same time, it was the motivation of individual fieldworkers that ultimately made the program successful. But fieldworkers were able to act only insofar as they were supported by the leaders and the members of their own communities: the program worked because individual ni-Vanuatu were interested in their own *kastom* and valued it. The ways in which the VCC developed the discourse about *kastom* enabled people to act. Specifically, through the radio programs and the workshops, the fieldworker program provided a way of talking about *kastom* that enabled people to act on it.

Women without *Kastom*

I have been building an argument, thus far, that the term *"kastom"* does not refer to precolonial knowledge and practice as a whole system—as "culture"—but rather to specific items, aspects, of that knowledge and practice. More importantly, *"kastom"* is a term that confers certain kinds of comparative value. During the colonial era, missionaries, government officials, and other expatriates used *"kastom"* (often as the English "custom") to distinguish local practice from what they identified as their own morally and practically superior practice. Islanders used the term but did not adopt its European connotations. They used *"kastom"* to signify the knowledge and practice that they either valued and wished to maintain or that they rejected in favor of Christianity and development. The term was applied to aspects of indigenous life that became symbolic of the difference between local and expatriate, to being naked as opposed to wearing clothes, to huts as opposed to houses, to the rituals of local life as opposed to the rituals of Christianity. Other indigenous practices such as cooking techniques, not made the explicit focus of morally evaluative comparison, were less likely to be labelled as *kastom.*

The independence movement of the 1970s explicitly valued *kastom* but introduced disputes about how it was to be enacted. Political parties proposed different approaches to the reclaiming of local practice. The syncretic innovations and transformations initiated by Nagriamel and the John Frum movement for example, were opposed to the largely rhetorical claims, made by members of the Vanuaaku Pati, for *kastom* as a symbol and as the basis for national identity. The success of the Vanuaaku Pati established this latter formulation of *kastom* in the newly emerging national self-characterization. Politicians attempted to formalize *kastom* through the creation of the National Council of Chiefs, which in turn attempted to codify *kastom* at a national level.

In broadcasting stories, songs, and ceremonies, radio demonstrated the depth and diversity of local practice. Islanders were genuinely interested in hearing this material, as is demonstrated by the volume of correspondence received by broadcasters. The 1979 First National Arts Festival developed the performative characteristic of *kastom,* providing a venue for the performance of songs, dances, magical skills, carving, and more in an occasion of extraordinary vibrancy and enthusiasm. After independence in 1980, the Vanuatu Cultural Centre took up the responsibility to give substance to the idea of *kastom* by addressing at a particular and local level, through the fieldworkers, questions about the documentation, preservation, and revival of local knowledge and practice. Influenced through their annual workshops by ideas from both anthropology and linguistics, the fieldworkers developed their own discourse about *kastom,* establishing ways in which local practices could be made meaningful and relevant in the new context of the nation. Radio continued to be extremely important to this process, since it was through the Cultural Centre's own program on Radio Vanuatu that the fieldworkers' discussions, and the knowledge and practice that they documented and revived, were made available to the nation as a whole.

Kastom is then the product of the interaction between expatriate ideas of culture and custom and ni-Vanuatu conceptualizations of their knowledge and practice. In precolonial Vanuatu, there was extensive trade in songs, stories, magical and sorcery skills, rituals, and other kinds of skills and knowledge, as well as in objects (Huffman 1996c). At a local level in many areas, it is this tradeable material that people most readily defined as *kastom* (Larcom 1982:333). In precolonial Vanuatu, trade was the prerogative of men. While women did sometimes make very substantial moves at marriage (sometimes even from island to island), in precolonial times men moved back and forth in trading expeditions. While women, in marrying, imported some skills and knowledge, the skills and knowledge that were traded belonged predominantly to men.

The term *"kastom"* can be applied in normal parlance to any set of practices. It is entirely possible to speak of *kastom blong ol waetman* (expatriate *kastom*) or even of *kastom blong Baebol* (Biblical *kastom*). It is, equally, possible to speak of *kastom blong ol woman* (women's *kastom*). There is, however, a distinction between this kind of usage and the sense in which the term is used to indicate ni-Vanuatu identity. Although it is possible to speak of *kastom blong ol woman, kastom* in Vanuatu until the early 1990s referred to male practice. The political disputes of the 1970s were predominantly a male affair, and the practices instantiated as *kastom* and performed on the radio and at the arts festival were primarily male. At least in part, this was because both political debates and radio programs used Bislama.

Until the 1970s, Bislama was the language in which people from different islands communicated with each other as they worked side by side in expatriate employment and was regarded as a language for these contexts only; it was thus primarily a language for men. Although about 10 percent of those employed on plantations were women, the great majority of people who needed to learn Bislama were men. In the early 1970s among the Sa of south Pentecost, men were unwilling for women to learn this language, arguing that learning Bislama would "make whores of our women" (Jolly 1994b:8). The translation of the Bible into Bislama, which Bill Camden began in the 1960s, was influential in broadening acceptance of the language. Radio was also significant, contributing greatly to the standardization of Bislama, which existed in a number of different dialects until the late 1960s. At least initially, radio use of Bislama influenced men more than women, since listening to the radio was primarily a male activity: women's domestic duties made it hard for them to sit down and listen to the radio, and men often listened to the radio in their communal spaces—the men's house or on the village plaza.

EXPATRIATE VIEWS OF WOMEN

Expatriates have often tended to see the status of women in Melanesia as unacceptably low. The Reverend T. Watt Leggatt, for example, writing in the Presbyterian publication *The New Hebrides Magazine* in 1910, says, "The outstanding feature of Woman's position on heathen islands is that of *Inferiority*" (1910:23; emphasis in original). Leggatt saw women's acceptance of this lot as a species of false consciousness: "if in course of generations they have reconciled themselves to the inevitable, and so fitted their necks to the yoke that it is really less galling than it seems to us, their condition is no less pitiable" (1910:22–23). In recent decades arguments among anthropologists about the status and role of women have been extensive, and oft rehearsed. In 1988 Henrietta Moore summarized part of the argument by observing that "even where more egalitarian relations between women and men exist, researchers are very often unable to understand this potential equality because they insist on interpreting difference and asymmetry as inequality and hierarchy" (Moore 1988:2). Her comments apply also to Leggatt and other colonial and postcolonial observers.

Marilyn Strathern introduced a new analysis of these issues into Melanesian anthropology through the publication of her influential study *The Gender of the Gift* (1988). Strathern's project is based upon her proposition that it is useful to understand Melanesian knowledge as fundamentally different from Western understandings. She uses a binary opposition between Melanesia and the West as a heuristic device. She acknowledges that there is no single "society" of the West, but rather uses "Western" to denote anthropological and feminist perspectives and modes of analysis; she suggests that "Melanesia" exists in the sense that the various communities defined by that term are "outgrowths and developments of one another" (Strathern 1988:309, 342–343). Her argument is complex, depending on a number of propositions, which she substantiates in detailed argument. One of the most important of these is the proposition that in Melanesia, "persons are frequently constructed as the plural and composite site of the relationships that produced them" (Strathern 1988:13). She suggests, moreover, that in Melanesia gender is a powerful metaphor, idiom, of relationship. Strathern considers the use of this metaphor beyond the simple constraints of biology, pursuing the way in which practices, actions, can be gendered as male or female. Observing that Westerners "find it almost impossible not to regard the sexes in a permanent relation of asymmetry" (Strathern 1988:330), she argues that in Melanesia "the asymmetry is always there, but men's and women's occupation of these respective positions [as agent or subject] is always transient" (Strathern 1988:332).

Strathern's arguments are helpful in breaking the stranglehold of expatriate perceptions of indigenous distinctions between men and women. Two issues are crucial. One is to grasp the extent to which the assumption of inequality in power relations between men and women is so deeply enshrined in "Western" thought. The second is to take hold of the suggestion that in Melanesia—and, specifically, in rural Vanuatu—a person is the sum of the net of relationships in which he or she is engaged. In east Ambae, a person is named differently in each of his or her relationships. The idea of a singular identity, enshrined in a singular name, is entirely alien to the indigenous system. In each relationship, a person has different responsibilities and obligations and different access to authority or power. Moreover, the kinship system is constructed so that it constantly ramifies to create a kin relationship between any two individuals. Two strangers from diverse areas of Ambae (or indeed from as far afield as Maewo or north Pentecost) can always establish a specific kinship relationship between themselves (for example, as sisters) and will act to each other on that basis thereafter. The suggestion that all men have power over all women misunderstands the specificity of each relationship in such a system—between a daughter and her father, a father's sister and her brother's son, or a wife and her husband.

I do not wish to imply that there were no forms of oppression, exploitation, and cruelty in indigenous practice in this region. Rather I want to point to the extent to which expatriate perceptions and influence located such oppression in a singular relationship between all women and all men. This is not an indigenous perspective. In discussing or recalling the past, rural ni-Vanuatu are far more likely to locate past forms of oppression in the spiritual dimension, to speak about fear of sorcery and about malevolent spiritual power as a dominating and destructive force in the community. Expatriates, generally dismissive of the spiritual realm as superstition, perceived and reported inequality between men and women. They did so in a way that makes it difficult to disentangle the variety of relationship forms that existed in the different parts of precolonial Vanuatu. Clearly, in some contexts and relationship forms, men exerted power over women against the latter's will. Strathern's suggestion of a shifting asymmetry, and shifting symmetry between subject positions rather than between individuals or categories, is helpful in elucidating the nature of relationships in the postcolonial context.

Another crucial assumption, read into indigenous practice in the archipelago by expatriates, is the distinction between public and private or domestic contexts and the further identification of indigenous male contexts as "public" and indigenous female contexts as "private." In many parts of the archipelago, indigenous practice allocated the domain of the *nasara,* the dancing ground or public plaza of a residential community, to men. It was on the *nasara* that much men's practice—songs, dances, rituals—was performed. Expatriates mistakenly perceived a spatial separation—between the men's house and dancing ground and the familial households—as a segregation of the public and the domestic, but in fact the spatial segregation did not exemplify a distinction between two such domains. In some parts of the archipelago women acted on the *nasara;* in others women had their own *nasara;* in all they had their own contexts of community action. Moreover, men were involved in what Europeans would regard as the domestic concerns of house and garden. For example, as Jolly observes, among the Sa of South Pentecost "the most central and public institutions revolved around the sacralisation of domestic life" (1989:222).

Many colonial-era expatriates were firmly committed to the distinction between public and domestic. Missionaries in particular believed that women properly belonged in the domestic domain of the household and deplored their participation in activities outside it. Thus missionary perception of the inferior status of indigenous women was "intimately linked to the observation that they did hard manual work outside the home" (Jolly 1991c:35). As Jolly argues, the creation of a female, domestic, house-centred, sphere was an explicit missionary objective: "wifely domesticity was . . . basic to their ideal of Christian civilisation" (1991c:32).

If missionaries condemned indigenous societies as granting women an inferior position, they also almost universally enshrined their own assumptions about male superiority in the structures they introduced. As churches were established, male missionaries were in charge; their wives held no formal positions. None of the churches permitted women to be ordained or to hold positions of leadership above men. The condominium government had a similar approach, appointing men as chiefs and assessors to broker relationships between specific communities and government agents. The condominium itself was staffed almost entirely by men. For all the rhetoric criticizing the status of women in indigenous practice, it was expatriates who established a formal inequality between all women and all men, on the basis of a public/domestic distinction that they introduced into colonial structures.

This observation draws me back to Strathern's argument. If persons are not individuals, but rather a "site of relationships," then the opposition between society and the individual, which is crucial to much Western thought, breaks down; "society" is not a set of controls over and against the "individual" (Strathern 1984:14), but rather the sum of the network of relationships in which the person engages. A distinction between society and the individual creates, in effect, the possibility of nonsociety: the individual can exist apart from society, in an asocial state, which is called nature. Western models regard the child as born in this natural state and as having to be drawn into society. Consequently, Western women, Strathern suggests, run the danger of appearing as less than full social persons, either because their creativity is understood to be properly in natural rather than cultural matters (such as childbirth) or because they belong to the narrower world of the domestic group, rather than the wider world of public affairs. Thus the distinction between society and the individual introduces a further crucial distinction between culture and nature, a distinction that leads to an association of men with culture and women with nature. Again, this kind of thinking leads to the expectation that men, and not women, are the holders of *kastom.*

The central characteristic of the Vanuaaku Pati model of *kastom,* which became the dominant model in Vanuatu from the mid-1970s, is that it established *kastom* in the colonially introduced public domain of politics and national performance. The connection between men and *kastom* forged during this era was also a connection between *kastom* and the public domain, which was itself dominated by men. The interpenetration of indigenous and exogenous ideas in the construction of this domain is complex. The slippage between the association of the *nasara* with men only and the allocation of the national public forum to men occurred easily and obscured the complex sets of relationships involving both men and women in various local contexts. The creation of a national public forum implicitly adopted Western models of the opposed domains of public and private or domestic, domains that were not relevant in indigenous contexts.

WOMEN IN THE NATIONAL PUBLIC FORUM

During the condominium era, the principal missionary and government activity with regard to women was the establishment of women's groups. Introduced mostly by missionary wives, women's groups were initially set up to teach the domestic arts (and especially the art of sewing fabric to make clothes) and to teach Christian beliefs and principles. In the 1960s the condominium government established a women's interests office, which was concerned with the administration of all women's clubs in Vanuatu. Office staff toured the islands giving advice to women's clubs and running training courses for club members (Aaron et al. 1981:133). After independence the women's interests office became the women's affairs office in the Department of Community, Youth, and Sports. Like the nongovernmental Vanuatu National Council of Women (founded in 1980), the office of women's affairs worked with women through the structure of both church and secular village-based women's groups.

During the 1970s a number of women attempted to introduce women into the public arena of the political process, through participation in the Vanuaaku Pati. Although these women continued to raise the issue of women in politics throughout the 1980s and 1990s, they remained in the minority. Two women—Hilda Lini and Grace Molisa—were particularly important. Hilda Lini, Walter Lini's sister, joined the Vanuaaku Pati in the 1970s and worked as coordinator of the Vanuaaku Pati women's wing and of young people's activities in the party. The Vanuaaku Pati women's organization was intended to "politicise women ensuring grass-roots support for Vanuaaku Pati policies" (Molisa 1980:265). Hilda Lini subsequently became a Member of Parliament.

Until her untimely death in 2002, Grace Molisa was a highly influential figure in Vanuatu, through her involvement in women's organizations, in the Vanuaaku Pati, and in the Vanuatu Cultural Centre. She worked with Walter Lini during the greater part of his prime ministership, mostly as his personal secretary. Her publications, and especially her feminist poetry, have been frequently quoted in studies of Vanuatu. These publications have been less important within Vanuatu than has her active personal advocacy. Molisa was strongly influenced by Western feminism during her studies at the University of the South Pacific during the mid-1970s, and her work reflects a complex mix of Ambaean attitudes, wider Vanuatu experience, and Western feminist perspectives. In 1980 she wrote an essay titled "Women," one of twenty-one essays about the new nation in a volume published by the new independent government (Molisa 1980). Her essay was primarily concerned with the involvement of women in the new nation. She discussed their participation in the Vanuaaku Pati, in the labor force, and in the

Fig. 9 Grace Molisa in her garden at Numbatri, Port Vila. 1994.

professions. She also commented on women's role in "traditional society": "Expected to be industrious, obedient, loyal, submissive, their investment in life and the future is having children, raising a family, and striving to give them a reasonable standard of welfare and prosperity. Constantly burdened, each woman hopes to create the best that is possible for her own social unit" (Molisa 1980:259).

Molisa's analysis implicitly accepted the distinction between public and domestic contexts. She recounted an Ambaean story about a woman who lived as a man and became a highly successful high-ranking chief (with ten wives), but who was eventually exposed (literally) as a woman when someone glimpsed her genitals, demonstrating "that women can undertake many tasks that have been the exclusive preserve of men" (1980:264–265). Molisa's poetry has often also bemoaned the essentially domestic tasks of women: "Women / cook, sew, / feed, clothe / housekeep / homemake / childbear / healthcare / passively / following / orders / instructions / commands" (1987:9). At the same time, her feminist abhorrence for domestic roles was moderated by her sense of the injustices of colonialism. In a speech made in 1978, she said, "Women's liberation . . . is a European disease to be cured by Europeans. What we are aiming for is not just women's liberation but a total liberation" (cited in Jolly 1991a:52).

Molisa was a driving force in the development of the Vanuatu National Council of Women, which was founded in May 1980 at the First National Conference of Native Women with the explicit objective of providing a network for women's groups throughout the nation. Although she described the VNCW as a "gathering of ni-Vanuatu women actively concerned about the exploitation, oppression, suppression, disadvantages, low status, lack of welfare and lack of well-being of the ni-Vanuatu woman and those in her charge" (Molisa 1991:68), Molisa rejected the suggestion that the VNCW was a feminist organization. Rather, she suggested, it was concerned with the welfare of women as mothers, as daughters, and as future mothers; the organization aimed for a humanist national development (pers. comm. 1992). Molisa's project was to bring women into the national public arena, and specifically the political arena. Her preoccupations reflected her position within the urban male-dominated political elite.

When the tenth anniversary of the VNCW was celebrated with a National Women's Festival, Molisa organized a five-day workshop on *kalja* (the use of the term reflecting her educational background). This workshop was offered to delegates as one among twenty-three other concurrent sessions, including Urbanisation and Employment, Sewing Machine Maintenance, and Health (Molisa 1990:33–36).[1] According to Molisa, VNCW leaders recognized that if the organization was to develop, it was "necessary to understand the national situation of women in each culture and each island in Vanuatu" (1990:21). Freely admitting that the workshop did not achieve its goals, and that she herself had not known how to run a "culture workshop," Molisa nevertheless saw the workshop as proving that women have *"kastom, kalja mo tredisin"* (1990:14). Her reflections on the workshop include an analysis of the male domination of *kastom* (which she here speaks of as *kalja*) during the ten years after independence.

> In the last ten years it seems that whenever our leaders have talked about culture they have only spoken about men. They suggest that men have rights in custom, culture, and tradition but women do not. Women are nothing. Men are something.
>
> When there are cultural activities at the national level most of the time only men are given the opportunity to take part. The Cultural Centre fieldworkers are all men. This means that a visitor or an ignorant person would be able to think that in Vanuatu culture is only a male thing. (Molisa 1990:32; translated from Bislama)

In an interview in July 1991, Molisa gave another reason why it was important to pay attention to women's participation in culture: "We've drawn from culture to make the struggle for independence meaningful, but knowing who we are and what we are isn't going to continue if present-day mothers don't have knowledge [about culture]" (pers. comm. July 1991). Thus Molisa's perception of ni-Vanuatu women as domestically burdened has been tempered by her increasing recognition of the importance of *kastom* to the status of women within Vanuatu and to the future of the nation itself.

CREATING WOMEN FIELDWORKERS

Molisa could speak with some authority about the work of the Cultural Centre because she served on its Board of Management during the 1980s. She asserted that for many years there was opposition within the

VCC to the idea of women's *kastom*. Kirk Huffman acknowledged that in this period women's *kastom* was largely disregarded, citing opposition from fieldworkers as one of the factors that inhibited the development of projects relating to women (pers. comm. 1993). There was one small project relating to women implemented in the mid-1980s; Nadia Kanegai obtained an Australian grant through the VCC to document female tattooing practices on Ambae. Kanegai's work resulted in a number of radio programs and eventually in a publication (1994). Generally, Cultural Centre staff, including Huffman himself, were content to focus on projects relating to men only.

Increasingly, however, some fieldworkers began to see the need for female counterparts. By the time the first moves were made toward founding a women fieldworkers' group in 1991, a number of men fieldworkers had already asked for women fieldworkers. Although the Cultural Centre itself is a national institution, working in the national public arena, the fieldworkers were working at a community level. Their grasp of local knowledge and practice was not generalized but highly specific; they worked within, and sought to document, the ways of doing and knowing of their own kin group. Although this knowledge and practice had altered in response to missionary and other expatriate pressures, it was nevertheless founded on indigenous models. In other words, the fieldworkers were in a position to recognize the crucial participation of women in local practice. Fieldworkers operated in contexts in which, while modified in numerous ways, collective "public" concerns continued to be essentially "domestic" and in which the contribution of women in certain subject positions was extremely important. Male fieldworkers were often barred from access to what the women in these positions knew.

Thus national political rhetoric and anthropological ideas about culture encountered specific local understandings of knowledge and practice through the fieldworker program. That encounter modified the idea of *kastom* itself. Specifically, when Cultural Centre staff and the fieldworkers talked about *kastom* they were not talking in general terms about the basis of ni-Vanuatu identity, as it was codified in Malvatumauri's custom policy, but were using the term to refer to the rich diversity of specific local knowledges and practices. In such a context, it became increasingly difficult to separate out men's practice, precisely because indigenous knowledge and practice was constituted in a series of specific kin-based relationships involving both men and women.

By 1990, when Huffman had resigned as curator and been succeeded by Jack Keitadi, the Cultural Centre had been under pressure
from other directions to initiate programs for women for some years.
Aid agencies that had funded VCC programs, and expatriates such as
researchers and museum colleagues, had made such suggestions. There
had also been steady pressure from Grace Molisa, as a member of the
Cultural Centre board, and other women in the government. In the
early 1990s, Kathy Solomon, the secretary of the Vanuatu National
Council of Women, told Jack Keitadi that the VCC should consider
women's *kastom* and institute women fieldworkers (Solomon pers.
comm. 1991). In addition, the Office of Women's Affairs in the Vanuatu
government listed the appointment of women fieldworkers as one of
its planning objectives (Helen Mitchell pers. comm. 1992).

By the time Huffman left, arrangements had been put in place to
employ a woman as VCC education officer. As outlined briefly earlier,
Nadia Kanegai had been studying in Western Australia for qualifications in education, and, in anticipation of her return, Huffman had
arranged, before leaving Vanuatu, for the Australian High Commission
to provide seed funding for the education officer position in the form
of a year's salary. Kanegai was to be the first woman employed in the
museum at a level above that of secretary. Kanegai returned to Vanuatu
in March 1990 and took up the position of education officer, but she
resigned after only a few days. Because by this time her gender had
become more important to thinking about the position than her
planned education officer duties, Cultural Centre staff and management board members saw a need to replace her with another woman.
It was this consideration that made VCC staff and the Board of Management receptive to the proposal that I provide in-country training
for a new appointee, as outlined in the Introduction.

When I returned to Vanuatu in July 1991 to undertake this research
and training program, I found that VCC plans for the project had
evolved further. The position no longer incorporated any education
officer component but had been entirely redirected to the documentation and revival of women's knowledge and practice. Appointment to
the VCC position had been held over until my arrival, and I found that
the appointee was allocated to work with me full-time. By this means I
became a full-time member of the VCC staff (albeit unpaid). The position was retitled coordinator, Women's Culture Project (WCP), and I
became the training officer, Women's Culture Project. My research

became the first WCP program, with the VCC goals of documenting and reviving women's textile production on Ambae. The long-term objective of the WCP was to establish a women fieldworkers group.

Without the formal agreement of the men fieldworkers, the Women's Culture Project could not go ahead. Grace Molisa attended the men's 1990 workshop to advocate this development. Being politically astute, and alert to the proprieties of female behavior in such contexts, she spoke with deferential respect to the fieldworkers, arguing for the institution of women fieldworkers (Darrell Tryon pers. comm. 1990). She talked about the *Kalja* Workshop at the National Women's Festival, which had recently taken place, emphasizing that many of the women delegates did not know (could not speak) about their own *kastom.*

When Molisa finished speaking, only one fieldworker, Aviu Koli, protested. Koli was the most famous and feared sorcerer in Vanuatu at that time (and was also the VCC's official sorcerer). He argued that women have no right to go onto dancing grounds or into men's houses and that therefore women should not be involved in *kastom.* This was a token protest only, as Koli himself admitted to Molisa immediately afterward. He came up to her privately and said that he had made the protest only to represent the standard male viewpoint on the issue, that in fact he did not himself accept the argument (Molisa pers. comm. 1992). By the time I attended the 1991 workshop, with Leah Ture Leo, the first trainee, there were no protests at all: a number of fieldworkers approached us to affirm their support for the program, and, sometimes, to suggest women in their own areas who might be suitable women fieldworkers.

At the time, my ideas about *kastom* were largely informed by anthropological accounts that had been published by that time, and I had little sense of the argument that I have made in the last few chapters. I did not, at the time, see the significance of Koli's protest against the institution of women fieldworkers, nor did I seek him out to ask him to elaborate further.[2] However, retrospectively, it seems to me that his protest came from the heart of the formulation of *kastom* at that time. He specifically associated *kastom* with those community spaces allocated to men—the *nasara* (or dancing ground) and the men's house. That is to say, he specifically linked *kastom* with predominantly male spaces, spaces that had come to be associated with the national public domain.

He assumed that if women are to become involved in *kastom*, then they must enter these male public spaces, and he argued that this would be inappropriate. Why he approached Molisa privately afterward is not entirely clear to me. However, it is possible to take his explanation at face value and to suggest that his own understanding of *kastom* went beyond this formulation, that he did indeed see his protest as replicating a standard perspective that he himself did not share.

While the fieldworkers collectively gave the seal of approval to the establishment of the Women's Culture Project, an individual fieldworker helped to establish the parameters of the Ambae project. The Ambae fieldworker, James Gwero, helped me to set up my fieldwork, making many valuable suggestions to me and Leah Ture Leo and introducing us to key people. Since participating in Peter Crowe's Oral Traditions Training Course in 1976, Gwero had become an active and important fieldworker. He had worked with Michael Allen, Peter Crowe, and Lamont Lindstrom and was well used to the priorities, and the apparent eccentricities, of academic research. He gave me some extremely sage and practical advice about the conduct of the project, the value of which became more and more apparent to me as my own experience grew. Most importantly, it was Gwero who introduced me to both James Anding, the president of the Ambae/Maewo Local Government Council (LGC), and Selwyn Aru, the Ambae/Maewo LGC secretary. Aru was himself familiar with the academic project, having studied at the University of the South Pacific, and had published about issues of land tenure and political developments in Vanuatu (see Arutangai 1987 and also Arutangai 1995).

The Ambae/Maewo LGC was crucial to the project, paving the way for us on Ambae in many different ways. For example, it was Selwyn Aru who requested that we approach the Ambae project from a regional perspective. That is, he expected that we would travel widely through the region to discuss the project with women in all districts. Nearly all the visits we made around Ambae were organized by or through the LGC and the Ambae/Maewo Island Council of Women. On several occasions we travelled with Gloria Tarileo, the women's affairs officer attached to the Ambae/Maewo LGC, who also supported the project. In our roles as VCC staff members we fell into the category of "government official" and were thereby granted a recognizable and acceptable identity. Since Ambaeans prefer to deal with outsiders through the distancing and formalizing mechanism of meetings, this status as government officials proved crucial to the implementation of the Ambae project. It was also, as I discussed earlier, staff of the LGC who, with villagers in east Ambae, urged the appointment of Jean Tarisesei as WCP trainee when Leah Ture Leo resigned from the position in December 1991. After Tarisesei joined the project, her connections with women through the National Council of Women network lent significant legitimacy to the project, as did her own considerable commitment to it.

From my very first discussion with the LGC I emphasized that the project was concerned with women. The local government presented the project as such thereafter, and this presentation affected the form of the meetings we had as we travelled around Ambae. My initial resistance to the formality of meetings subsequently gave way to the realization that but for them we would not have had any access at all to many of the women from whom we obtained substantial amounts of information. Visits to each district were generally orchestrated by the leader of the women in that area (usually the president of the Area Council of Women). A senior man usually appeared at part or all of the meetings to offer formal welcome and thanks, but in general the meetings were attended only by women. As I subsequently discovered, women do not often speak at meetings attended by men, so that this imbalance, which initially I regretted, actually proved to be critical to the kinds of information we were able to obtain. The women with whom we dealt were gratified by our interest in their knowledge and skills and monopolized the more informal contexts of our visits to their areas.

There was thus widespread support for the inception of the Women's Culture Project on Ambae. If the national rhetoric about *kastom* displaced women from its public space, in 1991 there was considerable interest, especially at the island level, on Ambae, in a reformulation of the concept to include women. This resulted from the positive influence of a number of key individuals—Grace Molisa, James Gwero, Selwyn Aru, and Jean Tarisesei in particular—but it also was effected through the supportive cooperation of women around the island.

◎ ◎ ◎ *4*

Ples

In the Introduction I made a comparison between the structure of an Ambae textile and the structure of this book. In that comparison, this short chapter functions like the central seam of an Ambae textile: it provides the point at which the two sides of my argument are joined. Ideas about place *(ples)* are crucial to the formulation of *kastom* in Vanuatu; they are also fundamental to Ambaean knowledge and practice. *Kastom* refers to what people know and do in the archipelago; at the same time, it is itself framed by that knowledge and practice. The relationship between *kastom* and *ples* is extremely important to the claim that women have *kastom* too.

IDEAS OF PLACE

Before the condominium, the archipelago now created as Vanuatu had no identity as a unit from the perspective of its inhabitants. Trade links between the Banks and Torres and the south Solomons, between central Vanuatu and western Polynesia, between Tanna and New Caledonia gave people known horizons that bore little relation to the group of islands now known as Vanuatu. Generally people understood themselves as belonging to a particular place. In the precolonial era this was often a very small area managed by a single landholding kin-group. During the condominium period few inhabitants of the archipelago perceived themselves as New Hebrideans, and quite correctly so, as "New Hebridean" was in fact a legally meaningless appellation (MacClancy 1983:105).

The way in which people's formulation of their place-based identity broadened during the colonial era occurred mainly through the labor trade, which tended to identify laborers on the basis of their island of origin. This means of identification was widely accepted and is now formulated in Bislama as, for example, *man Tanna* or *woman Maewo*. Even so, people had little sense of belonging to a wider polity. Vanuatu's first prime minister, Walter Lini, spent much of the first five years after independence building the idea of the archipelago as a unit, as a nation (Godwin Ligo pers. comm. 1997). This creation of the nation of Vanuatu involved the construction of an image of all the islands in the archipelago as a single entity. The endless maps of that Y-shaped string of islands—to be found on calico, towels, newspapers, and posters—are part of this construction of the nation. This image of the archipelago was also, especially through the radio, created verbally as a linking of islands, as "Aneityum *kasem* Torres."

If the idea of the nation as a place to which one belonged needed to be created, this is not because people attached no importance to place, but rather to the contrary. In most parts of the region, indigenous systems of language, knowledge, and practice involve strong affiliations to place, locally understood and expressed. This connection was first of all evident in language. Most Vanuatu languages utilize an absolute spatial reference system whereby location and movement are described in reference not to the speaker's own location (as in English) but in reference to the landscape. This is a common feature of Austronesian languages: all but three of the 113 languages spoken in Vanuatu are Austronesian. In these languages any reportage of location or movement is made with reference to the actual landscape in which one is. As Nils Bubandt comments of another Austronesian language, this linguistic strategy of locating the subject as a positioned social agent "creates the basis for a spatially defined sense of cultural belonging" (1997:132–133). This system is to some extent incorporated into Bislama grammar (Hyslop 1999:29).

In the spatial reference system of North-East Ambaean, which Catriona Hyslop has described, it is not possible to use a general verb meaning "go" to refer to movement in any direction; rather, "one must always pay attention to the features of the landscape, which determine the appropriate verb" (1999:25). The most basic feature of the landscape, which is crucial to spatial reference systems in most Vanuatu languages, is the distinction between going inland ("going up") and going toward the sea ("going down"). Movement is always connected to height. In North-East Ambaean, directional forms are used even when travelling over sea, where height differentials are no longer relevant. For the speakers of this language, all the islands to the south and east are considered to be "up," and all those to the north and west are spoken of as "down" (Hyslop 1999:38). One cannot speak of oneself or of another as being or as moving except in terms of the physical landscape itself.

The significance of place, especially as the basis for social organization and as a source of knowledge, emerges again and again in ethnographic accounts of Vanuatu. Although ideas about place are framed differently in different areas, a number of commonalities emerge. Thus, for example, locatedness is crucial to the organization of relationships. In many areas, group membership is framed in terms of common residence in a place as much as in terms of kin relationships. Joan Larcom, writing about the Mewun of south Malakula, comments that "while consanguinity may be one viable metaphor for Mewun relationships, it is overshadowed by the relational richness of contiguity—the focal idea of living together in the special sacred place of one's group" (1983: 186–187). She defines contiguity as "a relationship inspired by living on the same land" that is so significant that "non-agnates could, through marriage, gifts, food-sharing and adoption, be permitted to join a new *ples*" (Larcom 1982:334). Peter Lovell, discussing concepts of kinship in Longana, east Ambae, refers to the Longana saying that all coresidents are "born within one fence" and hence should "behave towards one another, and present themselves to outsiders, as if they were close kin" (1980:44). Both Margaret Jolly (on south Pentecost) and Mary Patterson (north Ambrym) agree that residence and nurturance can in effect create a form of kinship equivalent to genealogical connection (Jolly 1994b:96; Patterson 1976:133).

This is not to say that place substitutes for genealogical links, but rather that it is used strategically to create connections. Tim Curtis, also speaking about south Malakula, makes a similar point. He comments, "What is characteristic of this region . . . is the way people use the concept of *ples* (place) as a key metaphor through which their identities and associations are expressed and negotiated. . . . *Ples* is not just a locale or a physical situation, but a powerful idiom and a moral value that validates group affiliation" (Curtis 1999:60).

In south Malakula, a person's key place is the *nasara,* that is, the dancing ground to which they belong. Especially for a man, belonging to a *nasara* establishes rights to use land. Curtis reports that "a *nasara* is like a 'clan,' in that it is an exogamous social unit . . . claiming a common ancestral founder, but it is important to stress the spatial dimension of the term. It is also very much a place, where the founding ancestral spirit resides"; he also comments that "people acknowledge ties of *ples* when unable to trace a common human ancestor" (Curtis 1999:61).

Place is used not only to organize social relations, but also to organize knowledge. Lamont Lindstrom has made an extended study of knowledge on Tanna (1990). His work focuses on the production and control of knowledge in conversation. It is through knowledgeable talk, Lindstrom argues, that men on Tanna achieve political power. This knowledge is so closely linked with place that Lindstrom coins the term "geographic oeuvres" to describe geographic restrictions on who can talk publicly about certain knowledge. He defines a geographic oeuvre as comprising "text-like formulaic statements such as genealogical lists, stories, legends, songs, sets of local names for men, women, and pigs, maps of land plot boundaries, medical recipes, spells, and magical technologies" (Lindstrom 1990:80).

Joel Bonnemaison, also writing about Tanna, inverts this relation in suggesting that the Tannese feel they belong less to a social order than to a place, so much so that "if their social fabric were destroyed, the Tannese would lose none of their heritage—provided they kept the memory of their places" (1994:323). Thus "culture" becomes the outcome, the product of place: in "traditional thinking cultural identity is merely the existential aspect of those places where men live today as their ancestors did from time immemorial" (Bonnemaison 1984:118). Jolly makes a similar connection when she observes that for the Sa of south Pentecost, land "is thought to be the pre-condition of human culture" (1981:269). Such a link was formulated for Jolly by Bumangari Kaon of south Pentecost, who said, "Our *kastom* has been here like a banyan tree since the world broke open. It was here at the start" (cited in Jolly 1994b:21).

The importance of place is also made evident in the significance of ideas about roads.[1] Both *ples* and *rod* were and are deployed strategically and metaphorically at a number of levels. As metaphors, but also very often in practice, roads are about relationships. Many of the Bislama expressions about roads are about either the creation or the limitation of relationships. *Openem rod* often refers to creating a context in which a relationship can grow or develop. By contrast, a *pikinini blong rod*, an illegitimate child, is a child of the road, cut off from a place. It is not a good thing to be only on a road; one must be able to use a road in relation to a place. Bernard Deacon recorded that in Malakula, the place where a path entered a village was important at both a social and ritual level: this point was known as "the eye of the road" (1934:25), emphasizing the significance of the point of connection between road and place.

Place is a resource, a basis of social identity, a source of knowledge; it is also, of course, a source of all the necessities of life — of food and of the materials from which houses, clothing, and all other artifacts can be made. There were many different systems for the allocation of land for use throughout the archipelago, but in general land was held by groups and was allocated to individuals as need arose. Howard Van Trease comments that "traditionally, land was valued for what it symbolised at least as much as for what it produced" (1987:3), but this does not mean that land was an undisputed resource. Access to land could be a source of conflict in the precolonial era, and it was a constant source of friction in engagement with expatriates.

The independence movement linked land to *kastom*. In the meetings of the committee that drew up the Vanuatu Constitution, Walter Lini, then leader of the Vanuaaku Pati, said, "Land is the root of *kastom*. To deny customary owners their land would be to deny *kastom*" (cited in MacClancy 1983:303). The alienation of land was a key stimulus to the independence movement, and the reallocation of land to the people of the place was one of the key points of the new nation's constitution. The Constitution declares, at points 71 and 72, that "all land in the Republic belongs to the indigenous owners and their descendants" and that the rules of custom shall form the basis of ownership and use of land in the Republic."

Inevitably, this new formalization of this connection had an immediate effect on people's knowledge and practice. Paul Gardissat observed that the introduction of this legislation changed overnight the kinds of *kastom* stories people were prepared to tell him (pers. comm. 1997). Once the customary ownership of land was formalized, the stories that could be used to link people to places became a powerful resource in themselves and could no longer be freely told.

LAND, *PLES*, AND *KASTOM*

If the independence movement linked land to *kastom*, it made no particular distinction between land and place. Strictly, *"ples"* means "location," but, drawing on indigenous ideas about a person's place as central to who the person is, this Bislama word also embodies ideas about belonging and identity. The umbrella expression *"man ples"* (person of the place) was brought into wide currency during the 1970s. Derived from the formula for identifying island of origin *(man Ambae), "man ples"* was used to distinguish local people from all expatriates, perhaps especially from the British and French. The lack of specific geographic referentiality in the term made it an effective expression of a regional indigenous identity. While *"man ples"* could be used to express affiliation to a local landholding, or to an island, it was also used to express affiliation to the whole of the archipelago, and to the archipelago as independent nation. In the 1970s especially it encapsulated local claims to land in the context of land alienation for the whole archipelago. The independence movement linked *kastom* to *ples,* asserting the right of people to their land and to their local (place-based) knowledge and practice. Land and place are distinguished in Bislama. The Bislama for land is *graon.*

Although after independence national identity was expressed more precisely in the term "ni-Vanuatu," the term *"man ples"* has continued to have considerable currency. While it is used to assert ownership in land disputes, *"man ples"* more generally conveys the deep connection between people and place, between a person and his or her place. A *man ples* can be distinguished from expatriates by his knowledge and practice, by his *kastom,* and his *kastom* ensures and affirms his rights to his place. *"Man ples"* thus also reflects local understandings of the way in which knowledge and practice are derived from and connected to place.

The connection between *kastom* and *ples* in the ni-Vanuatu claim for independence was part of a global trend to lay claim to land on the basis of cultural connections. The last few decades of the twentieth century saw an increasing deployment of claims to land on the basis that it was inhabited by the claimants' ancestors, not only in settler colonial contexts such as Australia and New Zealand, but also in the Middle East and in Europe. The claim of cultures to places was a key basis for the building of new nations. François Aissav, in composing the Vanuatu national anthem, made this kind of claim in the first verse, *"God i givim ples ia long yumi"* (God gave us this place).[2] Likewise, in designing the Vanuatu flag, Malon Kalontas made a link to the archipelago itself. He commented, "At school I had learned that my country was shaped as a 'Y' . . . so I drew a 'Y'" (Ripablik blong Vanuatu 1994:3).

If there has been a global trend to lay claim to place on the basis of cultural connections, at the same time converse developments, such as massive population movements, have resulted in the disassociation of cultures from places. In anthropology this has led to an increasing focus on ideas about space, place, and landscape, which Gupta and Ferguson attribute in part to a loss of faith in the idea of "cultures" as bounded entities, a recognition that such boundedness is a more literary fiction than a natural fact. The days of ethnographic maps that located cultures in delimited spaces ("the Nuer" live in "Nuerland") have, they argue, passed (Gupta and Ferguson 1997b:34). Investigating how an ethnography beyond "cultures" might proceed they address "questions of place and the way that culture is spatialised" (1997a:3). In other words, because an isomorphism between place and culture can no longer be assumed, the relationship between them has begun to be problematized. They ask how "understandings of locality, community and region are formed and lived" (1997a:6). For them, this shift in perspective has a political dimension: "the presumption that spaces are autonomous has enabled the power of topography to successfully conceal the topography of power" (1997b:35).

Many researchers have taken a less political starting point, attending to "the way social knowledge is framed and vested in particular landscapes" (Fox 1997:1) and "the meaning imputed by local people to their cultural and physical surroundings" (Hirsch 1995:1). Such analyses of place and space generally attend to the language with which this material is discussed. Terms such as "landscape," "land," "place," "space," "ground," and "territory" are differently distinguished by a variety of authors. Hirsch, for example, focuses on the term "land-

scape," which for him entails a relationship between the foreground
and background of everyday life, in which landscape emerges as a cultural *process* (1995:5). This analysis of terminology attempts to distinguish the different ways people relate to places and leads to clear distinctions between terms such as "land" and "place": land becomes the
physical reality that can be owned and used, place becomes the focus for
meaning, memory, and knowledge to which a person might belong.
Even though *ples* and *graon* are different words, in the 1970s and early
1980s, this kind of distinction was not made articulate in Vanuatu. The
connection between *kastom* and *ples* was part of the justification for the
claim for local control over land. To belong in a place was, properly, to
own it.

Land ownership proved the subject of many disputes in the new
nation, all the more so as cash cropping turned land into a new kind of
economic resource and as population growth put pressures on fallow
ground. In the early 1980s Larcom (1982, 1990) argued that the attempt
to formalize local practices of land ownership, identified as *kastom*, into
principles that could be invoked in courts of law, had created a "legitimation crisis" in Vanuatu. She illustrated her point by documenting
dissension among the Mewun of Malakula about "the validity of past
practices and correct *kastom* behaviour" (Larcom 1990:187). In that
kastom validated the ownership of land, it became a resource for the
disputation of specific instances of land ownership.

It is here that the Cultural Centre introduced several new ideas into
the national discourse about *kastom*. Both Kirk Huffman and Darrell
Tryon have strongly opposed perspectives that suggest that the *kastom*
with which the Cultural Centre deals can be a source of dispute.
Although at one level Huffman always held that disputes and jealousies
are themselves part of *kastom*, he took care that the VCC was not drawn
into disputes about *kastom*, especially in connection to land ownership.
This attitude has become explicit Cultural Centre policy. In 1992, when
Jacob Sam Kapere taught Jean Tarisesei various aspects of VCC work,
he warned her to be alert in recognizing when she was being asked to
record "family business" as *kastom* and not to record information
about land. To do so would lead to rows. Kapere commented that it was
legitimate to record family histories, but that such recordings should
not be marked for public access in the audio-visual archive but should
have a restricted status and be available only to the families themselves.

VCC programs acknowledge a connection between *kastom* and place, but they are designed to avoid the detail of dispute about land ownership. The mediation of disputes about land and other matters has always been the responsibility of local community leaders (generally known as chiefs). Although some fieldworkers are also chiefs, the two roles are treated as distinct at the level of dispute mediation. In their VCC work, fieldworkers are expected to avoid entering into land disputes. Here the importance of the annual fieldworker workshops can be recognized: in them certain key aspects of the VCC view of *kastom* are annually rehearsed and affirmed.

There is a further aspect to the relationship between *kastom, ples,* and land. One of the preoccupations of early anthropological commentary on *kastom* was the degree to which the term could "mean (almost) all things to all people" (Keesing 1982:297). These early discussions tended to perceive this inclusiveness as a problem, commenting, for example, on the dissonance between national rhetoric and diverse local conceptualizations. Larcom, referring to the upheavals before independence, observes that

> *kastom* could divide as well as unify, as the Tanna and Santo secessionist movements demonstrated. . . . Since the revolts, the government has increased its commitment to a national body of *kastom* as a way of smoothing over local divisions. While a harmony of national and regional meanings would be crucial in any new nation, it is perhaps particularly so in Melanesia, where localism, potentially a force for division . . . is also a basic strength, creating for many citizens their sense of orientation and identity. (Larcom 1982:333).

The most significant development in the formulation of *kastom* since independence has been the affirmation of regional diversity within *kastom.* Largely as a result of the influence of the Cultural Centre, conveyed through Radio Vanuatu, *kastom* was constructed both as a source of national unity and at the same time as a legitimate expression of local identity. Huffman had a handwritten placard that read "unity in diversity" on the wall of his VCC office. Although in the cheerful chaos of that office the words had no striking effect, they seemed to sum up an attitude that Huffman implemented in all his talk about *kastom.* The idea of the diversity of *kastom* had already been implicit in the *kastom* radio programs that Ligo and Gardissat produced. When the VCC took over the program, this perspective was all the more evident: material submitted by fieldworkers for radio programs was explicitly characterized as the *kastom* of a particular place, rather than, for example, the *kastom* of a particular group or of the speakers of a particular language. The two national arts festivals (in 1979 and 1990) provided contexts in which regional differences in *kastom* could be publicly affirmed, and presented *kastom* as reflecting the diversity of practice in places. After independence, several islands such as Pentecost and Malakula celebrated the regional diversity within their shores in smaller arts festivals. The fieldworker program itself, which characterizes each fieldworker as knowing about, and working on, the distinctive *kastom* of his place, emphasizes the diversity of *kastom*. Each fieldworker speaks about the practices and beliefs of his own place. The formulation of *kastom* presented by the VCC emphasizes regional diversity within a national identity.

If the Cultural Centre discourages fieldworkers from dealing with place as land, in the sense of land ownership, they also do not deal with it reflexively as an ideology of belonging. Instead, the difference that place creates between people is the basis of the differences that the fieldworkers discuss. That is to say, since the visible and performative aspects of *kastom* are shared between the fieldworkers in workshop sessions, making knowledge communal and illuminating similarities in *kastom,* separate identities are defined by place. The Cultural Centre has thus introduced an implicit distinction between land and place in the contemporary formulation of *kastom.* Land, subject to ownership (however formulated), can be a source of dispute. While local knowledge and practice, invoked and disputed in conflicts over land, can be described as *kastom,* the *kastom* with which the Cultural Centre deals is explicitly characterized as uncontroversial. In the Cultural Centre context one fieldworker cannot dispute the knowledge and practice reported by another because each reports on his own place. *Kastom* is characterized by regional differences: different *kastom* derives from different places. This position is made possible by the existence of the Vanuatu National Council of Chiefs. Malvatumauri sets out the arbitration of disputes as a responsibility of chiefs at local and national levels. Thus it deals with *kastom* and land, while the Cultural Centre deals with *kastom* and *ples.*

This distinction has considerable importance for the VCC's program to extend *kastom* to include women's knowledge and practice. By disconnecting *kastom* from issues of land ownership, which in independent Vanuatu is characterized as a male practice (Bongmatur 1991:154), and identifying it instead as place-based knowledge and practice, the Cultural Centre defined *kastom* as something to which any ni-Vanuatu, male or female, could lay claim.

5

Ambae: On Being a Person of the Place

Leah Ture Leo and I moved to Ambae in August 1991 to commence the WCP Ambae project. After a series of visits to the Ambae districts of Nduindui, Lombaha, Longana, and Lolovoli, we moved in November 1991 to the Longanan hamlet of Vunangai, part of a collection of hamlets designated as Lovonda. We chose Lovonda, which is on the coast at the southern end of Longana, both for practical reasons (it is situated at the intersection of two roads, and there was a truck based there that we could hire) and because Jean Tarisesei lived there and was interested in and supportive of the project. Through a connection of Ture Leo's we were able to rent a very good house, owned by a hamlet member who lived and worked in Port Vila. Lovonda comprised then about ten hamlets, scattered over an area of about two square kilometers, linked by paths through fallow bush, coconut plantations, and occasional gardens. From the coast it was easy to see Pentecost and Maewo across the sea and, on a clear day, as far south as the island of Ambrym.

According to one of the stories about Ambae's origins, the island was created by the culture hero Tagaro. He was travelling from Maewo to Santo, taking yams to feed his pigs there. His canoe turned over in rough seas, and, impatient, he told it to stay where it was. The canoe became the island. From a distance, this is how Ambae looks: like a large upturned canoe, the long dome of the dormant volcano, Manaro, creating the curved bottom of the canoe. To the north and south of the island the land falls precipitously from cone to sea like the sides of the canoe, while to the east and west—the bow and stern of the boat—the land slopes more gently toward some plains. Ambaeans live on the coastal plains and on the lower slopes of the volcano.

Ambae is more than thirty-nine kilometers long and at its widest point, fifteen and a half kilometers across (fig. 10). The dome of the island, which rises to 1,496 meters, is almost always covered in cloud above about 450 meters, shrouding the uninhabited part of the island. In the flat curve of the very top of the island, in the crater of the volcano, two lakes lie side by side, one green and one blue, separated by a spit of land three hundred meters wide. A third and smaller lake lies at a lower altitude, slightly to the west of the two main lakes. Tagaro, fleeing from a man on Maewo whom he had enraged with a theft and an insulting practical joke, retreated forever into a cave by these lakes, and this place is the place of the dead. Most Ambaeans have never been there in life, although it is only a several hours' climb from the various "last places" —the highest and farthest villages. Shrouded in cloud, Manaro is also shrouded in other senses, dominating the known spaces of the coastal plains and its own lower slopes, itself aloof, unknown.

The coastal plains are now largely planted with coconuts. In some plantations secondary vegetation runs wild under the palms, but in

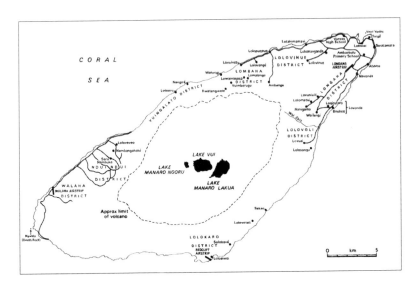

Fig. 10 Map of Ambae.

others cattle graze, and short-cropped grass stretches away under the trees as in a well-ordered park. Neat fences of cut stakes and barbed wire mark the borders of plantations, and where vehicular roads pass through them, there are barbed-wire and stake gates, sometimes with rough-and-ready cattle grids set underneath them. In the north and south of the island the narrow coastal plains are cut through with creek beds of smooth, worn stone, tumbled with boulders. When it rains in the hills these creeks suddenly become raging torrents, and there are many stories about people who were swept away by them. Higher in the hills luxuriant vegetation clings to steep ridges and plunging ravines. Walking along a narrow track one finds oneself on a level with the tops of tall trees growing only a meter or so away but from far below, and the sea seems vertiginously almost within reach, a long way down, but arching up to a high horizon.

The island's coastline is inhospitable, generally lined with broken volcanic rocks. Apart from a coral reef at the eastern point, the seabed falls steeply away from the land. Copra boats call only at a few safe anchorages along the steep and difficult coast. It is possible to travel around Ambae by copra vessel or small boat, but in the early 1990s the cost was substantial, much more than that of a plane ticket, and boats were only used to transport large numbers of people. Ambaeans are not

Fig. 11 Ambae, viewed from central Maewo in September 1999. Clouds almost always obscure the top of the island, where the volcano crater lakes lie.

oriented toward the sea. They rarely travel on it or fish in it. People living by the coast use features of the shoreline itself, most notably the freshwater springs that rise and fall with the tide and are found among stones at the shoreline, but the sea itself is in effect outside their territory.

Ambaeans divide the island into a number of named districts, each of which contains a section of coastline and which radiate from Manaro like uneven slices of cake. Before the influence of missionaries, employment, and education, these districts constituted territories beyond the borders of which their residents very rarely travelled. Indeed, W. Rodman reports that people did not even travel very far within them (1973:37). In the 1990s, many Ambaeans had travelled to other islands of Vanuatu, but they often had not visited districts other than their own. The population was concentrated on the coastal plains in the east and west, in the districts of Longana, Nduindui, and Walaha and in Lombaha. In 1989 the National Population Census recorded Ambae's population as 8,583 (Statistics Office 1991b:157), with a national population growth rate of 2.4 percent. Ambae villages always seemed full of tiny children; in 1989, 34.3 percent of Ambaeans (more than 2,500 people) were under ten years of age. The island is divided between Anglicans and members of the Church of Christ, with occasional Catholic and Seventh-Day Adventist outposts (Tarisesei 2000). Longana, where the WCP was based, is Anglican.

District boundaries are not clearly marked and are comprehended in nonspecific terms by most people.[1] From her study of landholding in the Longana district in 1978, M. Rodman produced a map that clearly shows the borders of land plots throughout the district but does not show the full length of Longana borders with adjacent districts. Longana borders are roughly defined by geographical features—the ravine of a creek bed, the tops of a spine of secondary volcanic cones. In fact at the time of Rodman's survey, the border between Longana and the Lolovinue district was under negotiation and was still disputed in 1982 (1987a:27, 56, 84). Thus although each district is known by name, its precise delineation would appear to be important only where cultivated land lies adjacent to settled areas of another district. While districts are framed by landscape, differences in dialect and practice, which are recognized by the inhabitants, occur from one to the next. The most significant differences are between the districts in the west and east, that

is, between the two districts to the west of the volcano Manaro (Walaha
and Nduindui) and all other districts, including the southwestern district of Lolokaro.[2] The people of Walaha and Nduindui are distinguished from those of the rest of Ambae by the language they speak
(Nduindui) and by some significant differences in their practices.

In the early 1990s the various districts were linked by several means
of transport. Vehicular roads joined east Ambae from the eastern border of Lolovoli to the eastern borders of Lombaha, while in the west
roads extended through Walaha and Nduindui both north to the borders of Vuingalato and south to the edges of Lolokaro. Four-wheel drive
utility trucks known as taxis were based in these districts; people hired
them to transport copra and sometimes to carry themselves on various
journeys. The greater part of the north and south could be reached
only on foot.[3] There were airstrips in Longana, Walaha, and Lolokaro.
Vanuatu's internal airline, Vanair, operated several services each day
except Sunday out of Longana and Walaha; planes landed at Lolokaro
twice a week, should there be passengers requiring them. Passengers
were predominantly ni-Vanuatu: government officials, school students,
and private individuals.

Although Ambaeans rarely entered one another's districts, they did
travel without hesitation to a number of locations that had become
common territory. These were associated with the postindependence
identity of Ambae as a single unit: the local government council headquarters at Saratamata in east Ambae, the three airstrips, and the small
commercial center of Lolowai. In 1991–1992 Lolowai was a scattering
of a few buildings on the shore of a beautiful bay created by a small volcanic crater at the easternmost tip of the island. It comprised a post
office, a hospital, a small fisheries extension center, the headquarters of
the Anglican Church, a place where vehicles could be mended, and four
or five trade stores.

Saratamata, the location of the local government council, the police,
and other government offices, is a few kilometers away from Lolowai,
on the road to the airstrip. Local government staff and other government employees (who work for the Agriculture Department, the Education Department, Fisheries, and the Development Bank) all have
houses there. When I first arrived there in August 1991 I found a neatly
maintained, peaceful settlement of about eighteen houses where the
Vanuatu and Ambae / Maewo flags were raised each morning by a uni-

formed policeman. There were only two expatriates resident in east Ambae at that time, a Japanese man from the Development Bank and a UN development adviser from Ghana. Both lived very quietly at Saratamata.

Vureas High School and Ambaebulu Primary School, both of which are boarding schools, were in the vicinity of Lolowai and Saratamata respectively. The Anglican Church also maintained two educational establishments, the Torgil Training Centre and Tunsissiro, where Anglican Brothers from as far afield as the Solomon Islands were trained, both of which lay between Saratamata and Lolowai. In this same area there were several hamlets of people from Pentecost Island who came to Ambae originally to work (for example, in the hospital), and stayed, acquiring land from local landholders.

In the early 1990s east Ambaeans quite commonly travelled to the Longana airstrip to send or take delivery of airfreighted parcels exchanged with relatives elsewhere in the country. They also visited the local government council and the post office to use the two public telephones, one at each, and to make purchases in the adjacent trade stores. These journeys were all a matter of a single day. The only place people

Fig. 12 Cargo boat in Lolowai Bay, east Ambae. September 1991.

felt comfortable to stay overnight was the hospital, where each district maintained its own resthouse. When people entered districts other than their own, they generally did so in connection with the common interests symbolized by Lolowai and Saratamata. They travelled with political campaigns, with church groups, or to attend government training courses being held in some particular village. They met and got to know one another on such journeys and at meetings, workshops, and training courses held at Saratamata and Torgil.

Outside these contexts, Ambaeans often expressed suspicions of people from other districts. I was often warned that I might be the victim of poisoning and sorcery when I travelled to another district, and I often heard criticism of people in other districts as being, for one reason or another, no good. In the past, Ambaeans practiced district endogamy (Rodman and Rodman 1978:38); in the 1990s marriages between districts remained an exception. Travel from district to district took place in the context of trade and ceremony. Men established relationships of patronage and assistance with men in other districts to facilitate their own achievements in the status-alteration system, which absorbed much of their energies. As the status-alteration system has declined in importance, these connections between men have become less significant.

There were thus two systems, or uses of space, on Ambae, in 1991–1992. The traditional system did not permit people to roam into each other's places but allowed formal travel and engagement between different areas based on trade in both goods and knowledge. The new contexts created by the condominium and the nation—the schools, the hospital, stores, roads, airstrips, and government offices—were excised from this system and operated independent of it, creating common territory where no common territory existed before. The exogenous distinction between public and private had thus been formalized spatially, in such a way that public space is the common space created by the new contexts of services and communications. All the land held and managed in the indigenous system, all the rest of the island, was effectively private and was not accessible to others without specific reason.

It is significant then, that the North-East Ambaean term used for a number of these common spaces is "*sara*." "*Sara*" is a word that appears in many Vanuatu languages to refer to a plaza or open space, sometimes in a settlement, sometimes separate in the bush. The word is often translated as "dancing ground," since these plazas are used for dancing as well as (or as part of) exchanges, ceremonies, and meetings. *"Sara"* has entered Bislama with a common Bislama prefix, becoming *"nasara."* In some areas of Vanuatu the *sara* or *nasara* is a highly restricted place, never used for anything apart from the ceremonies of the place, even for meetings. In some places, such as southwest Malakuka, a *nasara* is also the central embodiment of a land-owning group: one identifies who one is by naming one's *nasara*. In Ambae, a *sara* is not usually ritually restricted. It is a word that can be translated as "field," meaning "open space": describing the places where men's status-alteration rituals occur on Ambae, W. Rodman translates *"sara"* in that context to mean "ceremonial field" (1973:185).

Thus for Ambaeans, an open space in a hamlet becomes a *sara* when it becomes the site of a meeting, an exchange, or a ceremony such as a marriage; otherwise it is just the hamlet yard.[4] The word *"sara,"* then, is used for spaces where people meet outside the immediate contexts of residential community life. A *sara* was always under the authority of the senior man in the hamlet (who might be an accomplished and widely recognized leader), but it was, with roads, the most accessible of all places (M. Rodman pers. comm. Sept. 1999). It is thus the term closest in meaning to "public space" in North-East Ambaean. The word has also been adopted to describe some of the new spaces created in the colonial and postcolonial era such as football field (*sarai moli*, literally, "field orange," i.e., "field ball") and airfield (*sarai aka lolo*, literally "field for flying canoe"). It is also incorporated into the chosen name of the local government headquarters, Saratamata. *"Tamate"* means both "peace" and "law," so the name of the settlement means "field of peace/law." While the application of the word *"sara"* to these places evidently reflects on their character as open spaces, nevertheless, these are also the most accessible of spaces in the island, as *sara* were in the past. M. Rodman suggests that these new *sara* are like the former ones in that they are under the authority of the government (pers. comm. Sept. 1999)—ultimately the prime minister as leader of the nation.[5]

RESIDENCE PATTERNS AND LOCAL ORGANIZATION

In describing themselves, Ambaeans use a hierarchy of names. They identify themselves to other ni-Vanuatu as *man Ambae* or *woman Ambae*. To other Ambaeans they identify themselves as belonging to a district—*woman Longana*. To members of the same district they identify themselves by the hamlet in which they live—*man Loqirutaro*. This terminology suggests an identity between the different place-derived designations people use for themselves; all the places are of the same order. This concept of place is written into the languages of both east and west Ambae: "the word for place *(vanue)* can refer to the island *(vanue)*, the district *(loloevanue)*, the hamlet *(tokagi vanue)*, or to someone's piece of land *(mo vise vanue)*. *Vanue* is not land *(tano)*, it is lived space in which people and place are part of each other" (M. Rodman 1987a:35).[6]

Michael Allen, writing about west Ambae, makes the same distinction between *vanua* and *tano:* "Land when thought of as a substance, i.e., earth, is called *Tano*, but land as a social reality, i.e., in relationship to an individual or a group, is called *Vanua*" (1969:132). This distinction between *vanua* and *tano* to some extent parallels the distinction between place and land. The Bislama word *"ples"* is used by Ambaeans in the same way as *"vanue,"* to refer to the island, the district, an area of a district (as in the hill area of the Longana district), a village, or a hamlet. However, as Catriona Hyslop points out, in North-East Ambaean *"tano"* also embodies ideas of place in the sense that one is or becomes part of a place through eating the food that is grown in the ground there. Thus, when a woman is married to another area, that area is referred to as *tanona* meaning "her place"—the ground to which she is attached—not *vanuana* (Hyslop pers. comm. 1997). This usage again reflects the importance not just of residence, but of eating food grown in a place, to belonging there.

Commentators have conventionally made a distinction between "patrilineal west Ambae" and "matrilineal east Ambae" (see M. Rodman 1987a:27). Both Webb (1937:73) and Allen (1969:49) report, however, that west Ambaeans consider themselves to have lost the matrimoieties and matriclans they once had and to which people in east Ambae still belong—that they share a common identity with east Ambaeans the exact nature of which has been lost. My account in this and following chapters refers predominantly to east Ambae, drawing on data obtained in the districts of Lolovoli, Lolovinue, and Lombaha, but focusing on coastal Anglican Longana.[7] As it happens, Lovonda is a short walk down the hill from Wailengi, the village in which Margaret and Bill Rodman undertook anthropological fieldwork for many years. I draw on their publications here to supplement and illuminate my own data.[8]

Throughout east Ambae people are organized by their membership of dispersed exogamous matrimoieties known as Tagaro and Mwerambuto. Each moiety is further divided into dispersed matriclans. Matriclans are also named, the name referring to the apical ancestor of the clan. Membership of the moieties and the clans enables east Ambaeans to identify each other by kin terms even when an actual connection cannot be traced.[9] A person from one district entering a village in another needs only to establish the kin term to be used for one person there to be able to determine his or her relationships with all other residents. Thus when I travelled around Ambae the Longanan women who came with me would always explain to those we met who my adoptive Longanan parents were, so that my relationships with people in those villages could fall into place.

Moiety membership is critical to the way in which east Ambaeans who are residentially contiguous organize their relationships. By contrast, membership of the matriclans is not salient in everyday life. Allen argues, in fact, that "instead of reinforcing local solidarity, clan membership is used by both men and women in seeking followers, trade partners or protectors in remote communities" (1981b:17). People sometimes pursue a kind of intellectual interest in the history of the descent associations, in the stories of their founding ancestresses. In some cases, the ancestress is a figure from a myth (for example, the daughter of a culture hero), whereas in others she can be identified in the historical past. Thus a man who went to Queensland during the era of the labor trade (circa 1860–1900) returned with an Australian Aboriginal wife. Her descendants constituted a new matrilineal descent association: as a matter of nice irony it was into this descent association that I was myself adopted.

Clans are not significant in everyday life, but women are very concerned with the continuation of their more immediate female line, known as *garo* (rope) in North-East Ambaean, *laen* in Bislama. Women crave daughters and treasure them. They talk about this not so much in terms of the continuity of a matriclan but rather in relation to their own immediate family, the continuity from their mothers through their own and their sisters' daughters. I use the word *"laen"* in this sense, to refer to close relatives who are also joined by their moiety membership.

While a person's moiety identity is inherited from his or her mother, land is more often inherited from the father than from the mother's brother, and residence is patrilocal for men, virilocal for women. Land and moiety are therefore disassociated. Before mission influence changed settlement patterns, Ambaeans lived mostly in the hills in dispersed hamlets (W. Rodman 1973:37). In the 1990s hamlets were still built on the land of the senior male resident, but on land selected for its proximity to a church building. These hamlets might cluster together in such a way as to give the appearance of a village, but each hamlet had its own name and separate identity. A number of hamlets grouped together by their joint affiliation to a parish might have been identified by a single name, which served as a village name but which was generally derived from the name of one hamlet. Hamlets could also be built quite separately from each other.

Each hamlet is made up of the households of a number of closely related males, most often those of several brothers and their sons. It sometimes happens that there is only one household in a hamlet, but there may be seven or eight. A household usually comprises a man, his wife, and their children. Each household will have its own sleeping house and separate kitchen. W. Rodman reports that formerly hamlets shared a common cooking area and had a men's house (1973:37). Today only some hamlets have a men's house, but most have an open-walled shelter in which everyone may sit and that has a stone oven hearth used on communal occasions. Men usually also have some space (frequently under a tree) where they meet regularly to drink kava.[10] There is also generally an open area that is used as a *sara* when there are exchanges or other rituals to perform. Some hamlets have a more evident open area than others, a fact that today is likely to reflect how recently the hamlet hosted a major social occasion. Generally both hamlets and houses are private territory. Only specified categories of kin enter a person's house, and residents of one hamlet do not visit another hamlet casually. The pattern whereby people do not enter districts other than their own is reflected on a micro level by this ethos of residential privacy.

In most cases hamlets have nonresident members, usually men who are working elsewhere in the country but who retain their house in the hamlet and return for holidays, most often at Christmas. In some cases the man alone is absent; in others, both he and his family are. Children are often absent, at boarding school or living with relatives elsewhere. People also move about locally. Young men move out of their parents'

houses and find another building in which to live, often outside hamlet fences. Several members of a family will go and live at the hospital if
one of them is ill. A pregnant woman frequently returns to her mother's
hamlet for several months. During marital disputes, one spouse might
move to another hamlet for a period. Margaret Rodman studied "the
very high velocity of movement" in and out of a Longanan hamlet over
a period of eight months in 1978–1979 through a monthly census. She
records that from a base population of 68, 113 people arrived in or
departed from the hamlet of Wailengi during the census intervals (M.
Rodman 1987a:36).

Hamlet residence is also mobile. Margaret Rodman (1987b) records
a constant flux in the location of buildings within a hamlet, and the
hamlets themselves also appear and disappear. A major dispute between
hamlet coresidents may lead to some or all residents moving away,
either to new hamlet sites or to join relatives in another established settlement. A new hamlet will have its own name, and the combination of
people who live there may be different from the combination that
existed in earlier hamlets. Rodman argues that "a person's place in the
narrowest sense is his or her hamlet" (1987a:36), but if this is so the
affiliation between person and place cannot be so much with a fixed
point in the landscape, a hamlet site, as with the hamlet as a current
manifestation of the connection between person and *ples*.

Hamlet composition is fluid, and so is parish affiliation. When the
residents of a hamlet attend a particular church, then by that attendance
they make themselves part of a larger group, for which I use the term
"village." The village is the basic unit of the local government system
and is thus a secular as well as a church-based unit. Each village has a
village council, which organizes communal activities and from which
representatives are drawn who participate in the wider local government system. In the village in which I lived, the village council met on
Sunday morning after church, the only time at which (in theory) all the
residents of the village gathered together. Village councils, which have a
formal structure of office bearers (chairman, secretary, treasurer), manage secular, nontraditional activities such as the building of a community hall, for which they raise money through work parties and fund-
raisings, and also arrange communal events such as a joint meal on
Easter Sunday. Community halls and church buildings constitute common territory within a village, in much the same way in which Sarata-

mata and Lolowai are common territory for the residents of the various districts.

The structure of the Ambae/Maewo Island Council of Women parallels that of the local government council, and, at least in theory, each village has a women's club that feeds into an area council of women, and through the island council of women to the Vanuatu National Council of Women. Vanuatu was in 1992 setting up a similar structure for a National Council of Youth, and Malvatumauri (the National Council of Chiefs) is also arranged in a structure based on the chiefs in local villages. Neither of the latter two organizations had any presence in the village in which I lived.

Membership in parishes and hence in village councils is a matter of personal decision, and active involvement in them cannot be enforced. A perpetual theme of discussion is that of cooperation. I often heard Ambaean women discuss, for example, whether women in their own or another village cooperate sufficiently to be able to run a women's club. During my residence in the hamlet of Loqirutaro, Lovonda—whose residents attended the nearby Anglican church of St. John's and participated in the Havutu Village Council—several nearby hamlets broke away from the church of St. George's and the associated Waisilongi Council after a dispute with a man they considered too dominating and joined St. John's/Havutu instead. St. John's/Havutu accommodated the significant influx of new members without difficulty, and the catechist who came with them immediately started taking part in services at St. John's. It is even possible for half a hamlet population to be involved in one parish while the other half attends elsewhere. Parishes and village councils do not constitute fixed local groups.

If there is no fixed local group created by residence patterns or by parish and village council membership, there is also no fixed local group created by the way in which east Ambaeans organize their social interactions. Each person stands at a point in the network of both consanguineal and affinal relationships that connect the whole population of east Ambae. When a person decides to take part in one of the formal occasions of social life, that person makes a decision about which relationships he or she will privilege by the way in which he or she participates. In some cases the relationships people choose are obvious: a woman whose real brother is being married will take part in the marriage as a sister. In others the person has more distant and tenuous links with the various principals in the occasion and can actually choose which links he or she will enact. Thus one woman I knew was in a position to take part in a marriage both as a father's sister of the bride and as a sister of the groom. She decided to take the latter course, even though the bride's family had made a specific request to her, as a father's sister, to contribute a bush knife to the goods the bride was sent with to her new home. Her involvement was the result of her own decision.

Husbands and wives, members of different moieties, have their own set of relationships and do not necessarily act together, but rather on their respective consanguineal ties independently of each other. In the case just instanced, the woman's husband chose not to participate at all in the marriage and did not attend. In exchanges husbands and wives make presentations from their own independent resources, even on those occasions where they are acting in their role as parents.

Although the decision to participate in such an occasion is made possible by kinship relationship, the power of the relationship to invoke involvement is partially determined by residential proximity. In general, members of the same village support one another in all the small occasions of social life, drawing on the nature of their kin relationships to determine how they do so. This is a reflection of the ethic of coresidence (and coconsumption of the food of the place) as kinship, which I discussed in the last chapter. Kin who live farther afield tend to take part in the small events of social life only if they have very close kinship links or if the occasion is a major one such as a death or a wedding. The importance of residential proximity is also reflected in the fact that a woman who has married in from any distance is always allocated adoptive parents from within the immediate locality, that is, from a nearby hamlet. These adoptive parents act for her in the various exchanges and other ceremonies in which she is involved and are expected to provide moral support for her. On major occasions both her own parents and her adoptive parents may take part together.

Despite the ideology of coresidence as kinship, a person is always ultimately connected to the part of Ambae he or she comes from. This is not always the place where the person was born. Thus in a commentary on a fight between two sisters-in-law I was told that one of the women did not come from Lovonda, and that this explained her unacceptable behavior. The woman in question had married from a Longanan hill village about five kilometers away, but it was not her own birthplace that made her alien; rather it was that her *laen*, her mother, had come from a village in another district. The connection of person to place is not the product of his or her individual residence history. A person's connection to a place is both created and validated by the connection of his or her *laen* to it.

Thus Ambaeans do not construct any kind of social group that defines and maintains its boundaries against all others, as people do in other parts of Melanesia. Ambaean residential groups are flexible, and their kinship connections are open-ended. A person's affiliation to *ples* is strengthened or weakened by the connection of his or her *laen* to it. One of the ways in which *laen* is connected to *ples* is through holding rights to land, and I now discuss how land is held and transmitted.

LAND RIGHTS AND USE

Land on Ambae is not, strictly speaking, owned. As Margaret Rodman showed in her substantial study of land tenure and transmission in Longana (1987a), men do not own land so much as hold it. However, men can hold land in their own right, asserting their will over that of other people who have rights to that land. Land is also sometimes held cooperatively by a group of siblings under the guidance of the senior brother. Writing about west Ambae, Michael Allen provided a historical perspective on land that could apply equally to east Ambae. His comment referred to a time when the dominant interest of men's lives was their participation in the graded society, or *huqe:*

> In the days of the Hunggwe, land was of minor importance. So long as a man had sufficient for his gardens and large pig pens, he was satisfied, and for such purposes there was plenty of land available. The important heritable possessions were the dancing ground, men's house, slit gongs, textiles, pigs, and the various insignia of rank. Today, with the collapse of the Hunggwe and with the rise of a cash economy based on copra and cocoa plantations, and with status and authority in turn to a large extent dependent on having the money won from these crops to hold feasts, build stores [and so on] . . . land has in itself become . . . the greatest part of a man's estate. (Allen 1969:37)

Rodman emphasized the strategies men use to obtain large amounts of land for cash cropping. She was particularly concerned with the way in which the rights to hold land are transmitted after the death of a landholder through a series of funerary feasts known as *bongi*. In Longana, rights to hold land are in practice transmitted from father to son, less often from mother's brother to sister's son. Land rights transmission varies from district to district in east Ambae. My discussion here is restricted to the situation in Longana.

Rodman provided an extended account of the sequence of funerary feasts that take place every five days for one hundred days after a person's death, during which "[f]ood, mats, kava and pigs flow back and forth between representatives of the deceased's kin and his offspring" (1987a:45). A man's brothers control his land from the moment of his death. When a man dies, his sons, by giving pigs to his brothers, assert and establish their claims to his land, which otherwise the brothers will continue to hold. Other men, by assisting the participants in *bongi* exchanges beyond their capacity to repay, are able to acquire some of the land in the hundredth day ceremony, at which all debts must be repaid. By this means, some men in east Ambae have been able to establish sizeable coconut plantations.

Rodman's discussion of place was intertwined with her discussion of land ownership and was based on the assertion that a Longanan must hold land: "[P]lace is intimately bound up with land. . . . Over and over again, Longanans stressed to me the inseparability of being a Longanan and holding land: 'In Longana everyone *must* have a piece of land. There can *never* be a Longanan who has no land'" (1987:38). "Even Longanans without rank and with little influence over the actions of others must have the opportunity to hold land, if only as the most junior sibling in a landholding unit" (1987a:39).

But if landholding is crucial to being a Longanan, to having a "place," then the status of women as Longanans seems somewhat uncertain. In general women do not hold land in their own names: "When a woman marries, her husband replaces her father as her guardian and provides her with access to land, just as her father did while she was single. A married woman's place is her husband's place, and women without husbands need Longanan fathers or Longanan sons to secure their positions in society" (M. Rodman 1987a:41).

Rodman thus suggested that access to land, having a place, and having a position in society are multiple renderings of the single reality of belonging. I propose that these things can be seen not as equivalents of each other, but rather as being interconnected. Rodman talked here in terms not of landholding—since women do not hold land—but of access to land. I suggest that it is not holding land that contributes to one's identity as a Longanan, but rather the right of access to and use of land. The ways in which people have access to land are gendered. Land-holding and land transmission are male practices; men have rights to land either as sole landholders or as part of their sibling group, and men pass land on. Women do not hold land and do not pass land on in that sense. However, they do have access to land through their male kin— father, brothers, husband, sons. A woman is able to decide which of these land resources she will utilize, just as men also choose which part of the land that they hold they will use. Land use—that is, both use in the sense of finding land productive in gardens and animal husbandry and use through residence—is both a male and a female practice.

If male practice with respect to land concerns its ownership and transmission, there is also a distinctively female practice with respect to land. The idea of matrilineal descent is tied to the idea of location, and people work hard to ensure that a *laen* remains attached to the land. Because alternate generations in a male-focused hamlet belong to alter-nate moieties, in each generation a piece of land passes from one moi-ety to another. This alternation prevents a close tie between *laen* and land. The right to hold a particular plot of land is always transferring from one moiety to another, one *laen* to another. To counteract this effect in the longer term, men will always try to ensure that at least one of their sons marries a woman from their own *laen* so that their grand-sons will belong to the same *laen* that they do and thus have access to the same land; the connection between *laen* and land will thus be main-tained in the alternate generation. The connection between *laen* and location is highly valued. Significantly, although this connection rests partly with fathers in overseeing their sons' marriages, it is also seen as being a responsibility of women.

It is a responsibility of a woman to ensure that daughters are born to her *laen* and its land. Thus I heard criticism of a woman who had no sisters and who married an Australian and went to live in Queensland. She was criticized for not accepting her responsibility, as an only daughter, to stay and have daughters in her own *ples*. I, my maternal grandmother's only surviving granddaughter, was advised to return to my own home forthwith and have at least three daughters so that my *laen* would be continued in its *ples*. So that while a system that reckons descent matrilineally combined with predominantly patrilateral trans-mission of land constantly refigures the relationship of descent group to land, there is a strong pressure to tie descent to land where possible. Bearing children to a *ples* (that is, to a landholding) is female practice, and in this sense, women do pass land on. Men practice their relationship to land by having enduring rights to it. Women practice their relationship to land by bearing children to it. Both men and women practice their relationship to land by using it for gardens and by living on it. By correctly asserting that men hold rights to land, it is possible to emphasize the connection that men have to land in a way that obscures women's connections to it.

Rodman's discussion of land was based on a notion of Ambaeans as individuals with separate possessions and separate rights to land (a perspective that cash cropping is reinforcing), even though she acknowledged that individuals are linked by access to land: "Every place in Longana is identified with a chain of individuals in the past, with a network of potential claimants in the future, and with one individual (or, less often, with siblings acting as a unit) in the present" (M. Rodman 1987a:41). The focus on individuals obscures the essentially collective relationship Ambaeans have to Ambae, as holders and users of land. A reading of Rodman's material, which foregrounds the network of active and latent rights of access to land that Ambaeans possess, draws attention to the collective relationship they have to land and assists in recognizing women's connections to it. As Rodman herself remarked, "Men *and women* can broaden, reinforce, and even create claims to land through investment of their labor' (1987a:44; my emphasis).

Land use through the making of food gardens is not emphasized in east Ambae. Gardens are not the focus of any major ritual activity, and unmodified garden produce is not much used in any of the formal occasions of life. When food is exchanged, it is almost always cooked. Lovonda is set among coconut plantations on the coast, and residents' garden land is mostly six or so kilometers away, in the hills beyond the Longana airstrip. The hamlets did not empty each day as people went to their gardens to work.[11] Indeed, I knew one woman who never worked garden land at all. Instead, each morning she made fried yeast dough cakes, remotely resembling doughnuts, called *kato*, which she sold to other village members and which they often ate for breakfast. She used the proceeds to buy garden produce (yams, sweet potatoes, taro, plantains, leaf vegetables, beans, fruit). Although she was subject to sustained criticism for other aspects of her lifestyle, she was not criticized for this approach to providing for her family. Rodman's statement that "a person's place in the narrowest sense is his or her hamlet" (1987a:36) reflects the Ambaean focus on land use through residence rather than through productivity, which I also observed.

The focus on residence as a form of relation to Ambae is interestingly reflected in the existence of invisible people who reside in Ambae alongside Ambaeans. I was often told about these people (not to be confused with the "devils" and ghosts that also exist on the island), who can choose to appear to the island's visible inhabitants and with whom Ambaeans have an ongoing, if rather formal, relationship. In the past there were marriages between the two groups. In the 1990s the relationship balanced support and negotiation. Chief Marcel Tari, from hill Longana, once recounted to me a long negotiation with a group of invisible people (known as *vavi*) for the return of some cattle (they were returned). At a marriage I attended in 1995, there was a long halt in the presentation of textiles by the groom's family as puzzled women on the *sara* counted over and over again the most valuable textiles *(ngava hangavulu tavalu)* as they lay on the ground. There were too many, and no one knew who had given the extra ones. The next day the groom explained that it was the *vavi,* the invisible people, whose *laen* was close to his and who had consequently chosen to assist him.

Vavi live in known locations in the landscape. The land on which they live is owned by visible Longanans but tends to be land that is not cultivated. Thus in Longana *vavi* live in the hills above the highest settlements. In Lombaha, stories about another group of coinhabitants, known as *mwai,* place them at the coast, in an area that was previously used but not much settled. The idea of invisible coresidents reflects the relationship between Ambaeans and Ambae. It emphasizes the importance of dwelling in (see Ingold 1993) as a means of relating to Ambae. It is not Ambae itself that is important, the object of Ambaeans' attention, but people and land together, the one dwelling in the other. The existence of invisible people also reflects the distance inherent in Ambaean notions of land ownership. Land may be held by a man or group of men, but this same land may be the site of a hamlet of the invisible people, who have rights to that place.

The way in which land is constantly moving between moieties and *laen,* the way in which each piece of land is potentially subject to claims from many different people, the lack of ritual emphasis on gardens and garden produce, and the sharing of land with the invisible people—all these are factors that subvert the possibility that the holding of certain rights to some land defines the identity of the local group on Ambae. Nevertheless, the ways in which men and women practice their relationship to land are a critical factor in being a person of the place. These practices with respect to land are part of having a *ples.*

PRACTICE AND PLACE

The idea that space is socially constructed is one of the most well established anthropological "truths" (Gupta and Ferguson 1997a:40). On Ambae, a person's *ples* is (generally) the context in which he or she lives out his or her life.[12] It is the locations in which events took place and take place. It is the source from which he or she obtains food and other resources to be used in the various contexts of life. What a person does, what happens to him or her, happens in his or her *ples,* so that place and event are constituted as part of each other. Landscape becomes mnemonic; it reminds individuals of the things that happened there, both in their own lives and in the lives of their forebears. Ambaeans also consciously modify places to create this mnemonic effect, by, for example, planting special trees or shrubs to mark a place where a ritual has taken place. In the past, they also marked places to make announcements or spread news.

For Ambaeans, places have their own identity and importance, and people often understand or reflect on events in terms of the relation of event to place. While I was in Lovonda, two sisters-in-law, living in the same hamlet, came to blows over the upbringing of their children. Their case was put before local leaders in a *kastom* court hearing, and among other fines, one of the women was required to pay a particular type of pig, a *teveteve,* as a fine to the *ples* itself. A person who causes trouble in a *ples,* specifically in a hamlet, is usually made to compensate the place itself in this way. The leaders of the hamlet subsequently decide what they will do with the pig. In another example, at a wedding I attended, the father of the groom, in a speech presenting textiles and pigs to the bride's family, commented that many people had come to participate in the occasion. He said that this was because the hamlet was at a very important *ples,* the anchorage of Boeboe (the site of many myths and stories) and that people attended the occasion because they respected the *ples.*

Like Boeboe, locations in the landscape are often associated with stories. There is a special name, *tomtomu,* for the practice of telling of stories at night, in the house, to both adults and children. There are many different kinds of stories: very short stories that small children learn and can repeat, stories like fables, in which, for example, a king-fisher challenges a crab to a race around the island; stories of great moment and importance, about the origin of Ambae, the naming of places in Longana, the origin of women, the origin of kava; stories of journeys and stories that comment on Europeans, their advent and their difference. All these stories are set in Ambae, although they may refer to adjacent islands. They explain the history of specific locations and they also refer in passing to various landmarks. While some stories are restricted to certain people, it is not the case, as it is on Tanna, that such stories are the copyrighted property of the people of certain places to such an extent that they constitute "geographic *oeuvres* . . . the orga-nization of knowledge according to place" (Lindstrom 1996:127). A per-son from Longana is free to tell a story about a stone in a creek in Lolo-karo. Unrestricted stories that I recorded in Longana and broadcast in the VCC program on Radio Vanuatu were heard in other districts. People from Lombaha commented that their stories are "the same, but a little bit different." Knowing the stories that are distinctive to one's *ples* is a way of demonstrating that indeed it is one's *ples.*

Formerly, the dominant focus of men's lives was the *huqe,* a status-alteration system based on the exchange and killing of pigs, resulting in the acquisition of the right to wear certain insignia and to eat certain kinds of restricted food and the acquisition of social, political, and eco-nomic advantages. The east Ambaean *huqe* is distinctive among status-alteration systems in the degree to which it is focused on exchange (Blackwood 1981:44; Jolly 1991b:59). Men progress through a series of ten stages, alternating between *vavahegi* grades in which they exchange pigs with a sponsor and *mate* grades in which they kill a specified num-ber and type of pigs. The five *vavahegi* grades are not equal to the five *mate* grades that they intersperse; rather, "*vavahegi* occupies an inter-mediary and subordinate position between each of the five *mate* steps in the graded society" (W. Rodman 1973:169).

The *huqe* expresses an Ambaean preoccupation with order and ranking. Just as the *huqe* is a progression through ranked grades, so the pigs men kill are themselves classified into named, ranked categories based on tusk development. The upper canines of boars are removed so that the lower canines grow in an unimpeded curve, eventually reentering the jaw and growing out again to form a full circle. A pig that is well cared for may eventually have tusks that form two such circles. Each stage of tusk growth is named and valued. The different ranks of the *huqe* involve the exchange or killing of different categories of pigs.

In the past the *huqe* significantly affected the nature of Ambaeans' relationships to the landscape, even to the level of residence patterns. The political base of a leader *(ratahagi),* "although maintained by his skill as a leader in warfare and peacemaking, was established by his success in the *huqe*" (W. Rodman 1973:41). *Ratahagi* actively created a following of dependents, and before the advent of Christianity, people often altered the place in which they lived to live in the hamlet of a successful *ratahagi.* The *huqe* also affected movement through the landscape. Men made trading journeys to other districts to obtain pigs and certain textile types for use in the rituals, also travelling to other islands, such as Pentecost and Maewo, to trade for pigs. Rodman points out that in Longana even the more mundane resources needed for a rank taking had to be obtained in different parts of the district. He says that a "successful *huqe* demands copious quantities of taro, a lowland crop, kava, grown in the foothills, and firewood, found high on the slopes of the volcano," so that rank takers must negotiate with other residents of the district to obtain all the resources they need (W. Rodman 1973:183). Men sought not only resources but also supporters in other parts of Ambae: the involvement of a geographically distant, prestigious *ratahagi* brought renown to the rank taker. This contrasts with the connections men seek to make through marriage. Whereas until recently men sought marriages with women from their own district and often from nearby hamlets, they sought sponsors, assistance, and trade partners for the *huqe* from far afield.

W. Rodman's description of the *huqe* reveals the extent to which it is understood to have been developed in the landscape of Ambae. The very creation of pigs took place on Ambae. A culture hero, Tariboeaga, who lived as a recluse near Manaro, created pigs and was then taught by a spirit how to remove their upper canines so that they developed curved tusks. Tariboeaga introduced the pigs to men who until then had killed small animals such as rats and lizards in another form of the *huqe* (W. Rodman 1973:33–35). *Huqe* ceremonies imposed new associations on the landscape. The aspirant to rank would select the place, the *sara-to-be* where he would kill pigs, on the basis of one of several criteria: because of a dream, because a renowned ancestor himself killed pigs there, or because it was the site of a grave. Once the site is selected, the rank taker had to clear the *sara* of bush and scrub, ideally creating half an acre of packed earth hardened by the sun (W. Rodman 1973:185). The landscape was physically modified for a *huqe* and imbued by it with new associations and memories.

Rodman documented an efflorescence of the *huqe* when he undertook research in 1970–1971. In 1991–1992, only a few rank takings occurred in east Ambae. I attended only one, at which one of the speakers upbraided his fellows for being afraid to take ranks in the *huqe*. Apparently, men were afraid of the heavy obligations they would incur by taking rank. In 1991–1992, the principal focus of Ambaean interest and energies was marriage.

Like the *huqe*, marriage focuses on exchange, involving the presentation, by bride's and groom's families alike, of large numbers of textiles, food, and other goods. The form that marriage takes works out, among other things, a relationship between two hamlets. Marriage always commences with a pig killing by the bride. She takes one of the junior ranks in the *huqe*, usually but not always the second such rank that she has taken in her life. Unless, exceptionally, she is married to a man who achieves very high rank in the *huqe*, this is the last *huqe* rank she will take. The tusked jaw of the pig she kills to obtain rank is sent with her to her new home, visible evidence of the status she has achieved and the respect of which she is worthy. Her father arranges the pig killing with the explicit intention of ensuring that her new family will respect her. On the next day, the goods given with and to her are amassed on the *sara* of her hamlet, and a complex series of payments, mostly of textiles, is made to those who have helped her family with the wedding.

As these goods are heaped up on the *sara*, the bride's fathers and father's sisters place some special textiles on her head. Most of these are immediately removed and put with the other textiles going to her new home, but two or three are left on her head; she holds them in place by the fringes that hang over her forehead, separated from her head by a large green leaf whose name means "leaf placed on the head." The fringes obscure her face; the textiles cover her head and back. These textiles are known in Longana as *qana hunhune,* which translates roughly as "textile placed on the head." In putting a textile on his daughter's head a man conveys a message to his daughter's husband and family. Different textile designs have different known meanings in this context, concerning matters such as fidelity and stability in the marriage. The bride is fed a last meal, is dressed and decorated, and then she and all the goods that go with her are taken in ceremonial procession to her new hamlet. There, when the groom's family have presented the textiles and pigs they are giving to the bride's family, the bride is formally transferred to her new home. The groom's father's sisters carry her, her father's sisters, and the goods being given with her on their backs and on their heads across the ceremonial ground. Not until she enters her new house does she remove the *qana hunhune* from her head.

The covering of heads with textiles recurs in a number of formal contexts as a protective act. Allen reported that in west Ambae the head

Fig. 13 Placing *qana hunhune* on the head of a bride (Susan Woivire). Saraisese, Lovonda, east Ambae. May 22, 1992.

is regarded as the most sacred part of the body (1969:66), and I suggest
that this is also the case in east Ambae. When a girl's head is covered
with textiles during the central section of a wedding ceremony, she is
protected as she makes the transition from one place to another, while
she is in the vulnerable state of being temporarily "placeless." In part it
is the formal transition from one place to another that makes her a
married woman. Today couples often live together before marriage in
the husband's hamlet, but a woman does not belong there, even though
she bears children, until the exchanges and transfer of marriage make
her a *woman ples,* a "woman of that place." After marriage, even though
she may still use garden land belonging to her fathers and brothers, she
becomes a person of that new *ples.*

Women's capacity to make this transition from one *ples* to another
is a highly valued characteristic. When I asked Jean Tarisesei once about
the relationship between women and place she proffered a proverb: a
girl, she said, is like a branch of *nanggalat*—a stinging nettle tree; whatever the ground you stick it in, it will grow. A girl, this proverb suggests,
can thrive in any place, planted in any ground. Nearly any piece of
wood, stuck in Ambae's rich volcanic soils, will take root and thrive,
but a *nanggalat* will grow in the most inhospitable ground. Another
woman, Roselyn Garae from Lolovoli, expanded my understanding of
the proverb. She said that a *nanggalat* grows so easily that if you throw
a *nanggalat* stick (as you might, for example, to dislodge a mango growing high in a tree), no matter where it lands, it will take root and grow.
She said that the phrase that expresses this, *gai kugi kalato,* is a form of
respect to a woman, an honoring expression used on ritual occasions. It
is a strength in women that they can make the transition from one *ples*
to another, a strength that men do not have.

On Ambae, there is no role for a woman who is not married. Only
once a woman is married does she start to participate fully in adult life.
This full participation is signalled at marriage by the prefiguring of the
women's status-alteration ceremonies known as *huhuru,* in which only
married woman participate. *Huhuru* (to make red) refers to the dyeing
of textiles. (Textiles are always dyed a color described as red, although
store-bought dyes create a color closer to purple.) On the morning after
the wedding, the father's sisters of both bride and groom dye some
white textiles that the bride's mother has sent with her to her new home.
These textiles are given to the groom and his family. As will be discussed

in chapter 7 several years after the beginning of the marriage, the woman herself will plait a suite of textiles and on a nominated day will dye the textiles and present them to her husband, obtaining thereby a status similar to that obtained by men through the *huqe*. Marriage is associated clearly with the production of textiles, and it is through the production and use of textiles, particularly in exchange, that a woman becomes a productive adult.

Marriage is not, however, entirely sufficient to a woman's status as a whole adult person. Women should bear children. The bearing of children is very positively valued. Jean Tarisesei commented to me that bearing children makes women's bodies strong. Contrasting two elderly women, one of whom was childless, she demonstrated the truth of this dictum by comparing the vigor of the mother with the withered appearance of the childless woman. A group of young women will normally be addressed as "young mothers" (regardless of whether or not they are), and a childless young woman is in a socially anomalous position, marginalized by the absence of a child on her back or at her feet. When a woman bears children, she strengthens and reinforces her connection to her new *ples*. She becomes more and more connected to her *ples* as her children grow and have children themselves: an older woman with adult children and grandchildren is firmly incorporated into her *ples* in a way that a young wife is not.

The way in which the landscape of Ambae is saturated with stories and memories, the way in which Ambaeans live out their lives within the physical environment the island provides, makes Ambae the context in terms of which they understand who they are. Place and practice are part of each other. Early after my arrival on Ambae I was adopted by people who lived in one of the Longana hill villages, Leah Ture Leo's parents. I never lived near these parents, but retained amicable if somewhat formal relationships with them. From them I acquired a moiety affiliation and *laen* membership, so that any Ambaean could identify for me what kin term I should use for them. Some months later I moved to the village of Lovonda and began to participate in village life. Although adopted and resident, I retained my principal status as a government official, the person concerned with women's *kastom*.

Toward the end of my stay in the village, however, I attended a wedding and took part in it as a father's sister, placing some fabric (the usual alternative for the textile *qana hunhune* when given by father's

sisters) on the bride's head. The next day I learned that the women of
the village had approached the men and suggested that I should take a
rank in the *huqe*. The chief of the hamlet in which I lived approached
my adoptive father and four or five days later, timed to coincide with
one of the five-day feasts for a recently dead woman; I killed a pig and
thereby took a rank, acquiring a new name, the right to wear a particular textile type, and a new status. It was explained to me that because
I lived with them, had been adopted, and knew a lot about *kastom*, I
should *go insaed long kastom* (enter *kastom*) and become *tabu long hem*
(be initiated into it). By killing a pig I became fully Ambaean *(kam wan
ful memba long mifala)*, acquired a *kastom* name, and was thereafter
obliged to assist in exchanges.

   Discussing the event afterward, however, I was told that ideally, to
make me even more completely Ambaean, I should be married. This
did not involve marrying an Ambaean (I was to import the spouse).
Rather, the rituals of marriage, and in particular, the placing of textiles
on my head, would be the best way to properly incorporate me as a
woman Ambae. I infer that the rituals of marriage and in particular the

Fig. 14 "Entering into *kastom*": Amy Wesley fastening a *singo tuvegi* with
vovaho pattern around the author's waist before her participation in the *huqe*.
May 27, 1992. Photo: Jean Tarisesei.

placing of textiles on my head would incorporate me more fully into a *ples* (the adoptive home of my spouse) and therefore into the community. I should also bring my children to Ambae, so that they could take ranks in the *huqe*. At the same time, because my *laen* is not from Ambae, like the woman whose unacceptable behavior was explained by the origin of her *laen* in another district, my identity as *woman Ambae* will always be subject to the evidence of my ability to behave according to Ambaean practice.

What then is *ples* on Ambae? It is, I suggest, not so much that *ples* and practice are two aspects of the same thing, but that *ples* implies practice and practice implies *ples*. To become a *woman Ambae* is to be incorporated into a *ples* through practice. Territory demarcates the arena in which people live: they use land as they hold rights to it and know it as landscape. The characteristic way in which they do these things, and in which they live their lives, creates Ambae as *ples*. Men and women, equally, have an identity with Ambae as Ambaeans, but the way in which that identity is practiced differs. Men express their relationship to *ples* through holding land and using it, through marshalling the resources of *ples* (widely defined) in the *huqe*, and through knowing about the landscape. Women express their relationship to *ples* through marrying to a *ples*, through bearing children to it, and through their rights to use land from several sources, as well as by knowing stories about the landscape.

The equation of *ples* with practice accords with the hierarchical way in which the term can be used. It is possible to speak of the practices specific to a village, a district, the whole island. Differences to be observed at one level can be reconstructed as similarities, like the Longana stories that the Lombaha residents described as "the same but a little bit different." When practices are redefined as *kastom,* they retain this close connection to *ples.*

◎ ◎ ◎ *6*

Plaiting: "The Reason That Women Came into the World"

*W*_{*hen Ture Leo and I moved to Lovonda,*} Jean Tarisesei and other women set up a program for us by which we joined a number of groups of women who were meeting to plait textiles and participated in other community gatherings. The formality of this arrangement enabled us to observe that ethos of domestic privacy described in the last chapter, by which people do not enter each other's hamlets casually. It also mirrored the style of our visits to other districts, where, in each place we visited, we were always greeted by a meeting of women. By expressing an interest in textiles we were drawn into contexts that belonged, almost exclusively, to women.

In public contexts Ambaeans always maintain a spatial division between the sexes. On occasions that take place on a hamlet *sara,* such as wedding ceremonies, men always sit on one side, usually in the place where they drink kava, women on the other. At village council meetings and village court hearings, men sit close to the action, women at some distance. In church men and boys sit on one side of the aisle, women and girls on the other, while small children run about between. In everyday contexts within hamlets, the spatial division is less marked but still distinct. Men tend to gather in the area set aside for kava drinking, women under the shade of verandahs or in open-walled kitchens. Even when sitting in the same place, men and women keep apart. Only a husband and wife will sit together intimately (though still without touching). This physical separation between men and women is not reflected in a rigid division of household work. Both men and women cook, for example, and, though they do so less than women, men also look after small children. Both men and women work in gardens and process copra.

The nature of relationships between men and women is the subject of some debate. This debate usually focuses on two sets of relationships: that between brothers and sisters and that between husbands and wives. The relationship between brothers and sisters is often cited as the example par excellence of the changes in local practices identified as *kastom*. Brothers and sisters formerly practiced almost complete avoidance. Webb, writing in 1937, commented that brother and sister "are under a very strict rule that means that they must not meet under any circumstances" (1937:76). I was given several illustrations in Lovonda of the avoidance behavior formerly practiced. Brother and sister did not enter each other's houses, and indeed spoke to each other only from a distance. If a woman saw her brother on the road she had to immediately disappear into the bushes, looking fixedly away from him until he had passed. A woman could not eat food her brother had brought from the garden or food her brother had cooked. These prohibitions are no longer enforced. In Longana brothers and sisters no longer avoid one another. While it is daring for a brother to enter his sister's house, or vice versa, this may happen without occasioning much comment. Brothers and sisters also do speak to one another, but a certain formality and distance continues to characterize their relationship.

The avoidances that separate brother and sister were, and still are, mediated throughout life by the assistance they give each other. This assistance is often presented formally. Sisters are major contributors of textiles to the payment made for their brother's wife, and they also provide textiles to assist their brothers in other exchanges, such as during the *huqe*. Brothers provide food, especially pork, to their sisters. As Margaret Rodman discusses (1981), the principal return by a brother for his sister's gifts of textiles is effected through his child's participation in the junior ranks of the *huqe:* the pigs the child kills are given to the father's sisters. Rodman also draws attention to the gifts of food that pass from a brother's child to his or her father's sister, at the instigation of the child's father. She says that these gifts are "intended to counterbalance the assistance that the woman provides in raising her brother's child" (M. Rodman 1981:96).

The relationship between husbands and wives is one of sufficient interest and concern to prompt community discussion. Sunday services at the Anglican church of St. Johns, which I attended as a resident of Loqirutaro hamlet, comprised a liturgically based morning prayer followed by a free-form youth service, attended by the same congregation. The youth service was organized on a rotating basis by members of a parish committee and had a different program each week. Services I attended included a Bible quiz, the presentation of songs by small groups, the telling of *kastom* stories, even a community picnic. One Sunday in December 1991 there was a debate on the relationship between husbands and wives, on "our ordinary lives." The debate was held in Bislama for my benefit and that of a girl visiting from Malakula. The man organizing the debate divided the congregation into two halves, men and women at the back of the church speaking for women, those at the front for men. Although more men than women contributed to the debate, several younger women spoke, both for women and for men. The debate, which lasted about twenty minutes, canvassed the topic from a number of perspectives: *kastom,* Christianity, development. In doing so it raised several familiar subjects, notably the tension between husbands and wives caused by men's daily drinking of kava. It reached no formal conclusions, but a number of shared ideas were acknowledged. There was, for example, no protest mounted against the thesis that from the perspective of *kastom* men are the bosses, although the thesis that Christianity establishes the same relationship was lightly disputed.[1]

Much of the discussion concerned what women do; speakers commented that women cook, wash, have babies, look after one another in hospital (the contemporary equivalent of the menstruation huts in which women formerly gave birth). There were also some comments about what men do, both negative (men talk endlessly in the *nakamal,* drink kava, go to dances) and positive (men look after trucks, build houses). One younger man, speaking for women, emphasized contemporary developments in women's status. He commented that through the Vanuatu National Council of Women and other women's groups, women were developing themselves independently of men. He also argued that men now recognize that women are clever, that they can, for example, work as secretaries.

Several speakers commented that women can do everything men do, but that they can do one thing men can't do, which is to make textiles. Other traditional gendered activities were not discussed; no mention was made either of the *huqe* or of the *huhuru* or even of pigs. One man, speaking for men, commented, "Women need to know *kastom* —because if women don't make textiles, what will I be buried in?"

Men do not make textiles. They neither plait, nor do they dye. The production of textiles belongs to women alone, and it is a lifelong responsibility. In the era when birth took place in a menstruation hut within the hamlet, the birth of a girl was announced, in Longana, by the scattering of pieces of prepared pandanus on a public path leading down to the beach. The birth of boys was announced by the scattering of miniature bows and arrows. From their earliest moments, therefore, girls were associated with the work of plaiting. There are a number of stories about the origins and diversity of textiles around Ambae. In one of these stories, which I learned from Roselyn Garae, the different textile types were spread through east Ambae by the ten wives of the culture hero Tagaro.[2] This is part of what Roselyn said:

> The women divided themselves [into matriclans]. Then they agreed: "We are dividing ourselves up, but we recognize that we have one origin. We all know [the textile type] *maraha vinvinu*, we know [the textile type] *tavalu*. We can teach each other that whoever is born as a woman, she must plait, she must plait all these things which we have brought with us. This is the reason that women come into the world: so that they can plait. They can plait all the different textiles." (Roselyn Garae, National Audiovisual Collections WCP Workshop tape 7B)

TEXTILES

Dyed with store-bought dyes that produce not so much a red color as a rich purple, textiles add a striking and decorative note to formal social occasions, contrasting with the lush green environment against which they are seen. Laid out in great heaps on a hamlet *sara* during an exchange, folded for display beside a leaf-wrapped bundle of cooked food and given to an honored guest, or wrapped around the bodies of dancers, textiles act as a visual marker of special occasions. Textiles are also very much evident in the everyday life of a hamlet. People spread older textiles on the ground to sit on, and it is in the hamlet that women both prepare pandanus and plait: spreading prepared leaves to dry on convenient surfaces (a thatched roof, the top of a concrete water tank), sitting in the shade to transform a mass of spiky pandanus threads into the smooth surface of a woven textile. If special occasions are marked by the strong purple of dyed textiles, domestic space is more often characterized by the off-white of dried pandanus being processed and woven.

As a story from Lombaha tells it, pandanus first grew in the southern district of Lolovoli, at a place called Lolodomai. The nine sisters of a man called Tahigogona took leaves from the tree and from it wove textiles, which they sold to people who lived around about. But the nine sisters argued among themselves about who got the most pandanus. Tahigogona intervened. He broke nine branches off the tree and gave one to each of his sisters. He told them to go up to Manaro (the volcano), from where each was to follow a different line of hills down into a different part of Ambae. He warned them that they might be killed, but that perhaps they might meet a man who would point out a piece of land on which they could plant their pandanus. Perhaps some of Tahigogona's sisters were killed, but some were given places to plant their pandanus and so brought textiles to the district they had come to, to Nduindui, to Lombaha, to Lolovinue. One sister came down to the hill called Vui veveo above the Walurigi hamlet of Kwantangwele—the storyteller, Aganet Vuti, pointed it out, above his house, as he spoke— where she wove *qegavi* and *vola walurigi*. Another went to down to Nduindui, planted her pandanus, and wove the textile type *matai talai*. Today the descendants of Tahigogona's sisters, all members of a single matriclan, can be found in all the districts of Ambae and in all the districts women plait pandanus textiles.

This story offers an explanation for the different textile types produced on Ambae, differences that overlie the fundamental unity of pandanus textile production. There are over fifty named textile types on Ambae, and the complexity of their names, their distribution, their comparative values, and their local significance are considerable. As the story demonstrates, these differences are recognized by Ambaeans, and are important. The complexity of regional differences is allied to the complexity of the uses of these objects in each area. In each part of the island women plait up to about twenty-five named textile types, and each of these has a specific set of appropriate uses. There are pandanus textiles used in exchanges, to wrap the dead, to present to honored guests, to wear to mark achieved status in the *huqe,* textiles on which to sit or to use as blankets, textiles for specific points in rituals, textiles that are the focus of rituals. The differences between all these textile types are not apparent to the uneducated eye, but that there are significant differences can be established in the briefest of conversations with an Ambaean, and the use of a textile in the wrong context can be a matter of comment and condemnation.

Ordinarily, in common English, in publications and in museum catalogues, Ambae textiles are referred to as "mats," a term that, as I mentioned earlier, is generally associated with floor coverings in English. Bislama has, however, adopted the English term *"mat,"* and when speaking Bislama, Ambaeans will use *"mat"* to refer to woven pandanus textiles. However, in the Ambaean languages there is no single term that can be used to refer to all the different textile types. It is possible to refer to all these objects by the term for pandanus, *veveo,* just as one might refer in English to woollen articles, but this does not mean that these objects fall into the same category. There are *maraha,* which are high-value exchange items and which are used to wrap the dead. There are *qana,* which when new are used as exchange valuables of lesser importance and are used as domestic furnishings—to sit upon and sleep under. Once a *qana* has been used domestically, it is reclassified into a special category, *buresi,* and cannot thereafter be used in exchange or in ritual. A third category, textiles worn as clothing, has fallen into disuse with the introduction of European clothes. Textiles in this category still exist, but the distinctions between them and textiles in other categories are becoming blurred. Thus, for example, the women's clothing textile, *sakole,* is still made, but it is used increasingly as a *qana* (rather as someone might use a sarong as sheet or towel). Finally, there are the *singo*—textiles that are used to symbolize and confer status or rank.

My greatest difficulty in understanding pandanus textiles on Ambae was my uncritical use of the English term "mat" to describe them. My initial mistake was to assume a congruence of some kind between the English term "mat" and the Ambaean use of the Bislama term *"mat,"* to imagine that the term alluded to a coherent group of object types. I assumed that *"mat"* designated all textiles woven from pandanus. At a meeting in a village in the Lombaha district about six months after I started working on Ambae, I was astounded by an elderly chief who commented that one such object, known as a *wasmahanga,* is not in fact a *mat.* A *wasmahanga* is worn by men, folded over a belt and hanging from it, either at their front or back, to indicate achieved status in the *huqe.* It had not seemed to me to be markedly different from other textiles worn in the *huqe,* even though I had been puzzled about the category into which *wasmahanga* fitted. Struggling with the idea that *wasmahanga* is not a *mat,* I asked other people about it. Tarisesei and other women from Lovonda confirmed what the chief had said. A *wasmahanga* is not a *mat,* they said, because although women plait it, they do not use it. It goes by another road, used only by men. Although men use *qana, maraha, tuvegi,* and *singo,* these objects are identified as *ol mat*[3] because they are woven by, *and* used by, women.

The work of Annette Weiner has drawn attention to the important roles that many groups of people allocate to textiles. Her own ethnographic work highlights the significance of banana-leaf bundles and skirts to Trobriand Islanders (Weiner 1977), and she also discusses the importance of Samoan "fine mats" (Weiner 1989). In that women are often responsible for textile production, Weiner's emphasis on cloth draws attention to the often underrecognized contribution women make to the organization and mediation of relationships. However, in her enthusiasm for the importance of this contribution, Weiner suggests that cloth can be treated as a singular category. She defines cloth as including "all objects made from threads and fibres, such as Australian Aboriginal hairstrings and Maori flax cloaks, leaves such as Trobriand banana leaf bundles, and bark, such as Polynesian barkcloth" (Weiner 1992:157). Moreover, she and Jane Schneider, who jointly edited the volume *Cloth and Human Experience,* suggest that much can be claimed for cloth: "Throughout history, cloth has furthered the organisation of social and political life. . . . Cloth helps social groups to reproduce themselves and to achieve autonomy or advantage in interactions with others" (Schneider and Weiner 1989:1). As a generalization, this statement has some validity. However, the classification of Ambae textiles demonstrates that it is unwise to group objects together merely on the basis of a similar material form. Cloth should not be treated as a singular category, precisely because ethnographic specificities reveal substantial differences between the objects that such a categorization groups together.

Indeed it is dangerous even to accept what appears to be a straightforward translation from one language to another. If pressed, east

Ambaeans will translate the Bislama *"mat"* by the North-East Ambaean term *"qana."* To accept that *"qana"* can be translated by the term *"mat"* and hence by the English "mat" is to suggest that *qana* have a rather mundane role in contrast to other textile categories, such as *singo.* But the translation does not hold. Even though *qana* are used to sit and sleep upon, they are also in some cases highly significant in ritual contexts. *Qana* are used with *maraha* to wrap the dead; they are wrapped immediately around the body, evoking images of comfort and security that derive from their use as blankets. Today, people sometimes use blankets first and *qana* second, but the imagery holds. *Qana* are given at exchanges and are also presented with food to honored guests as a mark of respect. They are also used at many points in rituals, such as marriage, to protect individuals and to confer the ability to absorb knowledge. A bride covers her head with *qana* at her wedding; people sit on *qana* in contexts where they are seeking to learn important skills or information. It is therefore analytically unhelpful to think of *qana* as mats.

These issues are further complicated by the fact that Melanesians do not necessarily use names in the same way as English speakers do. On Ambae, names are not the immutable expressions of identity that they often are for Westerners. This is perhaps most evident with respect to personal names. People are rarely called by their personal names, especially once they become adults. Most people have both a language name and a christened name, and they may be known by either. People address each other frequently in terms either of the relationship between them (a person will address his or her classificatory grandparent or grandchild as *bubu,* for example) or in terms of particularly crucial relationships in their lives. Thus a woman is often addressed as the mother of her firstborn child—*retahii Ronnie* (mother of Ronnie). When men and women take grades in the *huqe,* they are given new names, and a person who holds a particularly significant position in the community may also be referred to by the name of the position by most people—*"jif"* (chief). People also use nonpersonal forms to address each other—like the mother I heard recalling the wandering attention of her small daughter by saying *"Tubui!"* (Woman!).

In a situation where personal identity is rarely at issue (since everyone is known), names are used creatively to reveal or suggest relationships, status, or some other aspect of who a person is. This is also the case with pandanus textiles. One particular textile can be referred to by a number of names: by the category name to which it belongs *(qana)*, by the individual object type name *(qana vululu, 'qana* with long fringes'), by the pattern stencilled onto it *(matanaho,* 'sun'), or by reference to some other characteristic. Thus since some *qana vululu* are left undyed and are known as *qana mavute* (white *qana*) ordinary dyed *qana vululu* are sometimes described as *qana memea* (red *qana*). Textiles can also sometimes be referred to by names used for that same object type in another district of the island. Ambaeans recognize an equivalence between some object types even though they have different names. Thus the textiles known in Longana as *ngava hangavulu* are called *sawea* everywhere else, and sometimes people in Longana refer to a *ngava hangavulu* as *sawea.*

For someone attempting to learn about Ambaean textiles, this variable naming is very confusing, but once the underlying framework is grasped, it becomes one path into understanding the creative and metaphoric use of these textiles. The way these objects are classified and named says a great deal about them, revealing some of the differences Ambaeans perceive between them. These differences are not, to the ignorant eye, immediately evident in the textiles' material form, for they share a set of similar characteristics, being generally long and narrow with a central seam. Many are dyed, either as a single block of color or with largely geometric patterns imposed on the central portion of the textile. Some have fringes of various kinds on the sides or ends, and some have openwork designs embellishing the textile at either end. Many consist of plain plait (one thread over another), but some have designs plaited into them using float weaves (where one thread passes over two or more opposing threads). *Singo,* which are small in comparison to most other textiles, incorporate overweave designs (designs created in low relief through a combination of float weaves and tied loops).

When asked to identify textiles and to explain what is different about them, Ambaeans refer to their uses. A *ngava hangavulu* is for the exchanges at marriage and for wrapping the dead. A *singo* is to be worn by people who have taken rank in the *huqe.* Uses nominated like this generally do not exhaust all the uses to which that particular textile can be put, but they are usually the most important ones. However, each textile type is distinguished from all others not by its use but by its form, by a combination of diacritic features. These are almost all related to the plaiting of the textile, not the dyeing. This is true even though one of the names used for a textile may be that of its stencilled pattern, and even though a textile may have a name that refers to the fact that it is not yet dyed. The feature most commonly used as a diacritic marker is the form and style of the fringes and selvages used on the textiles.

For example, the principal *qana* types are distinguished from each other by their side fringes. *Qana vulvulu* have long, fine fringes along their two sides, whereas *qana vivi* (*qana* with a *vivi* fringe) feature a short stubby fringe and *qana mwaho* (*qana* with a smooth edge) have a plain selvage edge in which the ends of the pandanus are turned neatly under the upper surface of the textile, and cut. This is not, however to exhaust the formal differences among these *qana* types. For example, there is a set range of stencil patterns appropriate to each textile type. It is not possible to put a *matanaho* (sun) pattern on a *qana vivi* but only on a *qana vulvulu*. Similarly the *qana vivi* pattern known in Longana as *vule* (moon) cannot be stencilled onto a *qana vulvulu*. There are also a number of other *qana* that are distinguishable by other criteria. *Qana hunhune* is the textile type placed on a girl's head at her marriage by her fathers and her father's sisters. It is always made with particular care and is usually smaller than the *qana vivi*, which it resembles; but the crucial characteristic of a *qana hunhune* is that it is made of only one panel and has no central seam. Each *qana* type has a characteristic size (*qana vulvulu* are usually about two meters long, for example), but they range between one and two meters long, and three-quarters to one and a half meters wide.

The distinction between *maraha* and *qana* is based on the different purposes to which they are put, but, again, this difference also lies in their appearance. *Maraha* are large textiles, the shortest at least four meters long, the longest up to a hundred meters. They are never dyed with stencilled patterns as most *qana* are, but only with a block shading of red dye (often more pink than red as they are dyed not by being boiled in the dye, but rather just dipped into it). The differences between them are largely a function of their length and width. The highest value *maraha* are referred to as casually as "long *maraha*," for the very obvious reason that they are very long. The most common long *maraha* is *ngava hangavulu tavalu* (meaning "one hundred lengths, one side"), which is always between eighty and a hundred meters long, a long, narrow, single panel. The short *maraha* known as *qiriqiri* average five meters in length and one meter wide; the different *qiriqiri* types are distinguished from each other by their side fringes.

In a system of this kind, where objects fall into recognized categories, it is tempting to look for a degree of order and consistency in the principles by which the categories are established. To do so would be a mistake. For a while I attempted to find organizational rules that operated with the infallibility of mathematics. The distinctions between pandanus textiles do not work like the rules of multiplication. The principles by which the objects within the four main categories are distinguished are complicated and inconsistent; an ambiguity is involved that is in fact important to how the textiles are perceived and used. Moreover, not all Ambaeans trouble to learn these distinctions clearly. The difference between *qana vivi* and *qana mwaho,* for example, is not one that all women recognize, although everyone can tell the difference between a *qana* and a *maraha.* The textiles that people are most at ease in discussing are the ones in daily use. In Longana, these are the *maraha* and *qana* used in exchanges and in the most common rituals and ceremonies. The textiles that are made to be worn as clothes are less well known; people would often refer me to an older woman for information about *tuvegi* and *singo.*

PLAITING

The practice of scattering pandanus threads on a path to the sea to announce the birth of a girl is a thing of the past. Today Ambaean children are generally born in Lolowai Hospital, and their birth is announced casually, by people returning to the village from the hospital. Often now girls do not become involved in plaiting until late adolescence. Occupied by kindergarten and primary school in their childhood, and having no need to contribute textiles to exchanges themselves, they remain disassociated from textile production. Not all children proceed to secondary school. Girls who do not, or who do so for only a few years, start to plait even before they are married as they begin to participate in the adult life of the community. They learn from their mothers, grandmothers, and other women resident in the hamlet. How much they learn depends on their individual interest. A girl who wants to learn will sit and observe skilled plaiters and imitate them. She may even find a textile she wants to be able to make and take it apart to see how it is constructed.

It is with marriage that a woman needs to know how to plait. All married women make textiles. Women who do not plait have no textiles to contribute to exchanges; since exchanges take place on most formal occasions of social life, a woman who has no textiles is excluded from social interaction. Without a textile to give, a woman would be embarrassed to attend. However, some women are more interested in plaiting than others; they take the trouble to learn how to plait more complex designs and how to cut a greater variety of the unrestricted *qegavi* stencil patterns. A limited number of women purchase or inherit the right to learn how to make the restricted stencil type called *gigilugi* and how to plait the powerful and important textiles in the category *singo*. All other women must purchase from them, with textiles or with money, the *singo* and the *gigilugi* stencilling when they need them. On an everyday basis, however, there is an equality in plaiting. When women sit down to plait the principal exchange textiles, they are able to produce equivalent products by means of common techniques.

In the past the prohibition that forbade men to have anything to do with textile production was strict. A man could touch a textile when it was finished, but he was not allowed to participate in any way in the production process, except in some cases as an observer. Tarisesei told me people used to say that if a man had anything to do with pandanus, he would go bald. I am not aware that there were harsher penalties than this, but given the strength of the prohibition it is possible that other penalties that are now forgotten or that I did not learn may have been invoked. The distinction has now broken down a little. A man may provide casual assistance to his wife—as she prepares pandanus for plaiting, for example—but men do not plait.

In the stampede to sell textiles to me for the Vanuatu Cultural Centre, Australian Museum, and National Museum of New Zealand collections at the conclusion of the Ambae project, a number of men cut stencils and helped their wives dye the textiles they hoped to sell to me. Their incentive was the inflated prices I was asked to pay for textiles, and that on the whole I did pay. The men cut nontraditional stencil patterns, using the unrestricted *qegavi* stencilling technique—a highly ironic conclusion to the WCP on Ambae. Possibly men felt free to take part in textile dyeing and to cut nontraditional stencils because they saw the textiles as being made for an entirely nontraditional purpose. I was seeking to collect as comprehensive a collection as possible of all the different stencil patterns. When I said that I was not interested in collecting the common patterns (which I had already acquired), and women did not know how to cut some of the more esoteric stencils to apply to textiles they had woven but not yet dyed, the men innovatively cut sand-drawing designs, never previously used on textiles.[4]

Three varieties of pandanus (*Pandanus* sp.) are cultivated in Longana. These are known locally as *veveo maeto* (black pandanus), *veveo biti* (small pandanus; the name refers to the shorter leaves of this variety), and *veveo mwaho* (a variety without thorns on the sides of the leaves). Of these, the first two are most commonly used. *Veveo maeto* produces a stronger fabric, which is longer lasting than *veveo biti* and which is used for *maraha*. *Veveo biti* is whiter, and takes dye better, and is used for *qana*. There is no rule; it is a matter of individual choice which variety is used. Women harvest pandanus leaves from trees to which they have access, in some cases trees they own personally and have planted on land to which they have use rights. Unlike the situation faced by Tahigogona's sisters, pandanus trees are an uncontroversial resource; I never heard any discussion about them, was never taken specifically to see them nor had them pointed out to me as I walked by.

The long, thin leaves of pandanus trees grow in large clumps, which sprout upward at the ends of branches; the base of each leaf grows closely around the others, like a celery stalk. Women harvest the leaves by pulling them away from a clump, working from the outside in. They trim the leaves at the tree and take the central portion to the hamlet. There they soften the leaves over a fire and then pare off unusable portions (such as the central spine). This produces long ribbons of green leaf, which are then split into threads so that they remain joined at the base of the leaf (fig. 15). The ribbons are soaked in water overnight and then spread in the sun to bleach and dry for several days. This preparation is the task of the individual, usually performed in an immediately domestic context. The prepared pandanus a woman produces is her own. Once prepared, pandanus is stored in the rafters of the kitchen or in the sleeping house until it is used. Pandanus is usually prepared with an anticipated use in view and is not usually stored for long.

The first thing women must do when they sit down to plait is to smooth out the pandanus threads, which are stiff and curled in on themselves at the end of the drying process. The ribbons are pulled tautly several times across the narrow edge of a tool such as a small half-coconut shell or the lid of a jar. This makes a scratchy scraping sound, not unlike the sound of a coconut being grated. The two noises are characteristic of Ambaean village life. In both cases the activity is generally performed with a rhythm of three actions and then a pause: three scrapes along one side of a pandanus ribbon, a pause to turn it, three scrapes down the other side. Coconuts are also grated with three downward movements followed by a pause in which the coconut is rotated slightly. People comfort babies by slapping them gently on their behinds or by bouncing them, in both cases with the same rhythm, three gentle slaps or bounces followed by a pause, often emphasizing the rhythm with a sort of staccato hum. It is a sound, a rhythm, associated with the security and peace of hamlet life.

When the plaiter has smoothed enough ribbons to be going on with, she joins them in pairs by laying one across another at the base of the threads and interlacing each thread with its opposite. These pairs are then joined side by side, initially held in place by the lower unsplit ribbons, which are roughly plaited together. This forms a long starting edge. These early stages of plaiting require little skill and are the ones in which men (these days), girls, and passersby such as I are most likely

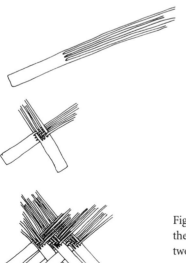

Fig. 15 The initial stages of plaiting: the split ribbon of pandanus, joining two ribbons *(benegi),* and then setting several pairs side by side *(belagi).*

to assist. Once the starting edge has been created, only women who are able to plait can proceed. The plaiter moves along this starting edge, gradually building up the fabric, a painstaking (but for the experienced plaiter, rapid) process in which each thread separately must be made to pass over or under the next.

In the large pandanus textiles woven in parts of Polynesia, such as Fiji, Tonga, and Samoa, the length of the fibres being used does not affect the width of the textile produced, as additional lengths of leaf are added into the textile as the plaiting progresses (Buck 1926:122; Ewins 1982:7). This never happens on Ambae. Rather, textile width is achieved by plaiting a second panel outward from the starting edge of the first. When the first panel reaches the desired width, the plaiter completes it with a selvage edge and then joins a new set of pandanus ribbons to the starting edge and plaits the second panel of the textile outward from it, so that the starting edge becomes the central seam of the textile. Nearly all textiles have two panels produced in this way, but never more than two. Since the longest prepared pandanus leaf is never more than about

Fig. 16 Harrison Hango plaiting a textile, Lolohihi, Lovonda, east Ambae. A pandanus thread is laid down and the opposing threads individually lifted, or pressed down over it. The lower and upper opposing threads are then separated to make space for the next thread to be laid down. August 1999.

three-quarters of a meter long, the largest textile is therefore never more that about one and a half meters wide and always has a longitudinal central seam.

Women say that plaiting is hard work, by which they mean not so much that it is difficult, as that it is time consuming and in some ways wearisome. Increasingly, large numbers of textiles are presented in exchanges; up to two thousand may change hands to seal a marriage. One middle-aged Longana woman commented to me that whereas in the past only one or two of the highest value textiles were given with the bride at weddings, she had recently attended a wedding at which forty had been presented. The number of other textiles presented is always proportionate to the number of high-value textiles, that is, of long *maraha,* so that this represents a very considerable increase in the number of textiles presented. The comparatively short life of textiles (no more than three years) and the preference for new textiles make the production of textiles an ever-present responsibility.

Plaiting is a sociable activity. Although women plait inside their own houses, they more frequently sit in a semipublic place such as a house verandah and talk to other people while they work. Often they arrange to sit together to plait, sometimes plaiting their own textiles together informally, sometimes gathering to plait textiles for one woman. This pooling of labor is occasionally organized as a more formal group, whose members take turns, plaiting the textiles of one woman on one day, those of another woman on another day. The woman whose textiles are being woven prepares the necessary pandanus in advance and produces a midday meal for her companions. On such occasions, women sit together in some communal space within a hamlet. Frequently more than one woman will work on one textile at the same time, so that plaiting is an explicitly cooperative activity, even though the finished textile is always individually owned. Village women's club plaiting is an extension of this pooling of labor; in this case each woman contributes pandanus as well as her labor and the textiles are owned by the club, to be sold to raise funds for club objectives.[5] Village women's clubs generally meet in a building belonging not to one hamlet but to the whole village, such as a community hall. In this case every woman contributes food to a communal midday meal.

In this sense plaiting is analogous to drinking kava. Women sit together to plait and talk. Men sit together to drink kava and talk. Just as women are excluded from men's kava-drinking sessions, men are excluded from women's plaiting sessions. By this means women are distinguished from men not merely by a negative definition—men drink kava and women do not—but by a positive—women plait textiles together. The opposition between textiles and kava takes a further form. Women are disdainful of men's kava drinking, not only with respect to the frustrations of living with a heavy drinker, but with respect to a characterization of kava as nonproductive. Several times women commented to me that it is women who make the formal occasions of social life because it is women who produce the textiles the exchange of which creates those occasions; men merely sit on the sidelines and drink kava. Men's action in drinking kava, in this formulation, becomes a response to their discomfort in the face of women's productiveness; indeed, one woman proposed to me that men drink kava at exchanges because they have nothing to do, since women are the principal actors. Of course, in the past, when men were absorbed by the *huqe* and devoted much energy to the production and acquisition of pigs, their presentation of pigs would have balanced women's presentation of textiles. In the 1990s, however, women are defined by their plaiting and demonstrate and assert that identity against men by displaying their productivity in exchanges.

Women's production of textiles is not only communal in that women plait together. It is also communal in that a woman, in making a *maraha* or a *qana,* is not making an object with which her name and labor will continue to be associated after it is exchanged. A textile is not more valuable because of who has owned it or made it (though the quality of manufacture may be recognized and admired). Individual textiles never have names and histories as do certain fine mats in parts of Polynesia (Linnekin 1991; Herda 1999; Kaeppler 1999; Schoeffel 1999). A textile once laid out on the *sara* is no longer associated with the individual who gave it or with previous owners, but only with the group of people contributing to the presentation; a group convened for the occasion that will never be exactly replicated. The textiles such a group gives are subsequently distributed by the recipients of the presentation among themselves and their supporters. The individual who receives a particular textile will give it again, usually without knowing who made it and with no reference to its previous uses in exchange. It is textile types that are important, not individual textiles.

Thus women in making *maraha* and *qana* are not making objects that will stand for them as individuals or, since Ambaeans do not form fixed residential or kin groups, as members of a group. This is a significant contrast to the situation in other parts of Melanesia. Maureen MacKenzie, for example, discussing the labor of Telefol women of Papua New Guinea in making looped net bags, comments that the bags are never disconnected from their makers. She says that "the string bag, as a product, is never alienated from the memory of the woman who looped it, for the bag *is,* metonymically, the producer" (MacKenzie 1991:150). Rather, in Telefomin, the net bag (or bilum) "is invariably thought of in terms of who made it, for whom, and on what occasion. . . . The bilum, once exchanged, is a constant reminder of she who made and gave it" (1991:152). Moreover, MacKenzie argues, "The woman's labour is not . . . constitutive of the value of the bilum, but of the value she holds for the person she will give the bag to. This is because Telefol women always loop bilums with a specific person in mind" (1991:151–152).

No such ties between plaiter and recipient hold for Ambae *maraha* and *qana*. A woman in giving a textile she has woven introduces that textile into a system in which her authorship will no longer be recognized; textiles do not represent an ongoing relationship between maker and receiver. In plaiting, a woman is not making an investment in her own separate status; rather she is making an investment in relationships; the fact that she contributes a textile to an exchange is more important than the textile itself. In giving a textile a woman may be, as a principal to the exchange, concerned with her relationships with the recipients of the gift. Alternatively, as a minor contributor to the exchange, she may be concerned with her relationships with the principals to the exchange whom she is supporting.

It is not only in presenting but also in making a textile that a woman invests in relationships. The time women spend sitting together plaiting involves mutual support and shared talk. In the European tradition, it is usual to distinguish the manufacture of a thing from its use; an object —a garment, a painting, or a coin, for example—is first made and then used. The period of manufacture, during which the object is incomplete, is a period in which it has no use, but is being prepared for subsequent use. Encounters with the manufacture of objects in other societies (the production of a painting in a traditional Australian Aboriginal context, for example) have introduced the idea that in some cases it is the manufacture of the object that has ritual significance; it is while it is being made that it has value. The *malangan* (funerary figures and masks) of northern New Ireland, for example, are displayed publicly for a brief period and are then destroyed (Küchler 1987:239). As Küchler's analysis shows, it is the reproduction of remembered *malangan* images that is of central importance. Once remembered and produced and seen by others who will recall it in the years ahead, the material image of the *malangan* should be destroyed. What is valued "is not the real sculpture, but the memory thereof" (1987:240)—a memory that is validated and transferred through the production of the image.

Ambae textiles do have an extended usefulness, a life, once they are completed. Nevertheless, they also have a particular kind of value while they are being made. Women making textiles are working to complete objects they will use to build and sustain relationships. But in plaiting they also invest in relationships they have with one another; for women, textiles being plaited are an *occasion* for relationships. It is not that the women locate in textiles meanings they invest in their relationships, but that the plaiting of textiles becomes the point around which these relationships are developed.

EXCHANGING TEXTILES

While women find value in making textiles together, they also find substantial satisfaction in presenting them at exchanges. Textiles are always presented in the same sequence. At major exchanges, such as weddings, men also present long *maraha,* usually *ngava hangavulu,* that they have obtained at other exchanges or that they have commissioned and purchased from women. Only men directly involved in the occasion make such presentations. These men move forward onto the *sara* carrying their gift of long *maraha,* which they unroll and lay out in piles. Then the men retreat from the ground and women move forward, carrying the textiles they are to present. At the largest exchanges, weddings, women carry these textiles on their heads folded into baskets known as *tanga bunie,* which they explained to me are like banks in the way in which they contain wealth. The sight of sixty to one hundred women pouring onto a *sara* to present textiles is dramatic and impressive. When they reach the center of the ground they let the baskets fall from their heads with a satisfying thud, expressive of the labor they have

Fig. 17 Jean Tarisesei and her kinswomen holding filled *tanga bunie* on their heads, just before carrying them onto the *nasara* to present at the wedding of Jean's brother Joseph. Note the rolled *ngava hangavulu* on the tops of the baskets. November 1994.

invested in their contribution to the exchanges, and start to unfold and lay out the textiles in great heaps.

The textiles are stored in the baskets so that they emerge from them in the order in which they are laid out; the first textiles to emerge from the baskets are the textiles that should be laid out first. Only women who are closely related to the principals of the exchange present long *maraha* as well as *qiriqiri* and *qana*. Other women present *qiriqiri* and *qana,* while women only remotely involved in the occasion will present merely a *qana* or two. There is a fixed order in which the textiles are laid out on the *sara,* and not only each textile category, but each textile type, has its place in the sequence.[6] In all contexts of exchange, *maraha* are considered to be more valuable than *qana,* and *maraha* that belong to the subcategory *ngava hangavulu* are more valuable than those that belong to the subcategory *qiriqiri*. This series of values is ordinal rather than cardinal (see Gregory 1982:49); a specified number of *qana* cannot be substituted for a *maraha,* nor can a specified number of *qiriqiri* be substituted for a *ngava hangavulu.* One or two pigs are often presented with textiles at major exchanges. They are tied to a stake driven into the ground at the end of the pile of textiles with which they are being given.

In some cases the textiles laid out on a *sara* are given in exchange for services or goods already provided. In other cases a return gift is made at the same time, the two gifts of textiles being laid out in separate parts of the *sara.* At marriages the textiles given with the bride are laid out on the *sara* of her own hamlet and are then folded and taken to the groom's hamlet, where they are carried across the *sara* with the bride but are not presented again. The payment for the bride is laid out on the *sara* of the groom's hamlet. In general, gift and countergift are not equivalent, but some debt remains to be discharged in goods or services at a later date. Ambaeans operate easily within the prescriptions for the textile types to be given on any particular occasion, knowing when it is appropriate to give *qana* and when it is necessary to give each of the different *maraha.*

Ambaeans derive an aesthetic pleasure from looking at heaps of new textiles laid out in presentation on a *sara.* At weddings, for which the women exchanging textiles have had adequate time to prepare, people note the preparations that have been made and attend to see the new textiles. New textiles, Jean Tarisesei commented to me, make an occasion alive.

Meaning and Material Culture

For women on Ambae, then, *maraha* and *qana* have agency in relation-ships of exchange, but the fact that a woman contributes a certain tex-tile type to an exchange is more important than the textile itself. It is more important that a textile is a *qana vulvulu* than that it has a certain design stencilled on it or that it incorporates particular in-weave designs, let alone that it was made by a particular woman. This is not to say that a textile, once completed and stored in the *tanga bunie,* becomes entirely like currency, having only an exchange value, even though it may be removed from the basket and used in a transaction in exchange for goods or services, or, for example to pay a fine. Women do make evaluative decisions about the quality of a complete textile, decid-ing when to give it and assessing, especially for a *qana,* whether it is well made and whether the stencilled design is clear and looks good. It is thus the context that gives the textile greater or lesser individual significance.

Despite the similarities, and the links, between them, all textiles are not the same kind of thing, and they do not all operate in the same way. Specifically, as I shall explain in more detail in the next chapter, *singo* operate quite differently from *maraha* or *qana.* Moreover, the same object, named differently, is a different thing, rather as a young woman, on having her first child, not only becomes a mother, but is afterward generally called by the name of her child. Similarly a *qana,* once it has been used in a domestic context, is redefined as *buresi* and can no longer be used in exchange.[7]

Exchange has been one of the key contexts in which Melanesian anthropology has addressed the significance of objects, even though, as several commentators have observed, these analyses have often focused more upon the relationships created or altered by exchange than on the objects themselves (Strathern 1990:38; Thomas 1991:204). Nevertheless because in many parts of Melanesia the material and the nonmaterial are often treated as continuous or equivalent in exchange transactions, it is from exchange theory that some of the more radical formulations of objects have been derived. Annette Weiner's study of banana-leaf bundles and skirts provided a new assessment of women's role in exchange, highlighting women's power and importance, but it also drew attention to the importance of these object types, which Western eyes easily overlook (1977). Nancy Munn's account of Gawan canoes demonstrated the transformation of one object into another over time (1977).

Marilyn Strathern, also working within an analysis of exchange, offered a yet more radical analysis of the role of objects. She argued that both persons and things have the social form of persons and that "relations and persons become in effect homologous, the capabilities of persons revealing the social relations of which they are composed, and social relations revealing the persons they produce" (Strathern 1988: 173). It is somewhat diminishing to the sophistication of Strathern's analysis to make the point I am making here. However, from her perspective, objects do not fall into a defined category at all. They are both transformed and transformable, created by or out of persons, embodying, effecting, and transforming relationships. Objects are subject to, obtain their significance from, and effect the form of the relationships in which they exist.

Alfred Gell implicitly built on Strathern's analysis in his proposal, set out in *Art and Agency* (1998), that an object be understood to have agency itself, to create effects.[8] In an extended argument, Gell demonstrated how objects exercise agency, mediating and entering into social relations between and with persons. This is a "kind of second class agency" (1998:17), dependent on the humans who make the objects, but Gell argued that it is agency nonetheless. Strathern, commenting upon this, observed that "Euro-Americans often think agency inappropriately personified when applied to inanimate entities, but that is because they link agency to will or intention." In fact, she remarked, "in terms of the effects of entities upon one another. . . 'things' and 'persons' may be co-presences in a field of effectual actors" (Strathern 1999:17).

For most of the Ambae project I determinedly sought meanings for textiles. I asked for stories of their origins, I asked about the meanings of the designs plaited into and stencilled onto them, I tried to elicit accounts of their significance. Eventually I realized that to the extent that such "meanings" exist, they are associated primarily with "small" textiles—with *singo* and the other clothing textiles. Over and over again, the answers I was given were names—the names of in-weave patterns, the names of stencil designs, the names of textile types. Only occasionally was I able to elicit a story of the development of a particular textile type. The *maraha* type *ngava hangavulu tavalu,* for example, was developed by a woman who lived near Navonda in the Longana district. Her invention was taken up widely through east and north Ambae, and the story is widely remembered.[9]

The importance of Strathern's and Gell's arguments is that obviating the distinction between person and thing and focusing instead on an object's effect draws attention away from a focus on meaning. It also highlights the fluidity of what persons and things are and raises the possibility of other ways of making connections and distinctions between them. This fluidity relates to the agency of both persons and things, and to their effects. By analytically obviating the distinction between persons and things, we may be freed to perceive other issues that it obscured. It is uncommon to ask what the meaning of a person is. We ask what the person does, or did, or who he or she is. These are the questions, it turns out, that it is good to ask about *maraha* and *qana*. By asking about the use of these things, what they do, one is able to elicit information about their effects. By asking what a *maraha* or *qana* is, one elicits names that reflect on its material form but that can also reflect on that object's current use and significance. What is important about these objects is not what they mean, but what they do.

◎ ◎ ◎ *7*

Dyeing: Designs, Power, Status

Plaiting binds women together in relationships of assistance, obligation, and shared labor. Dyeing, a process formerly associated with risk and anxiety, has a different set of associations. The process used to be hedged about with restrictions of various kinds, directed at achieving a clear stencilled image on the fabric. Groups of women dyed textiles together, apart from men and children and outside the hamlet space, generally by the sea, where there was easy access to salt water. When dyeing *maraha* and *qana,* they apparently gathered together to work on a number of textiles at once; the dyeing of *singo,* however, probably always took place separately.[1]

Significantly, it is through dyeing that women create and mark differences between themselves. These differences are tied to dyeing of *singo,* and in particular to the creation of certain designs that are the focus of the women's status-alteration system known as *huhuru.* Only certain women have the right to plait and dye *singo* and thus to act as ritual specialists in *huhuru* ceremonies. Another context in which textile designs were used to distinguish women from each other was, until the 1940s, through women's tattoos.

It is difficult to trace the exact significance of dyeing, as much of the knowledge associated with the dyeing of textiles is not much remembered. The older technology of dyeing using vegetable dye and a bark dye bath has been supplanted by a much more foolproof method, which relies on commercially available dyes and a galvanized iron dye bath. Tattooing is no longer practiced, although in the early 1990s there were women in their fifties and sixties who were tattooed as girls and who could describe the process. The *huhuru* rituals are still practiced, although it appears that, especially in Longana, some of the ramifications of *huhuru* are less significant than formerly. In talking to women about dyeing, I was constantly aware of a loss of knowledge and a truncation of practices.

Ambaean life is marked by a number of contradictions, such as that between women becoming part of a new place but never entirely belonging to it or that between the achievement of personal distinctiveness and status and the imperative not to "go too high"—become too different. In this chapter I discuss the different dyeing processes before outlining Ambaean ideas of rank and difference and describing the *huhuru* ceremony. The question of identity versus difference is related to the issue of place, for the security of being a person of the place creates the context in which the idea of difference is investigated and worked out. Indeed, each place has its own formula and scale of difference. There are notable variations in the way in which both the *huqe* and the *huhuru* are implemented from district to district in east Ambae (see Allen 1969:93). Here I focus on the *huhuru* as I learned about and observed it in Lovonda, Longana.

DYEING

There are three dyeing techniques in use on Ambae. The first involves simply dipping the textile in a bath of boiling dye. This technique is used to dye *maraha*. Since only red dye is used, this technique results in a wash of pink over the entire surface of the textile. All other textiles are decorated with designs applied to the central portion of the upper surface by log-wrap stencil dyeing, a technique unique to north Vanuatu. There are two kinds of stencilling techniques used: *qegavi*, used to dye *qana*, is known and used by all women; *gigilugi*, for *singo* and the women's clothing textile *sakole*, is used only by some.

In the *qegavi* technique, a stencil is cut from a sheet of prepared banana-palm spathe. The textile is tied around a special log *(gai wesi)* so that the central portion of the textile is stretched tautly over the surface of the log. The sides of the textile are folded down into a shallow groove that runs the length of the log, while the ends of the textile are tied at either end of the log rather in the manner of a Christmas cracker. Two stencils, with identical, symmetrical patterns, are bound onto the textile around the log so that they fit neatly side by side, one each side of the central seam of the textile. They are bound onto the log with a special rope made of the inner bark of the wild hibiscus (*Hibiscus tiliaceus*, Malvaceae), which is permeable to the dye. The whole is then placed in several inches of fresh water in a galvanized iron dye bath, into which it just fits, over a fire. When the water boils, store-bought powdered dye is added to it, and the whole is allowed to boil for about five minutes,

Fig. 18 Miriam Boe cutting a *qegavi* stencil with the *loloitavue* (conch shell) design. The material is scraped banana spathe. Vunangai, Lovonda, east Ambae. February 1992.

when the textile is turned over. When the dye is judged to have permeated the whole textile, a matter of fifteen to twenty minutes, the log is removed from the bath and the dyeing rope and stencils immediately removed from the textile. The stencils cannot be reused.

Commercial dye and an iron dye bath are reasonably reliable in producing a good image. The equipment used formerly was less reliable, and much more labor intensive. The dye was obtained by grating the bark of the root of a vine, *laqe* (*Ventilago neocaledonicum,* Rhamnaceae), different varieties of which were both cultivated and harvested where they grew wild in the forest. In Longana the roots were grated onto two leaf types, that of the fern *tutu* (*Sphaerostephanos heterocarpus,* Thelypteridaceae) and the tree *kalato* (*Dendrocnide larifolia,* Urticaceae), said to enhance the color of the dye. The dye bath was made of a single piece of green bark, cut from a tree and tied at either end so as to hold liquid. It was difficult to find bark without knotholes and other blemishes and to cut and carry it without breaking it. There was

Fig. 19 Ruth Garae tying a *qegavi* stencil around a textile over a dyeing log *(gai wesi).* The textile is pulled taut around the log and tied at either end like a Christmas cracker, the stencil being then bound tightly to it. Vunangai, Lovonda, east Ambae. February 1992.

always some uncertainty about whether or not the dye would take properly.

Although the commercial dye and metal dye bath are in common use, the old techniques are still known by older women. I twice saw textiles being dyed in a bark bath with *laqe,* once in Nduindui, where the process was demonstrated for my benefit, and once at the Women's Culture Project workshop when some delegates from Lolovinue demonstrated the technique to other delegates. In dyeing textiles for the National Film Unit camera, Lovonda women prepared *laqe* but added some commercial dye to enhance the color and used a galvanized iron dye bath. Younger women in the village commented that they had never before seen *laqe* being prepared.

Laqe dyes textiles a red the color of dried blood. The fact that the textiles are red is important; people often refer to them as red *(memea)* textiles. The red color produced using chemical dyes is quite different from that of *laqe,* closer to a reddish purple. Although they use this commercial red, women are not satisfied with it. They experiment with various techniques to make the color as dark as possible, for example by adding carbon from carbon paper, and Tarisesei and I were asked by women in Walurigi to help find a better, darker dye.

When trade stores have sold out of red dye, women urgently needing to dye *qana* will sometimes purchase and use another dark color, such as blue or green. This is an unusual strategy: *qana* in colors other than red are rare. They are tolerated in exchange, but are frowned upon. When I was given a green *qana* in return for a gift I made at a wedding, the woman who looked after my welfare in the hamlet took it away from me and brought me a red *qana* instead. She disapproved of the green dye. I never saw a *singo* or *maraha* dyed any color other than red.

Partly because dyeing is usually deferred until just before the first occasion of use, women generally arrange to dye their textiles together, making good use of the commercial dye that has been bought. They generally do so by using the hearth in a communal kitchen in the hamlet, although in the hamlet in which I lived, Vunangai, my nearest neighbor had a place outside her kitchen that she used specifically as a dyeing hearth. There seems today to be no particular objection to using the same hearth for cooking and dyeing. I never, however, saw a textile being dyed inside a private kitchen. The traditional technique involved digging a trench for the fire, the long dye bath supported above it; it would have been impractical to use a cooking hearth.

A textile may have been woven many months before it is dyed, may even, in an extreme case, be already starting to rot, but when it is dyed it is understood to be completed and is thereby constituted as a new textile. Dyeing completes a textile, making it exchangeable. Some textiles are given undyed, but they are never given as part of the heap of textiles laid out on the *sara*. Rather, they are given for a specific ritual purpose, like the *qana mavute* given by the bride's mother with her daughter, which are dyed the morning after the wedding in a prefiguring of the *huhuru*.

The women of Lovonda village did not observe any taboos in dyeing *maraha* or in cutting and applying *qegavi* stencils to *qana*. In the past, men were completely excluded from the process, but now men and children may approach women who are dyeing. While men were excluded, women were under an imperative to be involved: every woman had to have her own dyeing log. After her death it would become her canoe in the Ambae volcano crater lakes, which are the final destination of the dead. In the 1990s not all women have dyeing logs; a woman might borrow one and joke that she will have to share the canoe also.

I was never offered any exegesis, speculative or otherwise, associating dyeing with either menstruation or other reproductive issues. For example, no one ever made a connection between the dyeing red of the *qana mavute* the morning after the wedding and the (theoretical) loss of the bride's virginity. Equally, no one ever commented to me that the color of *laqe* is like dried blood, evoking both menstruation and the blood of childbirth. This silence may be a consequence of the various taboos that prevent women from talking about sexual matters in general discussion. A woman may not talk about sexual issues to her mother or sisters, but only to her father's sisters, with whom she has a close but serious relationship. It is the father's sisters of both bride and groom who engage in the somewhat ribald and competitive play around pigs and the "opening" of the young couple's new house at marriage. It is also the father's sisters who stay with the couple on their first night together to offer advice and information, including sexual instruction. Outside these venues, women's conversation is generally modest.

Although women may gossip about illicit sexual relationships, and are not embarrassed to talk about menstruation, they do not talk about sexual matters directly. This modesty may also reflect the influence of Christianity.

However, dyeing is linked to both menstruation and sexual relationships by the very effort with which they are kept separate. I gathered information from various parts of Ambae about the taboos and prohibitions that formerly applied to dyeing. In Nduindui I was told that in order to ensure that the dyeing was successful, women abstained from sexual relations with their husbands while preparing to dye textiles. They also took care not to speak to people they met on the road, for example when they went to the bush to get the bark for the dye bath. Menstruating women should avoid going near the dyeing process lest they become ill. These prohibitions suggest a mutually inimical confrontation between dyeing and social relationships, especially sexual relationships, making women's actions in dyeing textiles distinct and separate from other contexts. At the end of the century, however, the strengths of taboos and separations were constantly diminishing, especially with respect to the *qegavi* technique.

There are interesting parallels between this material and Janet Hoskins' data on indigo dyeing among the Kodi in Sumba, eastern Indonesia. Hoskins comments that "indigo dyeing is conducted as a cult of female secrets. Hedged by a system of taboos that forbid access to all men, and to women at certain stages in their reproductive cycles, older women practise an occult art that is associated with herbalism, midwifery, tattooing, and (more covertly) witchcraft" (Hoskins 1989:141). Hoskins suggests that for the Kodi, the separation between reproduction and dyeing represents "an effort to create a conceptual separation between two forms of creative production" (1989:150). On Ambae, child rearing and textile production were established as more broadly antithetical: I several times heard a myth about a woman who is so preoccupied with producing textiles that she neglects her children; the elder child, despairing for the baby, eventually drowns herself and the baby in the ocean. However, the taboos that specifically separate dyeing from reproduction seem to me to be also about removing distractions and enabling concentration. While at least today, dyeing on Ambae does not resemble "a cult of female secrets," it is nevertheless a context in which women are able to practice their knowledge and elaborate and develop their standing and maturity.

DYEING AND *SINGO*

The greatest number of restrictions and constraints applied, and continue to apply, to the *gigilugi* technique, especially as it is applied to dyeing *singo*. Not all women can produce *gigilugi* stencils; the art of using them is generally held by women who have also paid for the right to plait *singo*. Only a few women in a village have these skills. *Gigilugi* stencils are technically more difficult to produce than *qegavi,* though it is not the technical difficulty that prevents other women from producing them, but rather the fact that to do so one must acquire the right from another woman who has it and is willing to teach the skill. Women say that the right to plait *singo* and to produce *gigilugi* stencils is usually passed down "in families." This transmission is nearly always from husband's mother to son's wife. This is consistent with the fact that until

Fig. 20 Emma Martalini building a *gigilugi* stencil over a textile bound onto the dyeing log *(gai wesi).* As the stencil is built up it is held in place with pandanus ties. Later these will be replaced with a tightly bound dyeing rope. Vunangai, Lovonda, east Ambae. February 1992.

recently women seem to have learned to dye only after marriage; a woman may learn to plait from her mother, but she learns to dye from her mother-in-law. Women who cannot make *gigilugi* stencils must pay those who can if they want a *gigilugi* stencil applied to the women's clothing textile, *sakole,* or to an unranked *tuvegi* (a male clothing textile) that they have plaited. In the past, payments were made with short *maraha;* today they are usually made with money.

Gigilugi are not cut from a single sheet of spathe but built up using pieces of modified leaf stem. The leaf used is from a heliconia plant known as *robo gigilugi* (*Heliconia indica* Musaceae). Heliconia leaves are used extensively in Vanuatu to wrap food in cooking. *Robo gigilugi* is used for wrapping food, but Ambaeans identify this particular variety from among other heliconia plants as the one to be used in stencilling. The leaf stem is cut and the pith scraped away, leaving the thin outer surface of the stem. When the stem has been prepared, the textile is stretched on the dyeing log, and then pandanus threads are tied along its length at uniform intervals. Pieces of leaf stem are inserted under the ties and the pattern gradually built up. A few design elements, such as central diamonds, that require a greater surface of stencil are cut to size from prepared banana spathe and also inserted under the ties. When the pattern is complete, the dyeing rope is carefully bound over the stencil, the pandanus ties being removed as the rope is wound around it. The dyeing process is the same as for *qegavi* stencils.

Whereas the *qegavi* technique allows for the creation of free-flowing patterns, which can be based on spirals and circles, the patterns created by *gigilugi* are built up of diamonds and zigzag lines. These are the patterns that are so characteristic of *singo: gigilugi* stencils applied to *singo* highlight the overweave design, which is already part of the textile, and apply several pattern elements to sections of the *singo* plaited in plain weave. There is only one pattern of which I am aware that can be created using either *qegavi* or *gigilugi* stencilling. This is *taqangi bageo* (shark's belly), a design used on *qana* and especially on *sakole.* As with *qegavi* patterns, *gigilugi* patterns replicate a known template that exists insofar as it can be seen on other textiles. A certain variation is allowable within the template.

There are two kinds of *singo, singo maraha* and *singo tuvegi,* which are both distinguished by the use of a distinctive plaiting technique in their production: the pandanus threads are floated, wrapped, and transposed to create a raised effect, not unlike bas-relief, called *walivetu,* which I describe as overweave. This technique is complex: it is difficult, when looking closely at a *singo,* to trace the route of an individual pandanus ribbon as it loops, bends backwards, and reappears at a distance, all in a diagonal progression across the fabric. When a *singo* is dyed, the *gigilugi* stencil is cut to fit the in-weave design, so that the raised surface is highlighted with color. *Singo* is the only textile type in which the patterns stencilled onto the fabric are connected to the designs plaited into it, and it is the only textile type where these designs are significant to the textile-type template.

Singo tuvegi are the textiles worn to indicate rank in the men's status-alteration system, the *huqe.* Finely plaited and highly decorative, they are about a meter long and forty centimeters wide. Women wear them wrapped around their hips; men wear them hanging down from a belt at the front. The textile is presented to the grade taker by his or her classificatory father, with a branch of ritually significant decorative leaves, immediately before he or she kills the pig. The grade taker dons the textile, sticking the leaves in his or her belt at the back, and steps forward to kill the pig. Thereafter he or she has the right to wear the textile and the leaf type—a right invoked today mainly on the occasion of local dances. The textile is a sign of the rank that the grade taker has achieved, operating on the same principle as the hood on an academic gown. The relationship of textile to grade varies from district to district. In the Longana district the lowest grade, *vire* (which means "flower" or "to flower"), is symbolised by the *singo tuvegi* known as *vovaho.*

Singo maraha are also finely plaited, long and narrow, usually about one and a half meters long and thirty to sixty centimeters wide. These textiles are not worn but are joined to the highest-ranking textiles in the *maraha* category—the long *maraha.* All long *maraha* must have a *singo maraha* joined to one end to be complete. I once attended a wedding at which a long *maraha* without a *singo maraha* was presented (it was raining, so the textiles were not unfolded to be presented, allowing this absence to go undetected). When this deceit was discovered, the textile was immediately returned with a demand that it be replaced forthwith. Although a long *maraha* without a *singo* is not complete, it is not the case that the two are treated as being one unit. They are distinct entities. This is not least because any woman can make a long *maraha,* but only certain women have the right to produce the *singo.* A woman who

makes a long *maraha* must commission and pay a *singo* specialist to
make a *singo* for it. It seems that the *singo maraha* completes a *maraha*
rather as the taking of a grade and wearing of a *singo tuvegi* is a sign of
a person's becoming properly Ambaean.

Unlike *qana, maraha,* and the clothing textiles, *singo* are distinguished from each other by the designs they embody. The designs are
all based on motifs of repeated diamonds and zigzagging lines, the zig-
zags surrounding and echoing the form of one diamond and gradually
resolving to create the next. Although to the untrained eye the diamonds appear to be the key to these patterns, for Ambaeans it is the
lines that are important, the diamonds being merely the basis around
which the lines are formed. The word for these diamonds is *butogi,*
meaning "navel." The navel is understood to be seen from above. The
lines are called *rangagi,* meaning "branch." The ways in which the lines
zigzag distinguish the different named designs, and these differences
are very subtle: women recognize, but find it hard to articulate, the differences between them.

In Longana, three *singo tuvegi* are now known, of which two are
commonly made. The three are *vovaho, matai talai,* and *buto vudolue.*
The distinction between *vovaho* and *matai talai* lies in the way in which
the lines pass around the points at the apexes of the diamond. In *matai
talai* the lines follow the shape of the diamond as repeating V shapes. In
vovaho the lines surrounding the diamond are squared at the apexes,
and the further out from the navel they get, the longer these squared
lines become. The number of diamonds, the number of lines, and the
way one diamond is resolved into the next are subsidiary to the crucial
issue of whether the lines are pointed or straight as they pass the apexes
of the diamond. *Buto vudolue,* however, literally means "one hundred
butogi," and in this case there are many diamonds in the design, the
lines zigzagging and resolving from one to the next with considerable
visual complexity. *Buto vudolue* is the highest grade *singo tuvegi.*

There are four *singo maraha* designs now known and made in Longana. These are *singo tau marino* (*singo* from Malo), *gingini* ("to pinch
with the fingers"), *bebe* (moth/butterfly), and *bugu* (several triggerfish
species, family Balistidae). Although the key to distinguishing these
designs is also the shape of the lines, the number and disposition of the
diamonds is more significant. *Singo tau marino* is the same pattern as
vovaho, that is, it is based on squared lines around a diamond. *Gingini,*

likewise, is the same pattern as *matai talai,* that is, pointed lines around a diamond. These patterns have different names because they are used on different *singo* types, rather than because they are different. However, in *gingini* there should be two or three diamonds, navels, side by side. *Bebe* is the same as *gingini* in the disposition of the lines, but it is distinct because there is only one diamond at the center of each panel, not several side by side. Lastly, *bugu* is distinctive because the lines around the navel are not continuous, but appear as blocks of parallel lines that take as their reference point the sides of the diamond.

The crucial characteristic of all *singo* is that they are considered to be inherently dangerous, capable of inflicting various kinds of harm on those who handle them incorrectly, including their makers. All *singo* are subject to restrictions on their production, handling, and use. A woman who is making, or has even merely touched, a *singo* should wash her hands before she touches food or holds a child. To fail to do so would result in damage to the eyes and in boils and sores transmitted to herself and others through food, or directly to the child. A *singo* is dangerous from the moment a woman begins to make it and is in fact most dangerous during production. All the debris from its making, the bits and pieces of leftover pandanus and the rubbish from the stencilling process, must be carefully collected and buried at the foot of a fruit-bearing tree. The fruit of the tree can thereafter be eaten only by a person who has earned the right to eat the restricted food associated

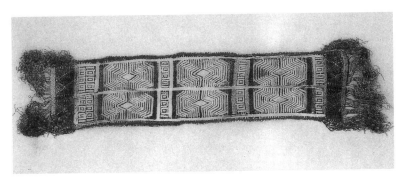

Fig. 21 A *singo tuvegi* with a *vovaho* pattern, acquired by the Australian Museum, Sydney, in 1899 (L:122cm; W:24cm). Similar *singo tuvegi* were still being made on Ambae in the 1990s. Register number E. 8402.

with that *singo* type. The power of a *singo* is such that a person should not even step over a long *maraha* that has a *singo* attached to it for fear of the harm it could inflict. I have found it difficult to elicit indigenous exegesis explaining the source of that power, other than that the power lies in the design (see also Bolton 2001c).

RANK AND DESIGNS

As is true for many parts of north Vanuatu, in east Ambae people operate within a preoccupation with order and ranking that is worked out in a number of different contexts. In the *huqe* men aspire to and achieve a progress through a series of ten grades, conceptualized as being of greater and greater height. Membership in these grades allows the men the potential for greater and greater political power and is signalled by various objects that they wear and by their right to eat certain restricted foods that are the privilege of the ranks they have attained. Michael Allen, surveying the *huqe* on Ambae in 1969, emphasizes the effort involved in achieving *huqe* grades. He says that they were achieved by "men who had the necessary means and skill to perform the complicated rituals at which [the grades] were assumed and in addition, the many lengthy and arduous tasks that had first to be accomplished" (Allen 1969:89).

In Longana the grades of the women's status-alteration system, the *huhuru*, are not established in a fixed order of achievement in the way that *huqe* grades are. It is not the order in which a woman makes *huhuru*, but the fact that she makes it for each *singo maraha* design and the flourish with which she carries off the ritual that accord honor to her. Like the *huqe*, the *huhuru* involves substantial personal labor, and requires both economic and social skills. For the *huhuru* a woman must plait a large number of textiles—a major achievement in itself—and must commission a ritual specialist to prepare a *singo maraha*. She must also prepare food and other resources to be exchanged and given as payment on the day of the ritual. Inevitably, to amass these resources she must draw on relationships of assistance and indebtedness with other women.

Men, women, pigs, and textiles are ranked. Although the different sets of ranks are at times seen to be equivalent to one another (as are *ngava hangavulu* textiles and *ala* pigs) and may symbolize one another, as a certain *singo tuvegi* indicates a certain type of pig, they cannot be substituted for one another. The different ranks are organized in separate and distinguishable hierarchies. Pigs are ranked into hierarchies with reference to the growth of the pig's tusk, textiles by their plaited form. Men are ranked on the basis of their achievements in the *huqe*, women by the number of times they have performed the *huhuru*. There is no ranking of the different hierarchies against each other. Women's ranks are not subordinate to men's ranks but are distinct from them, even though a woman's rank-taking ceremonies are often tied to her husband's progress through the *huqe*. A man may even stand a little in awe of his wife's achievements in the *huhuru*. A woman who achieves a high rank in the *huhuru* is said to have achieved seniority among women. In the same way, the different types of pigs and the different types of textiles constitute different orders of value.

Various avenues for status enhancement have been available for women in east Ambae. An important avenue for some women was tattooing. In the past, adolescent girls were tattooed with designs from neck to knee, or even in some instances to the ankle. The amount of tattooing reflected both the wealth of the girl's father and the rank of her proposed husband. Tattooing was a sign of status and brought honor to the girl herself. It required the marshalling of considerable resources since it involved payments to the girl's father's sisters, who did the tattooing, and since the girl killed a number of pigs during the process. Moreover, the tattooed designs were themselves statements, or messages, declaring the character and potential of the girl herself.

Tattooing usually took place over a period of about ten days, every alternate day a rest day. The girl being tattooed lay in a shallow trench on a white textile, in a specially constructed small house, and was tattooed using a mixture of the juice of the *angai* (a kind of Canarium almond) and soot, applied with a citrus thorn hafted to a stick. The process was extremely painful. Women today regret the passing of the practice because it brought honor to women, but they do not consider that it could be revived precisely because of the pain involved.

I did not find any woman who would speak to me in detail about tattoo designs *(bulu);* indeed, several women told me that there was only one tattoo design. However, in 1984 and 1985 Nadia Kanegai, a west Ambaean herself, recorded for the Vanuatu Cultural Centre a number of interviews about tattooing in Longana, Lombaha, and Lolovinue. Kanegai's research, which she subsequently published in a small illustrated booklet in Bislama (1994), suggests to the contrary that there were a number of designs, many of which had meanings relating principally to the woman's relationship with her husband. One such named design is *bulu gabani aka*. Kanegai defines this as referring to a binding pattern used to fasten the outrigger to the canoe and as meaning that the woman will support her husband through life as a canoe outrigger provides necessary support to the canoe (1994:37).[2] This design is the squared spiral, which, when it occurs on *qana*, is in Longana known as *vule* (moon).

There is a close correlation between tattoo designs and textile designs, including *singo* designs. Kanegai illustrates one tattoo, called *singo maraha,* which resembles both *gingini* and *matai talai* designs. She does not provide a further meaning for this tattoo, but she acknowledges that it is used on both kinds of *singo* and reports that when a girl tattooed with this design is married, the groom's parents must give a long *maraha* with this design on the *singo* to pay for her (Kanegai 1994: 38). In fact, Kanegai asserts that all tattoo designs are textile designs and that at the wedding of a tattooed girl, the groom's family must give textiles with her tattoo designs on them (1994:41). The connection between tattoos and textiles was made especially clear when a woman in her sixties, who had been born in Lombaha but married to Longana, looked at photographs of Ambae textiles held in the collections of the Field Museum in Chicago. She exclaimed with recognition when she saw one of the photos: the pattern was one with which she was herself tattooed.[3]

A traditional story, which I recorded in Longana, explicitly links the designs on a woman's inner thighs to her sexual relationship with her husband. The culture hero Tagaro detected an adulterous relationship between his wife and one of his followers when he found the designs tattooed on her thigh drawn in the dust by the adulterer. Formerly, when a girl was married, those who knew her thigh tattoo designs would secretly include textiles bearing those designs among the textiles with which she was sent to her husband. Kanegai records one hidden design, *bulu tabuniki,* the meaning of which is that the girl is ready for sexual intercourse—in other words, that she has reached puberty (1994:35). This design is specific to textiles from the Lombaha subdistrict, Walurigi, and the tattoo design may also be specific to Walurigi. Tattoo designs, like textile designs, were probably particular to the Ambae districts, to the extent that even when the designs were visually the same, their names and significance could change from place to place.

Designs, then, are crucial to all the different ways in which women achieve status. They are the focus of tattoo, they are achieved as the *singo tuvegi* that a grade taker obtains the right to wear in the *huqe,* and they are the focus of *huhuru.*[4] Moreover, some designs appear in all three contexts. The emphasis of the *huhuru* is on the dyeing of the designs, on the process by which they are made to appear. It thus celebrates women's power to make the designs that index, embody, and transmit status.

HUHURU

When women speak of the *huhuru* ceremony, they say that what is important about it is the *singo maraha* that lies at its center. It is from the *singo maraha* that women obtain the status that *huhuru* ceremonies confer. *Huhuru* means "to make red," an apt description of the ceremony, during which a woman dyes a specified number of *maraha,* which she subsequently presents to her husband. The woman making *huhuru* commissions a *singo* specialist to plait the requisite *singo maraha,* which will eventually be joined to the long *maraha* she has woven: the whole occasion is built around the dyeing of this *singo maraha* by the *singo* specialist.

Not being aware, when I began fieldwork, that a women's status-alteration system existed (for I had found no mention of it in accounts of Ambae), it took me a long time to recognize the importance of the *huhuru.* I was bewildered by descriptions of a *huhuru* ceremony given to me on my first visit to Lovonda, and I was subsequently further bewildered by the differing accounts I recorded in different districts. I gradually recognized that while women make *huhuru* in most districts, the events involved vary considerably from place to place. My account here is based on a *huhuru* I witnessed in Lovonda in February 1992. The women of Lovonda brought forward this *huhuru* ceremony, planned for later in the year, so that it could be filmed as part of the video about textiles made by Jacob Kapere for the Ambae project. In other districts the ritual is still highly restricted; because of regional differences I am not, in making a brief account of this version, revealing the secrets of others.

The first time a woman presents textiles to her husband is on the morning after their wedding. In this instance the *maraha* she presents are given with her by her mothers and are dyed that morning for her and her husband's father's sisters. This occasion is not one whereby the woman achieves status. It is rather understood as a prefiguring of the presentations she will subsequently make. It also represents the identification of a married woman with the production of textiles. On the first morning of her married life a woman produces new textiles (in that a newly dyed textile is defined as a new textile). In the presentation of those textiles to her husband and through them to his kin, she establishes herself as a member of the community of exchanging adults and as a source of assistance to her husband. This identification of a married woman with textile production is reinforced as a transition through the rituals of marriage. As I have already outlined, the day before a girl is married her father arranges for her to take a junior rank in the *huqe*. After the wedding she moves into a different system of status creation, the *huhuru*. Only the wife of a high-ranking chief is ever likely to kill pigs again, and then only once. A woman kills pigs immediately before her wedding and produces textiles immediately afterward. She thus enters the gender category "woman" in several senses at marriage.

Huhuru rituals involve the dyeing of a suite of at least eleven *maraha* (one long *maraha* and ten short *maraha* to accompany it), the preparation of food specific to the ritual, and an exchange of textiles between the woman and her husband and his family. In the Longana district the different *huhuru* ceremonies are distinguished solely by the identity of the *singo* that is dyed in it and the restricted food associated with that *singo* design. It is on the production and celebration of that *singo,* and specifically of its design, that the ceremony turns, even though the ceremony celebrates the woman's productivity in preparing the textiles she needs to mount it.

A woman who wants to take a grade in the *huhuru* must produce the necessary textiles herself (usually with assistance from close female kin) and must commission a *singo* maker to produce the *singo* to be joined to the long *maraha* she has made and, specifically, to dye the *singo* and prepare the food associated with it. At the conclusion of the ceremony, the woman presents the textiles she has produced for the ceremony to her husband (and hence his family) as a return for the textiles he and his family gave for her at her marriage. Indeed, women speak of making *huhuru* for their husbands, rather than of making it for themselves, although the status a woman achieves by making *huhuru* for her husband belongs to her alone. To take a grade in the pig-killing rituals, a man needs the textiles his wife gives him through the *huhuru*, so that a man's grade taking is dependent to some extent on his wife's taking a grade.

The *huhuru* ceremony I observed was of a woman from Longana called Lena Jasper. She made the ceremony for two *singo* at one time (which required her to prepare at least twenty *maraha*—a very substantial achievement in itself). Two *singo* specialists came on the day, each bringing the undyed *singo maraha* she had made. While they carefully worked on the cutting and placing of the stencils, other women helped Lena dye the *maraha*. The *singo* specialists dyed the *singo* and then prepared the restricted food. (*Singo* are joined to long *maraha* only after they are both dyed, reflecting their separate characters.) Then Lena, and those members of her family who were paying for the right to eat the restricted food associated with that *singo*, came, holding textiles over their heads, to look at the food. The *singo* specialists talked to them

Fig. 22 Two *singo maraha* just dyed, hanging folded over a clothesline to dry. Loqirutaro, Lovonda, east Ambae. May 1992.

about what was happening in the ceremony. The culminating moment for Lena was when the *singo* were removed from the dye bath. They became her responsibility at this point, and with shy but palpable pride, she removed the dyeing rope that held the stencil to the textile and both to the dyeing log and revealed the completed *singo*. This was the moment at which, perceptibly, the honor of the rank passed from the *singo* to the woman. She became a person of greater substance, worthy of respect.

Although there are, as I have described, only four *singo maraha* designs in Longana, there are three additional named decorative features that can be applied to any of the four. These features have a corollary in the ritual food prepared during the ceremony, but they are not integral to any grade. Rather, they are embellishments, both decorative embellishments of the *singo* themselves and also embellishments to the achieved status of the woman making the *huhuru*. They are called *mimi rawe* (urethra of a hermaphrodite pig), *vatu tawaga* (broken stone) and *golo vudolue* (one hundred tails). *Mimi rawe* refers to a slit woven into the center of the panel of the *singo*. Where the *singo* is being made to be joined to a *ngava hangavulu tavalu,* which is the long *maraha* with only one "side," one panel, then the slit occurs in the center of the panel. Where it is to be joined to any of the other long *maraha,* all of which have two panels, then the slits occur at parallel points in the center of each panel. *Vatu tawaga* cannot be made to be joined to a *ngava hangavulu tavalu,* for it refers to a slit in the central seam, between the two panels. *Golo vudolue* refers to the addition of woven strips extending from the end of the textile (rather as if the fabric had been split into five or so sections), each of which is resolved in fringes. *Golo vudolue* can only be added to a textile which is already embellished with *vatu tawaga*.

When I made a brief visit to Lovonda in October 1999, Evelyn Malanga was plaiting a *singo maraha* that a woman called Madeline Edgell had commissioned so that she could make *huhuru*. Madeline, a woman in her fifties with many children and grandchildren, had previously made *huhuru* only once before, and that time her *huhuru* had been based on the *gingini* design. This time she was making *singo tau marino*, that is, she was making *huhuru* based on a *singo maraha* with the *singo tau marino* design. The *singo* that Evelyn was plaiting was embellished with all three decorations. These made the *singo* much more substantial, more powerful, and Madeline, in making *huhuru* with it, would be significantly adding to her standing, to her position as a big woman in the community.

The details of the *huhuru* ceremony differ from district to district across east Ambae. This is a reflection of the differences in textile types in use in each district and of the degree to which the ceremony is still practiced. In particular, the sequence of *huhuru* ceremonies varies. In Lombaha women were able to describe five sequential ranks, distinguished by the textile types the woman must produce and the restricted food she earns the right to eat. In Longana, by contrast, the grades are not laid out in sequence. A woman achieves a higher status each time she performs the *huhuru*—the more times, the more honor—but she does not have to select the textiles she dyes in the ceremony in any particular order. In Longana, the crucial variation in the ceremony is the *singo* pattern itself.

Longana women who make *huhuru* do not acquire new names that mark their achievements as happens in the *huqe*. The *huhuru* does not involve clearly demarcated grades in the way that the *huqe* does. Nevertheless, a woman's achievements in the *huhuru* bring her respect and deference. This respect is of a kind not unlike that accorded in Western society to those who acquire academic qualifications: no attention is drawn to a woman's achievements within the *huhuru*, but where it is known it is respected. Women who do not perform *huhuru* can be criticized, and a woman who has not made *huhuru* for her husband will be ashamed. Older women who have made *huhuru* several times are said to be like chiefs among women. To some extent such women are powerful in a way that is a direct consequence of the *huhuru*. A man sometimes may be awed by his wife's achievements in the *huhuru*. Chief Marcel Tari of Longana told me how his first wife had made *huhuru* on the occasion of their building a new house. She had made a *ngava hangavulu vinvinu* to which two *singo* were attached, a textile so powerful that afterward some women were nervous about entering the house with this textile in it. Chief John Banga, of Kwantangwele in Lombaha, whom I also interviewed about textiles, spoke with fond pride of his second wife, a vigorous and animated young woman, who had already performed three of the four stages of the *huhuru* as it is formulated in Kwantangwele, performing all three on the one day, and had thereby achieved a high status.

It is partly because the Longana *huhuru* does not involve a specified hierarchy that I have introduced the term "status-alteration system" as an umbrella term to describe these ritual cycles. The term "graded society" was devised in the context of pig-killing rituals that involved named and marked grades. But not all the rituals by which it is possible to achieve status in north Vanuatu involve the acquisition of a specified position in a known hierarchy. Nevertheless, these rituals are seen as being equivalent, as the *huhuru* is equivalent to the *huqe*. In the Ambae case, as the Lovonda textile specialist Evelyn Malanga explained, this equivalence is based on the fact that in both, participants earn the right to eat restricted food associated with the grade: it is this, she said, that makes *huhuru* "the women's *huqe*" (see also Bolton 2001a).

WOMEN AND TEXTILES

When a *singo maraha* is joined to a *maraha,* it moves into another arena of use. The design on the *singo,* which is so crucial to the *huhuru* ceremony, is of no importance subsequently; instead, the completed *maraha,* having value in exchange, becomes significant. I found that people usually did not even know which *singo* were attached to the long *maraha* in their possession. Even the ill effects of handling a *singo* seem a little muted once it is attached to a *maraha.* The dangerous power of *singo* is most concentrated during the period of its manufacture. It is most potent while it is being produced, until it is paid for and, in the *huhuru,* the restricted food is made for it. Once it leaves the arena of production, a *singo* is not significant in the same way. This may not have always been the case, given that the more elaborated *singo maraha,* like the one Chief Marcel's wife used in making her *huhuru,* seem to retain some power after they have been dyed and joined.

The system I have outlined in this and the previous chapter is very complex. The variety of textiles, the variety of their names, the significance of certain plaiting and dyeing techniques, the central importance of designs, their explicit and metaphoric associations—all these things are aspects of the relationships that Ambaeans, and especially Ambaean women, negotiate with each other at many levels. In these relationships textiles do not operate as singular and unitary objects. In the first place, the textiles can be more important and powerful when they are only partially formed than they are when they are completed. As soon as two ribbons of pandanus are placed together with the intention that they should become a *singo,* they become dangerous to touch. Moreover, designs are detachable and replicable in other media. The same design may have a different name and a different meaning in different contexts, as the *singo tau marino* pattern on *singo maraha* becomes *vovaho* when it is applied to a *singo tuvegi.*

The very complexity of the textile and design system suggests that it is a venue for ideas about people and relationships that are only partially explored through words and are to a far greater extent explored through practice. Women do not readily analyze this system. When I spent an hour with the two most knowledgeable *singo* specialists in Longana, Eveyln Malanga and Emma Mwera, and with Evelyn's daughter-in-law Amy Wesley, seeking to clarify the difference between the different *singo* designs, Amy commented that the conversation made their heads ache because these were things that they were not used to talking about.

Women's practice of textiles, and their practice of designs, constitute a context in which they are able to explore and negotiate their relationships with each other and with the community. Textile manufacture draws women together, in plaiting and in dyeing with *qegavi* collaboratively. Textile manufacture also provides a context in which women are able to create differences, not only in that some women have skills others do not possess, like the ability to dye with *gigilugi,* but differences through which they acquire standing and respect. The dignity of Ambae women derives significantly from their sense of themselves as productive and capable, as having skills.

8

Making Textiles into *Kastom*

On my first full day on Ambae, which was in Nduindui,
James Gwero called upon me to make a speech to a meeting of women.
I was asked to explain why I had come to Ambae and what I was going
to be doing. This request established a role for me quite other than any
I had foreseen: I became a public speaker. In explaining why I was on
Ambae, I described the Women's Culture Project, outlining why it had
been developed and what Ture Leo and I were going to be doing. The
irony did not elude me: I found myself advocating to my audience some
of the very propositions I had planned to investigate. Instead of listening to women to ascertain what they thought about *kastom* and whether
they classified any of their activities in such terms, I found myself telling
my audience that they, as women, "had *kastom* too" (as well as men)
and that the textiles they made and used were *kastom* and were important. I became an evangelist. I found myself advocating that women
reclassify and reevaluate their practices and knowledge with respect to
textiles as *kastom* and that they then act on them as *kastom.* The Ambae
project offered contexts in which they could start to do so.

As the months went by and I spoke to meeting after meeting of
women, I came to terms with my role as advocate. I asked VCC staff to
explain to me the sorts of things I should be saying about *kastom* and
attempted as far as possible to reproduce the Cultural Centre line. I
observed the reactions of my audiences to the various points I made
about textiles and women's *kastom,* and I talked over the same material with individual women. I noticed which arguments made sense to

them and which made no impression. I gradually developed a speech that in the end I gave many times, albeit modified for each occasion. My theme was always the same: *ol woman ol i gat kastom tu, mo kastom blong ol woman hemi wan impoten samting*—"women have *kastom* too, and women's *kastom* is important." I tried to persuade Ambae women to see their knowledge and skills with respect to textiles as valuable, important, worth preserving through practice. I accepted that my role in fieldwork (in meetings and outside them) was active; I was not an observer, nor even a participant, but someone who made *new* things happen.

The role that I took as a Cultural Centre staff member is one often taken by expatriates in Vanuatu. Missionaries, government officials, educators, development advisers all introduce new ideas and practices. I, being none of these things, had a lot of difficulties with my role, not least because I did not want to overrate my influence. I attempted to minimize my own effect by reproducing the Cultural Centre discourse about *kastom* wherever possible and by being responsive to Ambaean reactions to the WCP. As the project developed, I realized the extent to which I was being used by ni-Vanuatu as what Keith Woodward described Huffman to be—an *animateur*—and as someone who facilitates change. Thus the understanding I developed about what *kastom* meant on Ambae became a matter of recording how people dealt with my activity.

From its inception, the VCC objective for the Women's Culture Project has been the documentation and revival of women's *kastom*. This objective assumes the preexistence of women's *kastom*: women's *kastom* exists; the work of the WCP is to ensure that it continues to do so. On Ambae I found this assumption to be both true and not true; one might say that things existed that could be called *kastom*, but that they were not so named. My naming of Ambaean textiles as *kastom* was greeted with recognition by my audiences, and yet at the same time it was a new idea. Indeed, when Tarisesei spoke about the Women's Culture Project to the 1992 fieldworkers workshop, she spoke about it in these terms (entirely at her own initiative). She said, "We talked to all the villages to make them realize that their *kastom* is important. They had *kastom* but did not realize that it was important." In speaking about textiles as *kastom* I, and other Cultural Centre staff who worked with me, gave them a new and welcome kind of significance.

This was but half of it. The implementation of the WCP on Ambae involved not only speaking, but also acting. The activities we undertook followed Cultural Centre precedents and were in some instances required of me. Radio programs and the filming of several videos were responsibilities that were more or less thrust upon me. The workshop that Tarisesei and I ran at the end of the Ambae project was not a Cultural Centre initiative, but was suggested by someone familiar with VCC practices as a suitable project for Australian funding. What we initiated through the WCP stimulated Ambaean women to suggest other ways in which they could act on textiles as *kastom*. The WCP acted on the new category "women's *kastom*"; it also provided and prompted new ways for Ambaean women themselves to act on it. In particular, it was women in Lovonda who suggested that we should film a *huhuru* ceremony and who decided to revive the practice of wearing textiles to perform traditional dances. They danced in textiles for the video; their delight in doing so led to the highlight of the whole Ambae project, and the last day of the workshop was devoted to dancing in textiles.

ATTITUDES TO *KASTOM* ON AMBAE

Chief Simon's account of the Women's Culture Project, which I set out in the introduction, draws attention to two connected but different aspects of the concept of *kastom* in terms of which Ambaeans first responded to the project. The first of these is the association between the practice of *kastom* and public occasions of national life. The second is the use of *kastom* as a way of describing precolonial life and those features of contemporary practice understood to derive from it. This second sense of *kastom* is bound up with ideas about loss.

The government's call for *kastom* dances that Chief Simon described was probably made with reference to the Second National Arts Festival held in Santo in 1991, at which teams from throughout the nation demonstrated *kastom* dances and other *kastom* practices from their own areas. The idea of *kastom* as a matter for national public ceremonial is well established on Ambae. At the Ambae/Maewo Local Government Council celebrations, held over five days at Saratamata in September 1991, activities throughout the week were interspersed with the performance of *kastom* dances by teams of men from different parts of the region. The celebrations were also marked by sports competitions (volleyball and football), string band[1] and choir competitions, night discos, and an agricultural show. The highlight of the latter was a pig from Maewo whose tusks were said to make three circles.

The Second National Arts Festival had a continuing influence on some Ambaeans during the year I worked there. Several Longana men who had been part of a dance team attending the festival continued to practice dances and songs every Saturday afternoon, meeting on a rotating basis in each other's hamlets. They hoped to be selected to represent Vanuatu at the South Pacific Arts Festival in the Cook Islands in late 1992. This group, which was led by Edgell Aru, of Lovonda, was regularly called upon by the local government council to perform a *kastom* welcome for visiting dignitaries such as the prime minister (on an election campaign). Several women had gone with the group to the festival to take the subsidiary role assigned to them in men's dances and to demonstrate some *kastom* ways of cooking. Some of these women lived in Lovonda. It was partly their familiarity with the category *kastom* through their participation in the festival that made them open to the work of the WCP and that in turn prompted me to base the project in Lovonda. The arts festival provided opportunities to practice *kastom;* it was also a context in which people talked about *kastom* and enhanced their sense of its importance.

A number of women who had a key involvement in the WCP had also been exposed to ideas about *kastom* through the National Festival of Women held in Vila in May 1990. Several Ambae women who attended the *kalja* workshop organized by Grace Molisa at this festival subsequently took an active role in the WCP. For example, the leader of the women in Lombaha, Jennifer Mwera, commented, the first time I met her, that she had listened to Molisa speak on the importance of *kastom,* had realized that *kastom* was important, and was now considering how children should learn about it. Mwera orchestrated all the WCP work in Lombaha, was appointed after the WCP workshop as one of the first VCC women fieldworkers (with Roselyn Garae of Lolovoli), and was also the source of some of the most considered and interesting commentary about *kastom* that I heard on Ambae. The women's festival also featured a "custom parade," in which all festival participants were involved. A number of Lovonda women attended the festival, including Tarisesei. Once again, their participation introduced them to ideas about *kastom,* linking *kastom* to national contexts.

The way in which, when I arrived in Ambae, *kastom* was linked to national public ceremonies but was not applied to all practices, is made evident by one example. The ceremony *huhu vuhe* (opening green coconuts), which celebrates a person's travel over water on a first visit to another place, was performed during my stay in Lovonda for a woman who had gone to Santo for the first time. She went as one of the team representing east Ambae at the Second National Arts Festival. Although the ceremony was referred to in Bislama as *wan kastom,* using the word as a noun to mean "a ceremony," this was not a self-conscious celebration of *kastom.* The woman went to Santo to demonstrate *kastom.* Her achievement in going was subsequently celebrated by a practice that belonged to her *ples* and affirmed her as belonging to it but that villagers did not understand as the practice of *kastom* in the same sense in which they understood performances at the festival.

The second sense of *kastom* to which Chief Simon's account draws attention is so central to the discourse about it that it could almost be said to be axiomatic. *Kastom* is connected to ideas about loss. Here the interaction between the various components of the concept becomes complex. In general, as Chief Simon's comments demonstrate, people understand the *practice* of *kastom* to refer mostly to public contexts of national life. As a category, however, it is also used to indicate practices that are seen to belong to or derive from the precolonial past. Here it becomes a way of talking about loss. Ambaeans often refer to *kastom* in this way. Chief Simon commented that he could not find ten young men who knew the dances. People often compare the different districts of Ambae in terms of the degree to which they still have *kastom,* by which they mean the degree to which they still know and enact the practices understood to derive from precolonial life. In this sense, *huhu vuhe* is *kastom.* I was often told, for example, that in west Ambae *kastom i lus finis*—"*kastom* is completely lost." When Ture Leo and I took up residence in Lovonda, the leader of the village, Chief Thompson, made a speech at the meeting to welcome us. He said that it was good that we had come because we could help to make sure that they did not lose their *kastom* and *kalja,* especially with respect to textiles. He directed us to talk to the young girls, so that they would learn to plait lots of textiles and know their names, lest things be lost when old people die.

This idea of loss is by no means straightforward. There are practices that I never heard mentioned, such as men's carving of wooden masks, that have receded entirely into the past. Then there are things that Ambaeans recognize as belonging to the lives of their antecedents but that they no longer practice, although they may regret their passing. Thus people often spoke of brother-sister avoidance as something of great importance that is being lost and the loss of which is to be regretted. At the same time, whereas Longanans, for example, recognize that people in other districts, such as the southern district of Lolokaro, live to a far greater extent than they do according to their local practices, they do not wish that they themselves were still living in this way.

Interdistrict jealousies may play some part in the way in which Longanans characterize people from the south, but the construction of those characterizations is significant. When Jacob Kapere came to make a video in Lovonda, men talked to him about *kastom* and related issues. One man spoke to him about the people in the southern districts. They marry too young, he said. They live in dispersed hamlets. They don't want to be developed. When they come to Lovonda they feel as if they have come to town. Kapere offered some interesting glosses of these comments. The people in the south, he said, are new to the world; the way they live is *wok blong Jimmy Stephens*—they were living traditionally, as the Nagriamel community advocates.[2] His interlocutor agreed. People who affirm *kastom,* who regret its loss, do not seek some return to an ideal past. Loss, here, is in part a nostalgia for the safely irretrievable. The man who spoke to Kapere did not want at all to live as Lolokaroans do. He did, however, strongly support the WCP and was in fact one of the people who dealt effectively with opposition to the project. Ambaeans want to retain those parts of their former practices that are consistent with the new ways in which they live and that affirm their identity. A nostalgia for some of the things that have gone is part of that identity.

Ideas of loss have another dimension, and that is the relationship between good and bad *kastom.* Here the influence of Christianity, and of colonial codes of appropriate behavior, comes into play. On Ambae, unlike some other parts of Vanuatu, *kastom* is characterized as something that exists alongside Christianity and that is validated by it. In almost every place I visited, meetings about the WCP were opened and closed with extempore prayer. In praying, people usually both thanked God for bringing the WCP to Ambae and asked him to bless the work of the project. People often made explicit parallels between their local practices and those about which they read in the Bible, implying a legitimate equivalence between the two. At the WCP workshop one woman quietly corrected my secular assumption that it would be possible to end the first day's proceedings without prayer. Thereafter, morning and evening, we prayed for the workshop.

The context in which I heard most about moral evaluations of *kastom* was tattooing. Tattooing, women said, was a good thing because it brought honor to women, and the missionaries were wrong to stop it. By implication, other practices had for good reason been brought to an end. It is part of the definition of *kastom* that the practices so identified should be valuable, and worth reviving. Currently unacceptable practices are not in this sense definable as *kastom,* even though in discourse the concept of "bad *kastom*" is used. In imitation of other VCC staff, I habitually made such moral evaluation part of my own discourse about *kastom:* the work of the VCC is to revive good *kastom.* However, I found it hard to elicit opinion from VCC staff about what "bad *kastom*" might mean or be. The proposition that *kastom* is by definition a good thing obviates the possibility that such a thing as "bad *kastom*" exists. There is much more talk about good and bad *kastom* in Vanuatu's urban centers, where there is among other things a far more uncontrolled use of sorcery, than there is on islands such as Ambae. In the towns, sorcery is explicitly identified as *kastom.* On Ambae, by contrast, sorcery is another area in which to observe the distinction between the practice of *kastom* and other local practices. There is sorcery on Ambae (I was often warned about it), but although it might be described in Bislama using the word "*kastom*" to describe it, it is not understood as *kastom* in the sense of a practice to be valued and revived.

The idea of loss has a further crucial aspect. People may safely mourn the loss of some precolonial practices, but they do not want to lose the *kastom* they still have. This is the sense in which Chief Thompson spoke about loss when he welcomed Ture Leo and me to Lovonda. He emphasized the importance of not losing what women still had, affirming the value of the project in terms of young women learning about textiles. His comments, and Chief Simon's failure to find ten young men, might suggest that older Ambaeans rail against young people's lack of interest in *kastom.* This is not, however, a regular theme of talk on Ambae. Although people recognize that education, especially secondary schooling, takes children away from contexts in which they could learn about *kastom,* there is little discussion about it as a major problem. This may be a function of the way in which the discourse about *kastom* in the 1970s and 1980s so firmly emphasized revival: young as well as old are understood to be committed to this objective.

Ambaeans seem most aware of the danger of losing *kastom* in speaking about their local languages. The term *"kastom"* is not applied to describe the local languages in Vanuatu—people do not talk about *kastom lanwis*—but they identify language as a crucial locus of *kastom.* They also identify language as expressing local identity equally with *kastom,* the two operating side by side. People are concerned that the infiltration of alien words into their languages represents an attack on the very essence of their distinctive regional identity. Thus I heard a discussion of the word *"na,"* which indicates words in Bislama drawn from local languages. In Bislama one speaks, for example, of *na huqe.* People comment on the way in which this usage has been carried back into North-East Ambaean, so that words such as tree names that in North-East Ambaean do not begin with *na,* but that do so in Bislama, are now often spoken in the vernacular with *na* as if it were a prefix. Such usages are common, but they are also commonly bemoaned.

"Kastom" itself is, of course, one of the words that has infiltrated local languages. In the North-East Ambaen language there is no term that translates *"kastom."* After she started work with the VCC, Tarisesei sought out and eventually came up with a word she considered a satisfactory gloss for the term, *"lulude"* (*lulu* means "to be tied up inside something"). She never, however, attempted to introduce this term as explication into Bislama accounts of the WCP to Ambaeans, nor was I ever aware of her using it in vernacular discussions about the project. Rather, her search seemed entirely personal, a private quest to validate her new role as WCP trainee. *"Kastom"* is a word that comes from outside and that people use within local languages to denote a category that has also been introduced. Tarisesei wanted to find a concept within her own local experience to which it could be said to be equivalent. It is perhaps in such terms that she made the statement I quoted at the beginning of this chapter: "they had *kastom,* but they didn't know it was important"—they had it, but they did not know to identify it as such.

When something is named as *kastom,* however, its character is changed; it is brought into a national context and given a new set of meanings and associations. The practices we defined as *kastom* were altered by that definition. It is tempting to hypothesize that some of the opposition to the WCP project on Ambae arose from a reluctance to allow such an alteration to take place.

OPPOSITION TO THE WOMEN'S CULTURE PROJECT

Ambaeans have always had a reputation among expatriates working in the archipelago as being intractable (Allen 1969:1–2; Rodman and Rodman 1991:10). One of the archaeologists working for the Vanuatu Cultural and Historical Sites Survey commented to me that he had heard from several ORSTOM researchers that Ambaean opposition made it difficult to work there. When a lone tourist got off a plane at Longana during my visit and walked into the nearest village saying that he had come to learn about *kastom,* he caused great consternation. The local government council asked the police to check on him and asked me if the VCC knew anything about him. He was given hospitality for some days, but he was not allowed to travel more widely around the island, was banned from taking photographs at the WCP workshop closing ceremony (then taking place), and was soon asked to leave the island. Without VCC and local government council support I imagine my treatment would have been much the same.

Women were deeply gratified by the news that the government of Vanuatu, through the VCC, had sent us to speak to them about their *kastom.* They were honored that their knowledge and activity in making textiles were held to be so important that we had been sent to say so. At that first meeting in Nduindui, the women, hearing news of our plans for the workshop (then a year away), asked how many of them could attend. When I said we had money to bring only two delegates from each area, they asked if more of them could come if they raised the money themselves. Throughout the project, this kind of enthusiasm was constantly in evidence. When we eventually held a meeting in a village where women were not interested in the project, in Wailengi, Longana, I was affronted and annoyed. I had got used to eliciting pleasure from my audiences. I was only marginally comforted by the women's affairs officer based with the local government council who went with us that day; she said that the people in Wailengi were against the government and that she, too, had difficulties there.[3]

In fact, the WCP was not greeted with universal enthusiasm on Ambae. In his account of the WCP, Chief Simon commented that men were suspicious of the WCP workshop, thinking that we had come to steal *kastom* and to make money out of it. This was a reaction of many men, although I rarely heard about such objections until after the event. Ambaeans who were convinced of the value of the project, sometimes people with whom I had no direct dealings (such as Chief Simon himself), dealt with these objections themselves, as an issue within the village or district community. They did not tell me about them, people commented subsequently, because they did not want me to be discouraged. In one instance I deduced from a suddenly tense atmosphere in a meeting that some objections had been raised. At a small gathering in the Lombaha village of Lolomalanga, organized by Jennifer Mwera and attended by two elderly senior men as well as a few women, one of the men asked Mwera and Tarisesei in the vernacular, in my presence, if I had not just come to make money out of *kastom*. He asked in the vernacular, they told me later, because he said he didn't want me to be offended by his question. Mwera explained to him that all I would obtain from the project was a "rank"—an educational qualification— and that this was like the *huqe*. At a pig killing everyone helps and everyone gets to eat the pig, but all the rank taker obtains is his rank. They would all benefit from my work; all I would get was the rank. Tarisesei and Mwera also told the chief that the project was for the benefit of Ambaean children. He was persuaded.

Such objections reveal another side to ideas about *kastom* on Ambae. They relate to indigenous thinking about the nature of knowledge, and in particular to how knowledge is related to *ples*. On Ambae, various kinds of knowledge can be exchanged in transactions in which the giver actually loses the right to use what he has sold. Language, for example, can be transferred in this way. When the people in Lolovoli bought some dialect words from Longanans, the latter actually gave up the right to use those words (see Hyslop 1998:1–2). Knowledge is in some instances regarded as a nonrenewable resource: if it is taken away, it is lost.[4] This is a Vanuatu-wide characterization, with which the Cultural Centre's Oral Traditions Project has engaged for many years. VCC policy is to restrict access to recordings of such material to its rightful owners and to encourage owners to transmit their knowledge to the next generation according to local practice. I found myself explaining this policy over and over again in meetings, responding to questions about control over recordings. News of the policy was received with great approval, especially by men.

The suspicion that we had come to steal *kastom* also exposes the extent to which Ambaeans connect *kastom* with *ples*. Kastom belongs in a *ples;* it should not be taken away. In Lombaha, where I was most conscious of objections to the WCP, I found that in some instances people were reluctant to record stories because they were suspicious of the Cultural Centre as resting place for their material; it was almost as alien to them as I was myself. Rumors abounded that the VCC would charge Ambaeans to obtain access to material recorded by the WCP. In all my time on Ambae I never once had to explain what the VCC was, no matter how remote the place I visited. Everyone had heard of it, even if they did not listen to the VCC radio program, and often people had met James Gwero, who has visited most districts in his years as a fieldworker. In most places, storage of material in the Cultural Centre was acceptable, and Lombaha objections to making recordings were generally easy to resolve, once I explained policies on restricted access to material and on the return of duplicate copies to the island when requested, free of charge. In other words, once the accessibility of VCC resources became apparent, problems generally disappeared. Some further reasons could be suggested for this willingness to store material in the VCC. The idea of documentation makes sense in a context where people fear loss; recordings are a form of insurance, preserving knowledge that can then be acted upon in the future. Moreover, I suggest that the VCC's national status can be seen to be formulated differently from that of other national institutions. In holding *kastom* from throughout Vanuatu, the VCC has also become an extension of, a part of, places all over *(ol ples)* the archipelago. It holds all places together.

Objections that the WCP objectives were to steal *kastom* and make money from it had also been raised in Lovonda. Both Tarisesei (before she joined the WCP) and a Lovonda member of the local government council, David Boe, dealt with the same objections with similar arguments. I had not come to make money; I had come to do something that would benefit their children. By the time I learned about these objections, most of the people who had expressed them were supporting the project. Thus one elderly chief, the senior man in the hamlet section in which I lived, argued at first that I had come to take away *kastom* but subsequently was so far converted that he was chasing women out of their houses to come and take part in the video about textile making. Boe commented to me that it was people without education who were opposed to the WCP, his comment reinforcing yet again the extent to which *kastom* is a product of contemporary national practice.

If I did not know about the strong objections some people made to the project, it was made clear to me again and again that the WCP was acceptable because we were making some return for the information we were recording, because the WCP "gave back." We gave back knowledge and information in the photographs of Ambae textiles in various international museum collections, which we always carried with us. We gave back by putting our recordings on the radio. We gave back in making the videos, showing the footage, and leaving copies on the island. We gave back by holding the workshop. We gave back in that women were honored that Ambae was the site of the first WCP project; Ambaeans considered that in choosing Ambae, the VCC had conferred a distinction on them. We would give back in the future by publishing information about textiles in a small booklet to be circulated on the island; Jean subsequently fulfilled this obligation (Tarisesei 1995).

The importance of giving back was made especially clear to me in the village of Kwantangwele in Walurigi (western Lombaha), where we spent three days in April 1992. The visit was arranged by Jennifer Mwera, but our time in Kwantangwele was organized by Father Mark Mwera, a Kwantangwele man and the local Anglican priest. On our first morning in Kwantangwele we were welcomed in a church service, at which Father Mark spoke. He said that while he was in the Solomon Islands in 1969, his father had died. The anthropologist Michael Allen was visiting Kwantangwele at that time. When Father Mark had returned home, he asked people about his father's funeral, but they had given him an unsatisfactory account of it. Father Mark recalled that he had written to Allen, now returned to Australia, and asked him about the funeral. Allen had sent a full account. With tears in his eyes, Father Mark went on to say, "He sent everything back. Other men wouldn't be able to remember the details, but I know. If I asked you how many textiles you'd covered the old man with, you'd say you'd forgotten, but I know. The record is still there. Lissant will be able to send things back." This was the first time, Father Mark said, that he had ever spoken about this. In Kwantangwele, we were overwhelmed by the wealth of information that people were willing to give us.

One district—Lolovinue—remained persistently closed to us. Although some women in Lolovinue district sent messages to us asking when we would come to talk to them about the project, and although we did in fact hold two meetings in the area, I never succeeded in getting to Lolovinue village itself. Rather, I found that meetings were always held within the cluster of coastal hamlets, at Lotahimamavi and at Lolomanganda, to which women from Lolovinue itself came down. The Lolovinue district delegates to the WCP workshop were accompanied by a man, the husband of one, who expected to attend workshop sessions and who directed some of their participation in the project. Various people hypothesized explanations for Lolovinue's inaccessibility: Grace Molisa, who was partly brought up there, told me that it is a place where there are "different attitudes, and a different range of freedoms" from other parts of Ambae, specifically from Lombaha. The assistant secretary of the local government council suggested to me after the WCP workshop that men are in charge in Lolovinue and that it was for this reason that the Lolovinue participation in the workshop was so guarded. It is possible that the meetings I attended in Lolovinue were, more than in other districts, a way to show courtesy but maintain distance.

ENACTING THE WOMEN'S CULTURE PROJECT

In implementing the WCP it soon became clear that the two objectives for the project, documentation and revival, are not equal. The process of documentation is in and of itself a *technique* for achieving revival. The attention we paid to women's knowledge and practices with respect to textiles drew women's own attention to those practices in a way that stimulated revival. This effect represents an alteration to, an extension of, women's knowledge and practices about textiles. In making textiles into *kastom*, we changed them.

On Ambae ideas about revival are the obverse of ideas about loss. What is in danger of being lost, or has been recently lost, can be revived as long as the right conditions are still in place. The concept of revival is well established in the national discourse about *kastom*, communicated through Radio Vanuatu, and it was entirely familiar to the Ambaeans with whom I dealt. What was in a sense not visible to Ambaean women was the specific material the WCP was there to revive. I found that it was often necessary to hold two meetings in any one village before women started to think about textiles in a way that enabled them to respond to our questions about them. One of the most effective ways of making visible the WCP interest in women's knowledge and skills about textiles was through the albums of photographs of textiles held in museums, which we carried with us. As photographs, the albums objectified textiles, placing them at one remove from everyday experience. As photographs of old textiles, many dating back to the beginning of the century, they demonstrated the continuity of textile production. As photographs of textiles some of which women recognized as Ambaean, but also recognized as different from what they plait today, they also demonstrated the need for revival.

Women were absorbed by the photographs and pored over them. They were particularly interested in and impressed by images of textiles that, from their acquisition or registration dates, were shown to be more than a hundred years old.[5] The photographs were mainly of *singo tuvegi* and *sakole* and of some other *qana*. Women were sometimes unfamiliar with the patterns on the *singo tuvegi* and *sakole* in the photographs; their unfamiliarity is perhaps a reflection of the contemporary emphasis on *qana* and *maraha*.[6] In one case a very skilled and knowledgeable plaiter in Lolovoli recognized a pattern as one that her grandmother had described to her but that she herself had never seen. If the photographs suggested that some textile types and patterns had fallen into disuse, they also reflected a striking continuity in textile forms and patterns throughout the century. Many textile types represented in the earliest collections are still being made on Ambae. For example, there is a *singo tuvegi* with a *vovaho* pattern in the Australian Museum collections, registered in 1899 (see fig. 21). The central design/pattern element is the same as that of the *vovaho* I earned the right to wear by taking a rank in the *huqe* (see fig. 14).

The very process of looking at the albums and of providing documentation for the photographs stimulated discussion about the names of textile types, and in particular about the names of stencil patterns. Often several women listened while older or more knowledgeable women discussed these names, and in this process the listeners learned things they had not known before. The albums stimulated the communication of information between women. They also provided a context in which it became possible for me to ask questions about different textile types, and their uses, and again the answers of knowledgeable women were often of interest to other women. At the second meeting Ture Leo and I held in Lovonda, one elderly woman, Emma Martalini, answered questions that stumped her younger companions. Some weeks later, at the Ambae/Maewo Local Government Council celebrations, I met Tarisesei, who had helped me ask questions at this second meeting (this was well before she joined the WCP as trainee). Tarisesei said that she herself had subsequently gone to ask Martalini more questions about the topics we raised at the meeting. In Kwantangwele many younger women were amazed to hear stories about the two textile types restricted to Walurigi, *wado* and *vola walurigi.* They knew the textiles, but not the stories associated with them.

Through the albums, the project affected, perhaps only temporarily, the suite of textiles made in various districts of Ambae. Women often asked us for photocopies of certain photographs or found a piece of paper and drew particular textile patterns. One woman from Kwantangwele, for example, looked at the photographs when I showed them to people at the Ambae/Maewo Local Government Council celebrations and asked for photocopies of several images, which I afterward sent to her. When Tarisesei and I visited Kwantangwele seven months later, she had woven a textile in imitation of one of the photographs.

A number of observations flow from such instances. First, contemporary plaiting skills are equal to the technical demands posed by the textiles in the photographs, although contemporary textiles are not as finely made. Second, women with such skills take pleasure in the challenge to use those skills in different ways, in this case in the reproduction of two-dimensional images as textiles. Third, in some cases these women were making "again" textile designs that were not indigenous to their particular district. Most textiles in museum collections do not have a more specific provenance than the general designation Ambae, and it was usually not possible for women to suggest more specific provenances. Women who marry from one district to another sometimes import textile types and textile designs with them, so that the transfer of textile types and designs from one district to another is not new. However, the production of textiles from the photographs introduces a new means of transferring them around the island. I never heard any woman comment on this innovation. Equally, the fact that the textiles they were creating from the photographs had no names or stories associated with them did not worry the plaiters. Women were content to recognize the textiles as Ambaean.[7] I do not know whether the textile types "revived" in this way have been adopted into the suite of textiles commonly woven in the different districts, or, if so, how they have been named.

In Vuimberugu in Lombaha people looked at the albums when I visited there in September 1991. When I returned the following May I found that a young man had asked a woman to plait a design he saw in the album as a costume for members of the local string band. The image was of a textile from the collections in the Museum für Volkerkunde in Basel (Vb4507); this textile had very long side fringes and was folded along the central seam, thus appearing in the photograph to have fringes on only one side. The textiles woven for the string band were as the image appeared in the photograph, having fringes on only one side. The young men wore them slung across their chests.

The Vuimberugu string band's textiles raise an interesting issue that was the subject of discussion among women involved in the project, that is, the question of innovation. Jennifer Mwera, of Lombaha, was persistently concerned that we record the "correct" stories about things. When, however, I suggested to her that it was part of Ambaean practice to adopt knowledge and skills from other districts, she immediately agreed. Innovation is also a theme that interested Grace Molisa. At the WCP workshop, which she attended and chaired, she argued that innovation is part of Ambaean practice and that women should consider continuing to make innovations in their plaiting. Molisa was here referring not simply to adoptions from district to district, but to more radical innovations, such as the transfer of openwork designs exclusive to textile production into the making of pandanus baskets.[8] Molisa's comments elicited no debate in the workshop session in which she spoke, and I did not hear any discussion about them afterward. Some innovations (rather than adoptions) in plaiting and in particular in *qegavi* dyeing were part of Ambaean practice before the advent of the WCP. I several times saw *qana* decorated with *qegavi* stencils that overall, or in part, incorporated words.

The idea that change and alteration is part of *kastom* provides a dimension to it that constitutes both challenge and threat to the VCC objectives of documentation and revival. *Kastom* itself is innovation, but it is an innovation that affirms ideas about revival and continuity, emphasizing replication of past forms and practices. Past forms and practices throughout Vanuatu have always involved trade and exchange in objects, knowledge, and practices. The VCC advocates the revival of practices that can be feasibly maintained under present circumstances —for example, encouraging people to put aside European clothing and perform ceremonies in local dress. But I never heard any VCC discussion about the extent to which new elements can be incorporated into practices defined as *kastom*. In fact, discussing with Jacob Kapere the interest of anthropologists in *kastom,* I mentioned that some commentators have suggested that *kastom* is created, a new thing. Kapere's response was anger. *Kastom* may be an introduced category, but the knowledge and practices it names are, crucially, defined as indigenous.

If *kastom* is a new category, it is a new category that is fitted onto existing forms. It took me some time to realize that it was always the production rather than the use of textiles about which women were interested to talk to me. When I moved to Lovonda the women there organized a series of meetings for me with the two women's clubs that met in the village and with smaller hamlet clubs; I went to sit with women as they plaited. Initially I asked them about the details of textile production because the process was there before me and because I considered that technical questions, being comparatively easy to answer, were a good place to begin. As time went by, I found that my inquiries about textile uses did not elicit the interest and information that inquiries about textile production did and that this was not a function of my focus, but of their interest.

Textile production was not an area to which the word *kastom* had ever been applied, even as an attribute. While the contexts in which textiles are used are so described (*kastom mared,* 'marriage') and textiles themselves can be referred to in the same way *(kastom mat),* nobody spoke about plaiting or dyeing as *kastom*. However, when I talked about textiles as *women's kastom,* women understood me to be extending *kastom* to a new area, and they identified that area as encompassing textiles in production and the *huhuru*. They were not as interested in the idea that the term *"kastom"* could refer to the presentation of textiles in exchange. I suggested that women had *kastom;* they agreed. But the knowledge and practices they were interested in identifying as *kastom* were different from those I had expected. By indicating that textiles in production should be identified as *kastom,* they revealed to me the importance that textiles in production have to their sense of themselves as women. They also made the congruence between *kastom* and local practice clearer to me. *Kastom* has value to them as a category because it enables them to draw attention to their practices in a new arena.

GENDERED *KASTOM*

At the very beginning of my research in Vanuatu, James Gwero, the Cultural Centre's Ambae fieldworker, said to me that although women make textiles, it is men who know about them. When I asked other Ambaeans about this they agreed with the proposition, but no one concluded as a result that I should be talking predominantly to men, not women. Gwero's comment suggests that women do not know about textiles. This seems self-evidently untrue: Ambae women do know about textiles since they both make and use them. What I gradually realized is that Gwero's distinction reflects not on whether women know about textiles, but on the way in which Ambaeans understand knowledge itself. It suggests that for Ambaeans, knowledge is a specific category into which not all instances of information possession fall. The information women hold about textiles is different from the information held by men, and the two categories of information are classified differently. Specifically, what women "know" about textiles relates primarily to their manufacture, and it is this that holds and absorbs their interest; it is this that they wished to redefine as *kastom.*

My opportunities to talk to men were somewhat limited by the way in which I was taken over by the Island Council of Women network, and it was only after I had been living on Ambae for about eight months that I began to have a few opportunities to talk to senior men about textiles and to obtain a little contrastive information about what it is that men know about textiles. Perhaps because by that stage I was absorbed by what women know, I was disappointed in what men could tell me.

Long interviews I had with two very senior men, one in Lombaha (Chief John Banga) and one in Longana (Chief Marcel Tari), seemed at the time frustrating in that they did not help me with the questions that by then bothered me, such as the relationships between the various textile types. Both men were primarily interested in textiles in the context of the *huqe*. They discussed how certain men used particular textile types in acts of innovative flair within the *huqe*, thereby bringing cachet to the men themselves, and to the textile type. They also both told me about trade in textiles—how men obtained the textiles they used in the *huqe* on trading expeditions to other districts. They both talked about textiles in the context of the full body tattooing of young girls; and in response to my questions, they talked about the *huhuru*. Here again, their perspective was different from that of women. It was Chief Marcel Tari who told me that formerly a woman's *huhuru* ceremony was generally tied to her husband's participation in the *huqe;* it had never occurred to any woman to explain this connection to me.

The phrase "women have *kastom* too" strongly enforces a gender divide in knowledge and practice. It implies a separation and a distinction. The proposition that women's *kastom* is different from men's *kastom* and that the two categories are closed to each other lies behind the fieldworkers' request for female counterparts. The foundation of the Women's Culture Project established this distinction even as it reformulated the concept of *kastom. Kastom* was redefined positively as referring to both women and men's knowledge and practice, but at the same time the redefinition enshrined a distinction between the two. Of course (as the fieldworkers would readily agree) there is a considerable body of indigenous knowledge and practice that people in either gender position can enact. However, the proposal to have two groups of fieldworkers elided that commonality in favor of a formulation of *kastom* as gendered. An alternative approach to the WCP would have been to attempt to redefine *kastom* as belonging to everyone.

The distinctions between men's and women's practice that I described in chapter 6 creates a context in which it is usual to speak about *ol woman* or *ol man*, grouping men and women into two separate categories. This usage is common. I often heard women speak about *yumi ol woman* (we [inclusive] women) and *mifala ol woman* (we [exclusive] women), and equally I often heard men addressing a group of women as *yumi ol woman,* identifying with them. At the same time, as I discussed in chapter 5, any individual's personal relationships are determined by the proscriptions and expectations of kinship. In each relationship a person has different responsibilities and obligations, and different access to authority or power. Moreover, knowledge and skills are mostly organized and transmitted according to kinship links (as is the right to plait *singo,* for example). These specificities actually run counter to the idea that there might be such a thing as men's or women's *kastom.* That is, while it is true that the production of textiles is something that women do, the specific details of the way in which they do so (who teaches a woman, what she learns to make, why she produces a particular textile type) is always a function of her particular relationships. Thus phrases such as *"yumi ol woman"* operate only when speaking at a general level—for example, in meetings or in broad-brush accounts of a community. The claim that women have *kastom* too is thus one that is made at a community level and that has application in the same context. As a concept *kastom* is not relevant in the same way at a level of individual relationships even while, of course, indigenous knowledge and practice significantly determine those relationships.

Although the idea of women's *kastom* was introduced by the WCP at the level of community rather than of individual relationships, it was not linked to any propositions about the equality or inequality of different sectors of that community. Women's *kastom* was at no point defined as being less important than men's *kastom.* Women's knowledge and practice were brought forward, and the ways in which men's *kastom* is dependent upon what women do was asserted. Kirk Huffman has suggested that the relationship between men and women's *kastom* could be compared to the canoe and outrigger—the outrigger absolutely necessary, balancing and enabling the canoe—and I made use of this metaphor in speaking about women's *kastom.* I was myself extremely careful not to raise issues of power and relative merit, but rather, in all conversations about the topic, to assume equality and also to speak with respect of men's *kastom.* In doing so I followed Cultural Centre practice, focusing on the value and importance of *kastom.* Crucially, this assumption of equal importance was at no point questioned by anyone with whom I spoke. While it may be that men assumed that women's *kastom* was less important, the crucial fact was that no one said so. The WCP argued that women have *kastom* too and acted on the assumption women's *kastom* is as important as men's. Nobody disputed either assertion.

Performing *Kastom:* The Video and the Workshop

Establishing that women have *kastom* too was not just a matter of rhetoric, but of action, and action on a community-wide, if not a national, level. We acted on women's *kastom* in three such contexts: by producing radio programs, by producing several videos, and by organizing a major workshop at Saratamata, which concluded the Ambae project.

The introduction of women's *kastom* was dependent on the radio, not only in Vanuatu as a whole, but also, specifically, on Ambae. Radio programs helped Ambaeans to understand the goals of the WCP. In general, I left the production of the programs to Tarisesei and Kapere, although the three of us did make a program about the WCP, emphasizing the message that women have *kastom*. Usually, however, the programs were devoted to broadcasting the stories and songs we recorded in the process of implementing the Ambae project. Although such material was already classifiable as *kastom,* requiring no stretch of categories, these programs drew Ambaean attention to local practice as *kastom*. Their value to the project was indirect. People were pleased to hear themselves on the radio, and the broadcasts gave a focus to, and a return for, the information we were recording. People came forward to record stories because they heard the programs, partly because they wanted to hear their own voices on the radio and partly because the programs provided a context in which audiotaping stories made more sense. Tarisesei and I sent audiotapes by plane to Port Vila for Kapere to broadcast, so that they were being broadcast while we were still on Ambae making recordings. Thus the programs went before us into parts of Ambae we had not yet visited, introducing the idea of the Ambae project before Tarisesei and I arrived to talk about it.

The making of videos also significantly affected women's perception of textiles as *kastom*. This effect was restricted to Lovonda, although, as Chief Simon remarked, the showing of the video footage had a much wider influence. Jacob Kapere visited Ambae three times to film footage for the Women's Culture Project. His first visit was made to film the textile-making process, the second to record a wedding, and the third to document the WCP workshop. Of these occasions, it was in the first that Ambaeans participated the most. While pleased that Kapere was filming the wedding, Lovonda residents simply allowed him, with assistance from Tarisesei and me, to film as he chose. Their interest was focused not on the filming, but on the ceremony itself. The third video project, filming the workshop, Kapere undertook entirely at his own discretion. But the first, the video about textile making, was in many senses directed by the women of Lovonda themselves.

Plans for this video were initially made while Ture Leo was with the project, when we first arrived in Lovonda. At a meeting called by Tarisesei to organize a program for our stay in Lovonda, I mentioned our plans to make a video, which I proposed should document textile making. The women at the meeting suggested that each stage of the textile-making process should be demonstrated by a different woman. Ture Leo proposed that they also act out some textile uses for the camera, a proposal that prompted some hilarity as they discussed how such a thing could be achieved. The women pointed out that about a month later a woman would be performing *huhuru* and suggested that this could be filmed.

By the time Kapere finally arrived to make the video, in February 1992, Ture Leo had departed the project, and Tarisesei had joined it. Much of the planning and negotiations that established what the women actually presented to the camera was undertaken by Tarisesei and other village women in contexts apart from Kapere and me. Tarisesei would tell us what women were suggesting. Ture Leo, Tarisesei, and I had spent some time making a list of women and a list of textile-production tasks to ensure that each woman in the village had a part to play, but this list was entirely disregarded. The women themselves arranged, without any apparent conflict, who did what, and we merely filmed what they presented to us, over a period of eight days. All the filming took place in the two sections of the hamlet in which I lived, Vunangai and Loqirutaro. Interest in the process grew over the week, as people watched the filming.[9] After the first few days' filming, one senior woman, a *singo* specialist with a lot of knowledge about textiles, decided to come forward and present the *gigilugi* technique for the camera. This woman had been criticized earlier for keeping her knowledge to herself and not sharing it with other women. In participating in the filming, she

Fig. 23 Jacob Kapere about to film a restricted segment of Lena Jasper's *huhuru*. To view the material he was filming he needed to hold a *maraha* over his head. Loqirutaro, Lovonda, east Ambae. February 1992.

went public with some of it, a development that received serious and pleased commentary from other village women.

The women decided to bring forward the planned *huhuru* ceremony they had mentioned in the first planning meeting (but which had still not taken place) so that it could be filmed. One of the senior women in Loqirutaro, Rose Boe, was the adopted mother of the woman performing the ceremony and was able to persuade the protagonists to bring the ceremony forward. I had been confused on a number of occasions by accounts of the *huhuru,* and it was not until partway through the occasion that I began to realize its importance to the women themselves. A wedding was also being planned at this time, whose principals came from the same hamlet (Narongleo) as those involved in the *huhuru.* While admittedly a wedding involves a great deal more organization than a *huhuru,* it is interesting to observe that no attempt was made to bring this way of using textiles forward to be filmed; in fact, that wedding took place a week after filming finished. The *huhuru,* which celebrates women's production of textiles, was important to them in a way that textile use wasn't. It was also, of course, an occasion in which only women were involved.

In speeches made at the textile exchanges with which the *huhuru* concluded, several speakers commented on the parallels between the *huhuru* and the *huqe.* Evelyn Malanga, one of the *singo* specialists who took part in the ceremony, said, 'Women, this is our *huqe*—with respect to *singo.* Men have the *huqe,* but it is important that we make this big ceremony, which is called *huhuru.*" One woman, listening to these speeches, commented to me, "When women kill pigs, men are involved, but when women make *huhuru,* they do it for themselves." I, through the WCP, identified textiles as women's *kastom,* but the women themselves saw the *huhuru* as its most important expression.

Women in the village decided to dance in textiles for the camera to finish the video properly. Rose Boe, who was also influential in the filming of the *huhuru* (and who was one of the women who had been to the Second National Arts Festival), suggested as a joke that they wear textiles to dance, but others took up the idea seriously. This was the first time in living memory that women had danced in textiles in Lovonda; usually they wore European clothes (sometimes with a textile over the top). The first time any woman had worn textiles by themselves was at the National Women's Festival in 1990 in Vila; then several women had put them on at the Second National Arts Festival in 1991 in Santo—that is, a few women had worn "traditional costume" in national venues. But they had never done so on Ambae. There was some debate about dancing in textiles. As one woman explained to me, some women didn't want to do it, but others said, no, we must so that we can display (*soemaot;* also "reveal") all the *kastom* textiles we've been showing all week. Several women commented to me afterward that they had been nervous about dancing in textiles because they weren't comfortable wearing them, were, in fact, afraid that they might fall off, but that having danced and realized that they could do it, they were eager to do it again. About eighteen women (and one man) danced a women's dance called *lenga* and acted out, within the dancing, the *kastom* story about a woman who was so preoccupied with plaiting that she neglected her children, who both died.

The women were exhilarated by the experience. Many people commented that although they had neither practiced nor performed any actions (such as drinking coconuts) to ensure that the dancing went well, the dancing was very good.[10] Women who had scrounged around to find textiles suitable to wear (not all of them had *sakole* ready to hand) would now make sure that they had the right kind of textiles for next time. Tarisesei audiotaped the singing with which the dancers accompanied themselves, and Kapere incorporated the recording into a radio program broadcast in the following weeks. When Tarisesei and I later went to Lombaha, Jennifer Mwera commented that she could hear in the recording that the women were dancing well. The idea of women's dancing as *kastom* was affirmed through the radio.

In speeches at a farewell ceremony for Kapere, which took place immediately after the dance, speakers expressed their pleasure in the dancing and discussed the impact of the video and, more widely, the impact of the WCP on village members. The president of the Havutu Women's Club said that in the past Lovonda women felt that other women (in other places) knew more than they did and that they were deeply pleased that we had chosen to come to them. They had had only a little *kastom,* but when we came and drew their attention to textiles and to *singo,* they had started learning more, had looked back to what their grandparents knew. She thanked Kapere and me for "waking us up." Tarisesei commented to me that Lovondans were pleased about the video because it made them feel important. She said that when you live your ordinary life in a village you feel unimportant; the fact that we had come to them and made the video made them feel valued.

The WCP workshop, held in June 1992 at Saratamata, the local government council headquarters, was the highlight of the WCP on Ambae. Tarisesei and I organized it, with advice and logistical support from local government council staff, and with the assistance and cooperation of many other people. Delegates stayed at the Anglican Church training center, the Torgil Centre, near Saratamata. Residents of Saratamata and other nearby communities were hired to build a shelter for delegates to eat in and to prepare and cook food. The Fisheries Department rented us their boat to bring delegates from Vuingalato and Lolokaro.

Thirty-nine women from every district of Ambae, and four observers from Santo, Malo, Pentecost, and Maewo, attended. There were far more delegates from Ambae than we had originally planned. Every time we succeeded in getting in touch with the leader of women in a particular district to discuss who would attend, we were asked to double the number of delegates. In districts in which we had undertaken a reasonable amount of work, the women who attended were those who had been involved in the project and consistently shown interest in it. Other districts, such as Vuingalato, sent either leaders of women or women who had some personal interest in getting to Saratamata. We had asked each district to send both older women who knew about textiles and younger women interested in learning about them, and there was a good age mix. Girls from Vureas High School attended two sessions. Grace Molisa attended and took on the role of session chairperson. We closed the sessions to men, but in fact four men attended. Jacob Kapere audiotaped and occasionally videoed the proceedings for the VCC archives. James Gwero sat quietly in one corner and at his own initiative took the minutes of the meeting for the whole week. The Anglican Church's Torgil Centre sent a young man to observe the sessions, and the chief from Lolovinue who accompanied his wife insisted on attending. None of these men spoke apart from James Gwero, who was asked to speak about being a fieldworker; otherwise they were all unobtrusive.

Imitating procedures I had observed at the VCC fieldworker workshops and at the Ambae/Maewo Local Government Council tenth anniversary, we organized an impressive list of community leaders to speak at the opening. Representatives of the local government council, the Anglican Church and the Church of Christ, the Ambae/Maewo Island Council of Chiefs, the Ambae/Maewo Council of Women, and the VCC all spoke. Whereas speakers at the opening ceremony represented local bodies, the closing ceremony, a public day, was attended by figures representing the nation. The deputy prime minister and minister for justice, culture, and women, the Honorable Sethy Regenvanu,

Fig. 24 Emma Taga from Kwantangwele, north Ambae, talking about the textile *singo matai talai,* which originates from Kwantangwele, at the Women's Culture Project Workshop at the local government council offices, Saratamata, east Ambae. June 1992.

accepted an invitation to close the workshop. Speakers also represented the Vanuatu National Council of Women, the Australian High Commission, the VCC, and the Anglican Church, as well as the local government council, the regional office of the Education Department, and the Ambae / Maewo Council of Chiefs. There was, in other words, widespread interest in the workshop not only among the delegates who attended, but more generally at a regional and national level. Some speakers at the closing ceremony, such as the representative of the Education Department, had asked permission to participate. Radio Vanuatu sent a reporter, and Regenvanu's speech was reported in the national news that evening.

Tarisesei and I had decided on the topics for the seven workshop sessions. One or more representatives from each district spoke on each topic. They discussed the suites of textiles produced in their districts, textile origin stories, textile designs and patterns, tattoo, the *huhuru,* and the events that formerly took place in women's lives from birth to death. The final session was an evaluation session in which women discussed the workshop itself. Delegates initially found it difficult to speak. Significantly, it was women such as Jennifer Mwera, who had attended the National Festival of Women and who had spent some considerable time working with the WCP, who were best able to marshal information in this way. However, other women who were personally interested in the material were also able to present a lot of information to the workshop. There was no conflict in the sessions over the information presented. Delegates accepted differences in the data presented as representing regional diversity. However, there was some discussion about such information behind the scenes. One woman who often spoke for Lolovoli proffered some information about the meanings of textiles that the Lovonda delegates (to whose opinions I had good access) privately disputed. Their objections may in part have reflected the mild antagonism to people from the south to which Lovondans are prone.

The delegates were most deeply interested in the session on textile designs and patterns. As each district representative stood up and exhibited particular textiles, pointing out features in the plait, all the other delegates leaned forward in their eagerness to see what was being pointed out. The response to this session was, I think, a reflection of the fact that women are used to articulating this sort of information and saw a practical use in learning it and of the fact that textile production lies at the heart of their interests. The session about life history also interested the delegates. Most speakers concentrated on birth, from the perspective of both mother and daughter, drawing attention to the way in which women were associated with plaiting from their first moments, through the use of pandanus as a symbol announcing the birth of a girl. The session on *singo* and *huhuru* was frustrating to me, as comparatively little information was presented. I only gradually realized that women were reluctant to talk in public about something that has significant restricted components. I was thus made aware that stricter restrictions relating to the *huhuru* and to *singo* are in place in districts other than Longana.

A lot of talk during the proceedings, in the evaluation session and afterward, focused on the complaint that the workshop was too short. Delegates felt that they were only just beginning to grasp the idea of the workshop as it ended, that they needed time to think more about the topics being discussed in order to bring forward more complete information. The workshop effected for them what the WCP and especially the video effected for the women of Lovonda: it made areas of their knowledge and practice visible to them in a new way. They wanted more time to think about it. Delegates requested another workshop, Jennifer Mwera commenting that it would be good if they could organize it without any white assistance. Women also said that they had learned new things; they exchanged information with each other in the workshop. These new things included information about textile types, in-weave designs and stencil patterns, stories about textile origins, and information about aspects of women's lives in the past, such as the practices associated with birth and tattoo. The assistant secretary of the local government council commented to me that the workshop should have had better participants with more skills and knowledge; to achieve this, he said, we should have done more work in villages before the workshop.

The last day of the workshop was its highlight. Observing the effect that dancing in textiles had had upon Lovondan women, I had decided to include dancing in textiles in the closing ceremonies of the workshop. I did so, at least initially, as a way of giving further expression to Lovondan women's exhilaration at the dancing for the video and to stimulate them to prepare the appropriate *sakole* so that they would have them ready to wear on other occasions. This idea grew over the months preceding the workshop, so that when the day came there were seven dance teams, six representing Ambae districts and one made up of Pentecost women living around Saratamata and Lolowai.[11] Approximately 250 Ambaeans came to Saratamata for the event, most of whom were women and children. The dancing was exciting to watch, and many people exclaimed that it was the first time they had ever seen women dancing in textiles. Given that men had always dominated *kastom* in Vanuatu, so that women had only ever danced in support of men in public ceremonies, this was a historic event not only for Ambae, but for the nation. It was the first public occasion affirming women's *kastom* through practice in this way.

It seems to me that the key to understanding the women's exhilaration at dancing in textiles lies at least partly in the discussions Lovonda women had about whether or not to do it. They decided to dance in textiles to display, to reveal *(soemaot),* their skills and knowledge in making textiles. As I have argued, textile making is very important to women's sense of themselves and is the context in which they achieve status and respect. If textile making is crucial to their sense of themselves, then by wearing textiles women display on their bodies evidence of the productivity that makes them who they are. From a Cultural Centre perspective, the fact that women danced in textiles, for the National Film Unit camera and before the deputy prime minister, affirmed the redefinition of textiles as *kastom* and women as the possessors of it.

Chief Simon's account of the workshop draws attention to the features of it that influenced the wider community. First, the presence of Sethy Regenvanu provided an affirmation not only of the workshop, but also of what it represented, by the very source that has always validated *kastom* in Vanuatu—the government. Just as Walter Lini and other national leaders (including Regenvanu, in fact) had affirmed the importance of *kastom* to national identity in the 1970s and 1980s, so now a national leader was affirming a new aspect of the discourse about *kastom*—that it is something women also have. Second, Chief Simon commented on the dances: "Every man smiled and was glad." It was not merely that women were *said* to have *kastom,* but that they demonstrated that they do by putting on textiles and dancing. They acted. Third, we showed a rough cut of the video footage of both the textile-making process and a wedding we had filmed. Watching their own practices on the screen objectified *kastom* for the audience, giving them an opportunity to see it in a new light. As Chief Simon reported, the next morning opposition was overturned: men commented that the workshop was a good thing and that they must help women with their *kastom*. We had reidentified women's practice as *kastom*.

The Women's Culture Project, in talking about and acting on certain women's practices on Ambae, objectified those practices and made them visible to Ambaeans, particularly to women, defining them anew as *kastom*. The extent to which this process made these practices visible is evident in a comment made by Jennifer Mwera, in a conversation with Tarisesei: "We used to think that these things were unimportant *(bifo yumi ting se samting nating)*, just part of everyday life, but now we see that they have value."

◙ ◙ ◙ *Conclusion*

Women with *Kastom*

S*everal weeks after the Saratamata workshop* the Ambae project concluded, and Tarisesei and I returned to Port Vila. In August 1992 we went as part of a large Vanuatu delegation to a week-long conference, "Developing Cultural Policy in Melanesia," held in Honiara, Solomon Islands, where we spoke about the Women's Culture Project (Lindstrom and White 1994). At a meeting of the delegation after the conference, Grace Molisa spoke about the development of the WCP. She commented that while the contribution of women might be recognized at village level (here thinking of the negotiations of everyday life), at national level in Vanuatu "we go beyond a single language group to a new organization, a new territory." At this level, she observed, "women are missing. When men talk about *kastom* at this level they omit women; they pretend that women don't have *kastom*." She went on to say, "If we make women's work of no importance *(samting nating)*, then much will be lost."

The role that the independence movement and the Cultural Centre created for *kastom* was to attribute value. The reasons for the attribution of value differed. The independence movement attributed value to *kastom* in order to assert the distinct and separate identity of the indigenous citizens of the archipelago, as a basis for nationhood. The Cultural Centre attributed value in support of that objective, but it also attributed value to *kastom* on the basis of a museological and anthropological assessment of the importance of cultural diversity in and of itself. In response, rural ni-Vanuatu took hold of the idea that their own knowledges and practices are important and, through the fieldworker program, began to develop locally specific senses of the value of their own *kastom*. Thus if *kastom* was constituted in the new national context, the idea of *kastom* was worked out, and its ramifications extended, at the local level.

This tracking between the national and the local was equally true of the creation of the idea of women's *kastom*. This is what Grace Molisa's comments make clear. At the local level, both men and women participate in local knowledge and practice, whether or not these things are defined as *kastom*. At the national level, until 1992, the expression and affirmation of *kastom* focused almost exclusively on what men know and do. Molisa, and other women operating at the national level, for example in the Vanuatu National Council of Women, recognized that women were absent in the national constitution of *kastom* and saw this as a problem. The importance of Molisa's remarks was that she recognized the effect of the national on the local level: "if we make women's work of no importance, then much will be lost."

If it had not been demonstrated with reference to specific knowledge and practice, the claim that women have *kastom* too could only have been made rhetorically at the national level. The importance of the Ambae project was that it demonstrated the claim with such unanswerable clarity. The indisputable importance of textiles on Ambae, and their absolute identification with women, was critical to the assertion that women have *kastom*. In that Sunday debate on gender relations at St. Johns, Loqirutaro, described in chapter 6, people commented that making textiles is the one thing that women can do that men can't do. Ambae textiles are a highly visible feature of Ambaean life. Once textiles had been identified as *kastom,* their constant presence became a continuing reminder that women have *kastom* too. Textiles would have had less potency as a demonstration of women's *kastom* had they been less significant, but the depth and complexity of the Ambae textile system, and the extent of its reach into all aspects of local practice, made textiles a visible reminder of the complexity of what women make and know.

If the choice of Ambae textiles as a focus for the first WCP project was so apposite, this was perhaps more a matter of good fortune than of good planning. Whereas VCC programs were influenced, through Huffman, Tryon, and others, by museology, anthropology, and linguistics, the WCP was further informed by my own specifically museum-anthropological concern with objects, and with their significance to their makers and users. It was I who wanted to focus on objects: the Cultural Centre Board chose Ambae. Grace Molisa, in advocating the focus, hoped that we would document the vital role of textiles in regional trade, an aspect of textiles that, because it was controlled by men and because it had largely died out, Tarisesei and I actually hardly considered.

The significant further aspect of the Ambae textile complex was that it lent itself so readily to the new, postindependence role for *kastom:* as performance. Because they could be worn, and specifically worn as *kastom dresing* (traditional costume) for dances, textiles could be translated directly into a performance context. At the end of the filming for the video about textile production, the women of Lovonda themselves decided to dress in textiles and dance for the National Film Unit camera: as they said, to display, or reveal, their *kastom.* At the end of the Saratamata workshop, women from across the island dressed to dance in textiles in a kind of impromptu arts festival at which, as Chief Simon put it, "every man smiled and was glad." Women asserted and demonstrated the claim that they have *kastom* too by dancing in textiles, and that claim was accepted readily by those present. Moreover, by making the videos, both about textile production and about marriage, Kapere, Tarisesei, and I affirmed the new performative dimension to textile production and use.

Analysis of *kastom* has often concentrated on what *kastom* represents, asking about the relationship between culture and its externalization as a symbol (Keesing 1982:300), and as a consequence focusing on the accuracy of that representation. This focus sometimes resulted in those commentaries that describe *kastom* as inauthentic or spurious (Philibert 1986:2; Keesing 1989:20) or in the conclusion that *kastom* is polysemic (Jolly 1992:340). In other words, many analyses attend to the content of *kastom,* addressing the range of the material to which the term refers. What engagement in the Women's Culture Project taught me is that, partly as a result of VCC programs, the important thing about *kastom* is not what it describes, but what making that description does, what can be achieved by applying the word *"kastom"* to aspects of what people know and do. It is not so much a question of what aspects of ni-Vanuatu knowledge and practice can be described using that term as what effect using that term has on that knowledge and practice and what possibilities and opportunities doing so presents. In other words, if theoretical developments in material culture studies, discussed at the end of chapter 6, emphasize the agency, rather than the meaning, of objects, this emphasis on agency can also, most helpfully, be applied to concepts. It is not what *kastom* means that is important, but what it can achieve, what its work is.

CONTINUITY AND CHANGE

As it is constituted through the VCC, the work of *kastom* is to attribute value; and it is to attribute value in the new context of the nation. It is also, however, to attribute value in this new context in order to create a continuity at a local level. Jennifer Mwera, comforting me in the face of the objections to the WCP made by the old chief in Lolomalanga, Lombaha, said that I must not be discouraged, that she and Tarisesei were concerned with the WCP because they had to find a way to link the past to the future. This is not a changeless continuity however, rather, it is a processual continuity, involving transformation.

When practices are redefined as *kastom,* they are altered, and new occasions are built around them. These are both imposed (as the WCP imposed the making of radio programs and videos and the holding of the workshop on Ambae) and also developed by the people whose practices are so redefined. There were several alterations to knowledge and practices with respect to textile making in Lovonda as a result of the WCP. The first was an explicit goal of the project from the perspective of the VCC: the transmission of knowledge. The elderly woman who came forward during the filming of the textile-making video to demonstrate techniques she had formerly kept secret was communicating something she might otherwise have taken with her to the grave and making use of a new context to communicate it. Chief Thompson, the chief of Lovonda, emphasized the importance of the transmission of knowledge in a speech made in farewell to Kapere when the filming of this video was finished. Chief Thompson commented that the WCP had encouraged older people to reveal some of their knowledge. He said it is no good if someone knows something and locks it in their minds like clothes in a box, where no one can see it; rather they should tell it to someone else. "If you die," he said, "everything will be lost."

At the end of my time in Ambae, I interviewed a number of Lovonda women for a radio program about the impact of the WCP. Many of them reported that they had learned something new, such as a plaiting technique, because of the project. The WCP created a series of new contexts and new relationships in and through which knowledge could be transmitted. Inevitably, this altered (perhaps only temporarily) established practices of knowledge transmission. Certain kinds of knowledge, as a resource, were formerly only transmitted in fixed conditions (such as was the skill of making *singo*). The possession of such knowledge conferred distinction on, and was a source of remuneration for, the holder. Contexts such as the video and the workshop provided new ways of transmitting knowledge between differently situated persons, and new ways of conferring distinction.

Kastom also provides new ways in which honor can be conferred. As Jean Tarisesei commented, Lovondans were pleased about the video because it made them feel important. More generally, the people whom I addressed in meetings about the WCP were pleased because the government of Vanuatu had chosen to initiate the project on Ambae. *Kastom* had been used by ni-Vanuatu as a source of status since the 1970s. It is interesting that when I asked Keith Woodward, the British Residency official, about the development of the concept of *kastom* during the 1970s (Woodward left the country in 1978), he actually reformulated my questions specifically in terms of the status *kastom* can confer (pers. comm. 1993). Was I asking, he inquired, at what point people in Longana—who went on taking ranks in the *huqe* throughout the colonial era—started to consider doing so to have a significance over and above the acquisition of rank? At what point did they see it as a means of enhancing their status in another way? Similarly, in an interview about the Oral Traditions Project published in *Pacific Islands Monthly* in 1988, Huffman commented that "in certain areas . . . having a video made of a ceremony is looked on as validating your ceremony" (Rothwell 1988:15). Filming an occasion enhanced the person mounting the occasion in the eyes of his or her neighbors. The practice of *kastom* can confer honor.

At the same time, these new formulations of *kastom* can also introduce forms of fixity to past fluidity. As I mentioned in chapter 4, the connection between *kastom* and place has sometimes been asserted to the point of challenge—a certain ritual, for example, cannot, by this argument, be performed outside its place (see Jolly 1994a:140). And as

I discussed in chapter 8, the claim that women have *kastom* too strongly reinforces a gender divide in knowledge and practice, drawing a distinction that was often far less clear in local practice. Ironically then, the claim that women have *kastom* too at once subverts the colonially introduced gender distinctions that linked women to the private or domestic sphere and men to the public and introduces new distinctions by implying that all indigenous knowledge and practice can be gendered as either male or female.

WOMEN, *KASTOM*, *PLES*

The interpenetration of indigenous and exogenous ideas in the construction of *kastom* is at its most complex in relation to ideas about place. In chapter 5 I argued that the European and colonial emphasis on land ownership obscured east Ambaean ideas about gendered relationships to land. I suggested that bearing children to a landholding is female practice, and in this sense, women do pass land on. Men practice their relationship to land by having enduring rights to it; women practice their relationship to land by bearing children to it. Both men and women practice their relationship to land by using it for gardens and by living on it. The colonial interpretation of such systems accounted men as landowners and discounted women's relationships to land, and this perspective has been upheld by ni-Vanuatu since independence.

The independence movement clearly associated *kastom* with land. A circular setting out the aims of the newly founded New Hebrides National Party (later the Vanuaaku Pati) declared that "[New Hebrideans'] culture and their ways of life are in immediate danger of large scale settlement by Europeans" (cited in Van Trease 1987:207): local culture is in danger because of the large-scale expatriate settlement of land. This is a link not just with land, but with land ownership. *Kastom* is tied to the ownership of land. Women are by this association separated from *kastom* because women very rarely hold or own land. A discrimination between *ples* and land is not made explicitly in Vanuatu. However, the effect of the VCC policies was to make such a distinction in practice, both by disassociating *kastom* from land disputes, and hence from land ownership, and by operating on the basis that each place has its own *kastom*.

The VCC definition of *kastom* as the practice of different places crucially reflected many local conceptions of the relationships between practice and place. In many areas ideas about place are central to the organization of social life: they often inform the very formulation of kinship. When the VCC acted on *kastom* in a way that differentiated practices by *ples,* that action was itself a reflection of local practice in many parts of the archipelago. However, while the connection between *kastom* and *ples* is part of the discourse about *kastom,* that essential connection is not formulated as itself *kastom.* The fieldworkers do not deal with ideas about place reflexively as an ideology of belonging, but rather that the difference that place creates between people is the basis of the differences in practice that the fieldworkers discuss. As with the fieldworkers, so more generally with respect to the discourse about *kastom.* The way in which people are tied to their *ples* is not discussed as a *kastom* practice, but the tie itself underpins the discourse. The perhaps unintended consequence of this is to make it easier for women to be recognized as having *kastom. Kastom* derives from *ples.* Landholding is a male practice of *ples.* Women have other practices of *ples.* Therefore, women have *kastom* too.

The knowledge and practices that Ambae women chose to designate as *kastom* in response to the Women's Culture Project were not all derived from the precolonial past. Although women spoke of traditional dyeing techniques using the vegetable dye *laqe* as *kastom,* no one suggested that dyeing textiles with store-bought dye made the textiles something other than *kastom.* Rather, the women with whom I worked welcomed the definition of their present practices as *kastom,* recognizing them as belonging to and exemplifying their districts, their island, their *ples. Kastom* can be understood as equivalent to neither culture nor tradition. While the legitimation of *kastom* is that it represents an identity that has historical continuity, *kastom* does not prejudge where the best exemplars of that identity lie, in the past or in the present. It is possible for ni-Vanuatu to identify as *kastom* practices that did not occur in the precolonial period.

NEW RELATIONSHIPS

The formulation of *kastom* as the diverse practices of *ples* is specifically significant in the national context. Jennifer Mwera once remarked upon an essay by an Ambaean boy studying at Malapoa High School in Port Vila. The student had written that *kastom* is like a *nakato,* a hermit crab, because "we walk about inside it." Mwera commented on the truth of this metaphor: "You don't see it when you stay in the village, because you have the shell, but when you go to Vila you realize it. People come and ask you about your *kastom* and you don't know, and they say you're not really from Ambae." *Kastom* makes *ples* evident, and *ples* has been formulated as a key basis for social identity within the new nation of Vanuatu. The importance of this is to do with the elaboration of relationships.

To say that *kastom* is not so much about identity as it is about the elaboration of relationships is in a sense self-evident: clearly, identity is only meaningful in relationships. However, relationships involve considerably more than identity. Changing social conditions in Vanuatu that have resulted from the impact of the Western world have both reduced the potency of traditional relationships, such as trading partnerships, and introduced a new range of potential relationships between ni-Vanuatu. People needed to find new terms in which to negotiate and elaborate these new relationships. By emphasizing a common possession of *kastom,* national leaders initially provided grounds for largely ideological relationships of commonality among the many different groups in the archipelago. After independence ni-Vanuatu used *kastom* as a way of expressing individual difference in national contexts: hence the idea that *kastom* is like a hermit crab—you can walk about inside it.

The idea of *kastom* as a means of elaborating relationships also throws light on the new venues in which *kastom* is expressed, such as arts festivals. Such occasions brought people together in ways that enabled them to establish new connections and to share knowledge, without dislocating them from the identity and relationships that frame their lives in the village. It was perhaps those people who were not much exposed to contexts outside the village who did not see the value of *kastom* and were resistant to having their practices so defined. Where there was no occasion to form relationships outside the immediate area, then there was no need to formulate one's practices as *kastom.*

In the early 1990s, islanders made use of *kastom* to reframe their identity and to build relationships when they saw themselves operating in a national context. Such national contexts include not only towns such as Port Vila, but also the nationally created contexts of local government council regions and the postindependence self-consciousness of islands such as Ambae as a whole. *Kastom* was used by Ambaeans to formulate both differences and similarities between the different districts of the island, as being "the same but a little bit different." The extension of *kastom* to women enabled them to operate in these contexts independently of men. It enabled them, metaphorically speaking, to step forward onto the national *sara.*

If my account of this process seems unduly rose-colored, I think there are some reasons for this. *Kastom* provides interest and entertainment. For women on Ambae, the WCP was enlivening to have around. People enjoyed thinking about it; they were pleased to hear themselves on the radio and see themselves on video. It gave women a new and positive affirmation of a major aspect of their daily lives. And they enjoyed dancing in textiles. At a national level *kastom* has facilitated some highly enjoyable occasions, such as the national arts festivals. If people can lay claim to an identity grounded in the place, then they are at liberty to transform the very practices on which they base their claim. Romanticism is inherent in, indeed necessary to, this process. Indigenous practice in itself was not a sound basis for unifying the archipelago, but laying claim to that practice was a way to negotiate the transformations of independence. If *kastom* was one basis of the new nation, then the claim that women have *kastom* too was a claim for women's participation in the nation, as well as a claim for their contribution to the ongoing practices of rural communities.

Kastom altered the practices to which it referred. It conferred a new status on existing practices, brought about the revival of others, and modified both by assigning to them new purposes and meanings. In this sense, the definition of practices as *kastom* was a process similar to that of applying a *gigilugi* stencil to a *singo*. The stencil outlines the design woven into the fabric of the textile, drawing attention to it. It also adds a number of new elements and transforms the textile with color. In the dyeing of *singo* with *gigilugi* in the *huhuru,* an Ambae woman confers honor and status on herself. In redefining textile making as *kastom,* Ambae women transformed those practices and conferred a new kind of honor on themselves. By identifying their production of textiles as *kastom,* women were able to step onto the national arena and unfold and display their practice as *kastom.* By this means they made it possible to form new relationships derived from their own places, within the nation of Vanuatu.

Epilogue

The first women fieldworkers workshop was held in Port Vila in 1994 and was attended by ten women. Women fieldworker workshops have taken place annually thereafter, directed by Jean Tarisesei and me, and the group has grown steadily in size, reaching approximately forty in 2002. Women fieldworkers have hosted and supported researchers, initiated and participated in video projects, contributed to radio programs, and revived almost-forgotten practices in several different parts of the country. Some women fieldworkers have participated in linguistic and archaeological training programs, and several took part in workshops discussing aspects of condominium history. When a new Vanuatu Cultural Centre building opened in 1995 with a mini arts festival, an Ambae women's dance group was among the participants. In 2000, women's groups from various parts of the archipelago were included among those representing Vanuatu at the Pacific Arts Festival in Noumea.

Jack Keitadi left the Cultural Centre in 1993, being replaced first by Chief Willie Bongmatur Maldo and then, not long after, by Clarence Marae. In 1995 Ralph Regenvanu was appointed as Cultural Centre director, and under his leadership the institution has grown and blossomed. Projects in archaeology, linguistics, ethnomusicology, the ethnography of marine resource management, and colonial history have all been developed. All of these involve and depend on the participation of fieldworkers, both men and women. In 1997 the Cultural Centre developed a major initiative with young people, first in Port Vila and latterly in rural areas: the Vanuatu Young People's Project (Mitchell 1998). Darrell Tryon continues to direct the annual men fieldworkers workshops, and Kirk Huffman makes annual visits to Vanuatu, usually timed to coincide with the men fieldworkers work-

Fig. 25 Jennifer Mwera *(right)* and Roselyn Garae. Both were deeply interested in the Women's Culture Project on Ambae, and both subsequently became women fieldworkers. They are photographed here at the third women fieldworkers workshop. July 1996.

shop. The fieldworker program has become famous in the region. In 1999, for example, the Cultural Centre made presentations about the program to a Pacific Islands Museum Association meeting, as several regional museums hoped to emulate it.

During the decade in which the women fieldworker program has grown and developed, women's organizations in Vanuatu have moved away from a commitment to *kastom,* developing instead a discourse of women's rights drawn largely from Anglo-American feminist concerns but prompted by the problems faced by urban women in the context of significant population growth. These developments have led to some disconnection between rural women and organizations such as the VNCW. Political instability marked much of the decade, with increasingly frequent changes of government and a lack of strong leadership: the commitment to *kastom* has become decreasingly significant in political discourse. The Cultural Centre remains a widely respected institution within Vanuatu and has considerable influence.

The statement that women have *kastom* too no longer needs to be asserted. It is widely accepted and understood. But as an urban, educated elite develops, and as a large population of mostly unemployed young people grows in Port Vila and Luganville, the new challenge for the Cultural Centre is to link rural understandings of *kastom* to developing urban contexts. For the fieldworkers, this is about finding ways to make the practices of their places provide meaning and value for the next generation.

Notes

Introduction

1. I am indebted to Ian Coates for this quotation (1999:20).

2. I use the term "Western" throughout this book as a heuristic device, creating an artificial opposition by which to draw attention to the material I am discussing.

3. Jacob was at this point called Jacob Sam; Kapere was added to his name in about 1998. However, since he is now known as Jacob Sam Kapere, I have chosen to simplify his identification by using his current name throughout this book.

4. Monographs concerned primarily with the anthropology of Vanuatu are Bonnemaison 1986a,b,c (Tanna); Brunton 1989 (Tanna); Deacon 1934 (Malakula); Guiart 1956a (Santo), 1956b (Ambrym), 1958a (Santo), 1958b (Tanna); Humphreys 1926 (southern New Hebrides); Jolly 1994b (Pentecost); Layard 1942 (Malakula); Lindstrom 1990 (Tanna); M. Rodman 1987a (Ambae), 1989 (north Vanuatu); Tonkinson 1968 (Efate); and Vienne 1984 (Banks Islands).

5. Chief Simon's talk, which he gave on July 29, 1992, was recorded by the Cultural Centre as part of the fieldworker workshop proceedings. It is now in the National Audiovisual Collections held in the VCC.

Chapter 1   History/*Kastom*

1. As I recall, I met only one man (an elderly professional from Ifira, the island in Port Vila harbor) who was dismissively antagonistic to *kastom*.

2. When Walter Lini, a key figure in the independence movement and Vanuatu's first prime minister, died in 1999, there was an extraordinary outpouring of grief throughout the nation. Young people in town were a striking exception to this. They did not share this grief and could not understand it (Jean Mitchell pers. comm. 1999).

3. As William Rodman (2000) points out, not all the Nagriamel supporters based in other parts of the archipelago were as committed to *kastom* as were those based at the Nagriamel headquarters at Vanafo.

4. Woodward, former political adviser to the British Residency, commented to me that until the 1970s there were in fact very few francophone New Hebrideans. The French Residency had difficulties finding francophone New Hebrideans to serve on the Advisory Council. The francophone political movement was dependent on the involvement of French nationals to a greater extent than was the National Party dependent on British citizens.

5. *"Tok haed"* is somewhat inadequately defined in Crowley's dictionary as metaphor. It is a technique of using humble analogies to express difficult ideas or secret information. The use of *"tok haed"* is allied to the idea of respect.

6. Terms in other Melanesian pidgins that translate *kastom* are *kastomu* (Solomon Islands) and *kastam* or *pasin tumbuna* in Papua New Guinea.

Chapter 2   *Kastom* in the National Arena

1. This chapter is based on a number of sources, including interviews with Paul Gardissat and Godwin Ligo, interviews with VCC staff and board members past and present, including Woodward and Huffman as well as ni-Vanuatu staff such as Jacob Sam Kapere, Jack Keitadi, and Willie Roy and also twelve of the forty-six VCC fieldworkers; VCC archives, both paper and audiotape (National Audiovisual Collections); and my own observations made while assisting the VCC from my position at the Australian Museum 1978–1990 and while working for the VCC (September 1989, March 1990, July 1991–August 1992). Short of disguising the identity of the country itself, it is not possible to disguise the identity of the people involved in the VCC for anyone with any familiarity with either the country or the literature relating to it. As a result, my account has had to be written tactfully, omitting some material not directly pertinent to my argument. A rather more rosy picture of the VCC may result from this process than is perhaps warranted, although the account is accurate in essentials.

2. I interviewed Paul Gardissat on July 29, 1996 and February 14, 1997. Information in this section is also drawn from Gardissat's personal archives and from a recording of an interview with him broadcast on Radio Vanuatu on June 28, 1981 (Gardissat archives).

3. Gardissat and I converse in Bislama. His economical expression of this idea was *"festaem we kantri i luk kantri"* (interview, July 29, 1996).

4. In 1995 a new purpose-built museum was opened on a site opposite the

new Parliament House, adjacent to the Malvatumauri buildings. All the VCC sections except the library moved into this building.

5. In common parlance within Vanuatu, the library and archives are always known as such, while the museum and other departments (including, for example, the Vanuatu National Film Unit and the Vanuatu Cultural and Historical Sites Survey) are always referred to as the Cultural Centre. I adopt this usage in my discussion.

6. The funding arrangements for the project become even more confused in the light of a report in the VCC museum files in which Crowe suggests that he personally funded the training course he ran (Crowe n.d. [1977]).

7. This project resulted in *Big wok: storian blong Wol Wo Tu long Vanuatu* (1998), co-edited by Lamont Lindstrom and James Gwero.

Chapter 3   Women without *Kastom*

1. Molisa defines *kastom* as "something which we all accept as a good introduction into our way of life," *kalja* as "the knowledge given to us, the people of the place: the thought and experience of our people from the past continuing into the present," and *tredisin* as "the knowledge which people have passed down from generation to generation. Tradition is born in the place, it is alive in the place, it is always with the people of the place. . . . Tradition, like the ground, was here yesterday, today, and will continue to continue" (1990:14–15).

2. Koli died in 1994. He was the subject of a film made in 1993, *The Return of the Sorcerer,* produced and directed by Peter Obrist and Waltraud Erhardt for EOF Films, Munich.

Chapter 4   *Ples*

1. I am indebted to Jean Mitchell for drawing my attention to the importance of the idea of roads in Vanuatu (see Mitchell 2002).

2. The official English version of the anthem translates this as "God gave us this our country fair." The French version is, mysteriously, completely different: "Les enfants de toutes les couleurs / partageant le ciel immense."

Chapter 5   Ambae: On Being a Person of the Place

1. Ambaeans sometimes also discriminate smaller district divisions within their own areas, but these divisions are not recognized by people from other parts of the island. Thus the east Ambae district Lombaha is sometimes understood to subsume and sometimes to be separate from the adja-

cent northern district of Walurigi. Unless otherwise indicated, when I refer to the Lombaha district I include Walurigi within it.

2. A. S. Webb, writing in 1937, records that the inhabitants of these two areas were known as the Meraeulu (east, literally "people from above") and the Merabeo (west, literally "people from below") (1937:73). As mentioned in chapter 4, the North-East Ambaean language uses a complex spatial reference system that relates all places on the basis of height. In this system, the northeast of Ambae is treated as being higher than the southwest, hence the characterization of the people of the east as being higher than those of the west (see Hyslop 1999).

3. During the mid-1990s a road-building program significantly extended the reach of vehicles around the island.

4. A man once commented to me that to make space for the rituals of his own wedding (then in progress), he had had to uproot some excellent tomato plants, which had been growing in the hamlet's open center. Such informality is perhaps a reflection of changing times.

5. I am grateful to Catriona Hyslop for reflections on the meaning of the word "sara."

6. According to Catriona Hyslop's orthography for North-East Ambaean (not available to Rodman when she made this observation), "tokagi vanue" would be "togagi vanue," and "mo vise vanue" would be "mavisei vanue" (pers. comm. 1999).

7. I spent some months exclusively in Lovonda, but after Tarisesei joined the project, we made a number of visits to other districts to fulfill the expectations of the local government council. None of these visits was for longer than one week.

8. Bill Rodman focused his research on the huqe, the men's status-alteration ritual sequence, which was the principal focus of men's lives until the 1980s. Margaret Rodman's Ambae research primarily concerns land tenure and cash cropping.

9. Margaret Rodman has identified the east Ambaean kinship terminology as Crow Type II (1981:85)

10. Kava is drunk almost exclusively by men. In the past it was used mostly during the formal occasions of social life, but many men now drink it daily. Its consumption has become a matter of considerable controversy at all levels of the community in Vanuatu, as a heavy drinker is rendered sleepy and ineffective the next day.

11. Lovonda, where people rely both on cash crops and on other forms of income generation, may not be typical of the rest of Ambae in that regard.

12. The greater mobility people have had since independence is of course making this less and less the case.

Chapter 6   Plaiting: "The Reason that Women Came into the World"

1. The leader of the debate, Alan Garae, concluded it with a short sermon on the topic based on his own reading of the Bible, from which he quoted extensively. He identified men as the boss of their wives, but emphasized the equality of men and women, citing references such as 1 Corinthians 7:1–5: "For the wife does not rule over her own body but the husband does, likewise the husband does not rule over his own body, but the wife does," and Acts 2:18 (which quotes the book of Joel): "Yea on my menservants and my maidservants in those days I will pour out my Spirit; and they shall prophesy." He argued from the story of the Fall that women were the first to know, and that for this reason men should take their wives' advice.

2. Roselyn Garae told this story at the Women's Culture Project workshop on textiles. Roselyn is from the small northwestern district of Vuingalato district but married to Lolovoli. I am not sure where the story itself comes from.

3. *Ol mat* is the Bislama plural of *mat*.

4. Sand drawings are designs drawn on the earth that illustrate stories. In contrast to the angularities of many textile patterns, sand drawings have a flowing curvilinear line. Men, women and children all make sand drawings although there are many ritually important sand drawings the knowledge of which is restricted (see Huffman 1996b).

5. Monica Allen, Women's Interest Officer in the British Residency of the New Hebrides from 1968 to 1976, in describing her work in building up women's clubs in the archipelago, commented that the clubs she promoted were a development of indigenous organizations. Women's clubs are a development of textile-plaiting groups (Allen pers. comm. 1993).

6. The only time this order is reversed is at death. A body is wrapped first in *qana* and then in *qiriqiri* and finally in *ngava hangavulu.* As a result of this sequence, the *ngava hangavulu,* as the outermost textile type, is at the bottom of the pile, so that in a sense the order is not reversed at all.

7. In this case, the textile may be still identified individually as a *qana.*

8. Strathern has remarked upon the similarity between Gell's argument and

her own deployment of terms in *The Gender of the Gift* in one of her sub-sequent publications (1999:17).

9. I discuss this story, and the story of several other textile innovations, in Bolton 1996.

Chapter 7   Dyeing: Designs, Power, Status

1. A myth about the origin of the Lombaha textile type *vola walurigi* reports that textiles were dyed by the sea (Bolton 1999b:47). This practice is also documented by Walter for central Pentecost (see 1996:104).

2. Catriona Hyslop advises that *"bulu gabani aka"* actually means not the outrigger but the sail of the canoe. Kanegai is a speaker of the Nduindui language, rather than of North-East Ambaean, and thus could have mis-taken the translation. Nevertheless, the metaphor of the woman as outrig-ger, supporting and enabling her husband, is a common one. Not being able to unpick the process by which Kanegai came to her definition, I cite it as it stands.

3. The textile in question was Field Museum registration number 132709.

4. Designs are also worked into other elements of the costume of a high-grade *huqe,* for example, in large shell-bead armbands and belts.

Chapter 8   Making Textiles into *Kastom*

1. String bands are very popular in Vanuatu. Groups of young men playing a variety of stringed instruments (mostly guitars) produce a distinctive style of rather tinkly music, singing songs that canvass themes characteristic of popular music in most places (such as matters of the heart) and that also often celebrate Vanuatu itself.

2. Of course, the Nagriamel community itself lives according to a complex mix of practices from precolonial, colonial, and postindependence sources, drawing on local practices from throughout the archipelago. Nagriamel has had a significant influence on some parts of Ambae, especially the hill villages of Longana, in encouraging people to reinstate a number of local practices that had been banned by the Church of Christ (see W. Rodman 1991, 2000).

3. I also suspect that although we had negotiated the date for our visit with Wailengi women in advance, we had done so at cross purposes. We arrived just before a girl started to kill pigs as a preliminary to her marriage, and we were thus an interruption to the real business of the day. However, oppo-sition to the WCP in Wailengi continued after this visit. The village is a few

kilometers up into the hills from Lovonda. Lovonda residents occasionally reported further Wailengi criticisms of the WCP.

4. I am indebted to Kirk Huffman for this insight.

5. The use of numbers to mark years, and their chronology, is well understood on Ambae. People looking at the albums usually noted the year of registration or acquisition in the accompanying documentation themselves, and commented on it.

6. I do not know whether the bias in favor of *qana* and *singo* in museum collections acquired over the last hundred years reflects changes in the suite of textile types made on Ambae, is a result of the kinds of textiles that Ambaeans were willing to sell to collectors, or reflects the interests of the collectors themselves. *Maraha,* large textiles without stencilled patterns, may have appealed less to European purchasers. Ambaeans may also have been reluctant to sell them. Whatever the reason, I have not found long *maraha* (either *ngava hangavulu* or *vatu kule*) in any museum collection.

7. Some photographs were of textiles that women did not recognize as being Ambaean. In several cases they recognized them as belonging to another island, most particularly, Maewo. In others they simply did not recognize the image as Ambaean.

8. Although women in Longana do not plait baskets, except for the huge baskets, *tanga bunie,* in which they store textiles and in which they bring them to major exchanges, women in the northern districts do plait small baskets for use in carrying personal possessions.

9. Many Lovondans recognized Kapere, whom they had seen filming events of national importance both on Ambae and elsewhere (for example, at the Second National Arts Festival). Part of the excitement of the week was generated by his presence, which for many Lovondans constituted something of a brush with fame. Overall, my own status on Ambae was substantially enhanced by the fact that I was able to bring Kapere to the island on three separate occasions.

10. The success of the dancing was such that some found it necessary to find further explanations. One woman came to me privately some days later and attributed the success of the dancing to *paoa blong yutufala*—to Kapere's and my "power" as VCC people. In Kirk Huffman's construction of the Cultural Centre, the idea that we might actually have such power was entirely acceptable. It was consistent, for example, with Aviu Koli's status as the VCC sorcerer. Both instances illustrate the way in which the VCC, under Huffman's direction, attempted to incorporate or to discover *kastom* in its institutional practices.

11. Teams came from Lolokaro, Lolovoli, Vuingalato, and Lombaha and Lolo-vinue (who danced together), and there were two teams from Longana villages, one each from Lovonda and Navonda. With a little supplementary aid from the Australian High Commission, I managed to stretch the workshop budget to pay for transport for all the dance teams to come to Saratamata and to feed them while they were there. Approximately a hundred women came to the workshop just to dance. A team from Nduindui cancelled at the last moment because of a death in the district.

Glossary

Note on pronunciation: all letters are pronounced as in English except g = k, k = ngg, q = nggw. Ng is pronounced as in the English "singer," not "finger."

belagi	The secondary step in plaiting, where paired pandanus ribbons are joined side by side.
benegi	The preliminary step in plaiting, where two pandanus ribbons are joined together.
bongi	Funerary feast; also means night, and night as in a countable unit of time.
buresi	Textiles in the category *qana* that are no longer used in exchange, but that have been used for some other purpose within the house (for example, as a blanket); also a woman who has been tattooed.
garo	Rope; also, immediate descent group.
gigilugi	Stencilling technique in which the stencil is built up using short lengths of cut leaf stem. This is a restricted technique, which only some women may use and which is mostly applied to *singo* and to *sakole*.
huhuru	Female status-alteration system in east Ambae, for married women (literally, "to make red").
huqe	Male public status-alteration system or graded society in east Ambae.
laqe	Vegetable dye from the root of a vine (*Ventilago neocaledonicum,* Rhamnaceae) that was formerly used to color all textiles.
loloitavue	Inside of a conch shell trumpet.

maraha	Category that includes high-value exchange textiles; also used as an alternate name for any textile in that category.
maraha vinvinu	High-value exchange textile in the *maraha* category (literally "joined *maraha*"); also known as *ngava hangavulu vinvinu* ("long *maraha*").
matai talai	Textile worn to mark achieved status in the *huqe* (literally, "eye of the clam shell," or "clam shell adze blade"; full name: *singo tuvegi matai talai*).
memea	red
mimi rawe	Slit woven into the center panel of a *singo maraha* (literally, "urethra of a hermaphrodite pig").
ngava hangavulu	High-value exchange textile in the *maraha* category, either single or double panel.
ngava hangavulu tavalu	High-value exchange textile in the *maraha* category, single panel (literally, "ten lengths, one side"); also known as "long *maraha*."
ngava hangavulu vinvinu	High-value exchange textile in the *maraha* category, double panel (literally, "ten lengths, joined"); also known as "long *maraha*."
qana	Textile category that includes medium-value exchange textiles that can also be used as domestic furnishings and that have some specified ritual uses; also used as an alternate name for any textile in that category.
qana hunhune	Textile in the *qana* category that is placed on a bride's head at marriage (literally, "*qana* placed on the head").
qana mavute	Undyed *qana vuvulu*.
qana mwaho	Textile in the *qana* category that has a smooth selvage edge (literally, "bald *qana*").
qana vivi	Textile in the *qana* category that has a short, stubby side fringe.
qana vulvulu	Textile in the *qana* category that has long side fringes.
qegavi	Stencilling technique using a stencil cut from banana palm spathe; also the name of a textile type from the Walurigi subdistrict of Lombaba.
qiriqiri	Textile in the high-value exchange category *maraha;* usually about five meters in length; different types

	distinguished mainly by the form of their side fringes; sometimes also known as "short maraha."
sakole	Women's clothing textile.
sara	A plaza or open space, generally, but not always, in a hamlet.
singo	Textile used to signify achieved rank or status.
singo tuvegi	*Singo* that is worn usually to signify achieved status in the *huqe.*
singo maraha	*Singo* that is attached to high-value long *maraha.*
tamwata	Peace and law.
tanga bunie	Large basket in which textiles are stored.
tano	Dirt, ground, earth, land; also place, as in "my place."
tavalu	High-value exchange textile in the *maraha* category. Abbreviation of *ngava hangavulu tavalu;* also sometimes known as "long *maraha.*"
tuvegi	Abbreviation for *singo tuvegi,* the textiles worn to signify achieved rank in the *huqe.*
vanue	Place, as in village, district, island, country.
vavi	Invisible people who cohabit the landscape of east Ambae with Ambaeans.
vatu kule	High-value textile in the *maraha* category; also sometimes known as "long *maraha.*"
vatu kule mwera	Male *vatu kule;* also sometimes known as "long *maraha.*"
vatu kule vavine	Female *vatu kule;* also sometimes known as "long *maraha.*"
veveo	Pandanus; prepared pandanus leaves; pandanus in the process of being plaited.
vola walurigi	Textile from the Walurigi subdistrict of Lombaba; literally, "design from Walurigi."
vule	Moon; name of a spiral design applied to *qana vivi* and *qana mwaho.*

Bibliography

Aaron, D. B., et al. 1981. *Yumi Stanap: Leaders and Leadership in a New Nation.* Suva: Institute of Pacific Studies, University of the South Pacific.

Allen, M. R. 1964. "The Nduindui: A Study in the Social Structure of a New Hebridean Community." Ph.D. thesis, Australian National University.

———. 1969. Report on Aoba: Incidental Papers on Nduindui District Aoba Island, New Hebrides, ed. C. Leaney. Vanuatu National Library collection.

———. 1981a. "Innovation, Inversion, and Revolution as Political Tactics in West Aoba." In *Vanuatu: Politics, Economics, and Ritual in Island Melanesia,* ed. M. R. Allen, pp. 1–8. Sydney: Academic Press.

———. 1981b. "Rethinking Old Problems: Matriliny, Secret Societies, and Political Evolution." In *Vanuatu: Politics, Economics, and Ritual in Island Melanesia,* ed. M. R. Allen, pp. 19–34. Sydney: Academic Press.

Allen, M. R., ed. 1981c. *Vanuatu: Politics, Economics, and Ritual in Island Melanesia.* Sydney: Academic Press.

Anderson, B. 1983. *Imagined Communities: Reflections on the Origin and Spread of Nationalism.* London: Verso.

Arutangai, S. 1987. "Vanuatu: Overcoming the Colonial Legacy." In *Land Tenure in the Pacific,* ed. R. Crocombe, pp. 261–302. Suva: University of the South Pacific.

———. 1995. "Post-Independence Developments and Policies." In *Melanesian Politics: Stael blong Vanuatu,* ed. H. van Trease, pp. 261–302. Christchurch; Suva: Macmillan Brown Centre for Pacific Studies, University of Canterbury; University of the South Pacific.

Barlow, K. 1990. "Collections, Sources, and Further Research: Some Examples from the Lower Sepik." *COMA Bulletin* (Australia) 23:12–21.

Barlow, K.; D. Lipset; and L. Bolton. 1988. *Trade and Society in Transition along the Sepik Coast: An Interim Report on Anthropological Research in the East Sepik and Sundaun Provinces, PNG, July–August 1986.* Sepik Documentation Project. Sydney: Australian Museum.

Bedford, S.; M. Spriggs; M. Wilson; and R. Regenvanu. 1998. "The Australian National University-National Museum of Vanuatu Archaeology Project: A Preliminary Report on the Establishment of Cultural Sequences and Rock Art Research." *Asian Perspectives* 37:165–193.

Blackwood, P. 1981. "Rank, Exchange, and Leadership in Four Vanuatu Societies." In *Vanuatu: Politics, Economics, and Ritual in Island Melanesia,* ed. M. R. Allen, pp. 35–84. Sydney: Academic Press.

Bolton, L. 1993. "Dancing in Mats: Extending *Kastom* to Women in Vanuatu." Ph.D. thesis, University of Manchester.

———. "Tahigogana's Sisters: Women, Mats, and Landscape on Ambae." In *Arts of Vanuatu,* ed. J. Bonnemaison et al., pp. 112–119. Bathurst: Crawford House Publishing.

———. 1998. "Chief Willie Bongmatur Maldo and the Role of Chiefs in Vanuatu. *Journal of Pacific History* 33.2:179–195.

———. 1999a. "Radio and the Redefinition of *Kastom* in Vanuatu." *The Contemporary Pacific* 11.2:335–360.

———. 1999b. "Women, Place, and Practice in Vanuatu: A View from Ambae." *Oceania.* Special issue: *Fieldwork; Fieldworkers: Developments in Vanuatu Research* 70:43–55.

———. 2001a. "Classifying the Material: Food, Textiles and Status in North Vanuatu." *Journal of Material Culture* 6.3:251–268.

———. 2001b. "The Object in View: Aborigines, Melanesians, and Museums." In *Emplaced Myths: The Spatial and Narrative Dimensions of Knowledge in Australian Aboriginal and Papua New Guinea Societies,* ed. A. Rumsey and J. Weiner, pp. 215–232. Honolulu: University of Hawai'i Press.

———. 2001c. "What Makes *Singo* Different: North Vanuatu Textiles and the Theory of Captivation." In *Beyond Aesthetics: Art and Technologies of Enchantment,* ed. C. Pinney and N. Thomas, pp. 97–115. Oxford and New York: Berg.

———, ed. 1999. *Oceania.* Special issue: *Fieldwork, Fieldworkers: Developments in Vanuatu Research* 70:1–8.

Bongmatur, W. 1991. "Report blong Offis blong Malvatumauri: National Council of Chiefs of Vanuatu." In *Museums and Cultural Centres in the Pacific,* ed. S. M. Eoe and P. Swadling, p. 154. Port Moresby: Papua New Guinea National Museum.

Bonnemaison, J. 1984. "The Tree and the Canoe: Roots and Mobility in Vanuatu Societies." *Pacific Viewpoint* 25:117–151.

———. 1986a. *La Dernière Ile.* Paris; Arlea: ORSTOM.

———. 1986b. *Gens de Pirogue et Gens de la Terre.* Vol. 1: *Les Fondements Géographiques d'une Identité: l'Archipel du Vanuatu.* Paris: Editions de l'ORSTOM.

———. 1986c. *Tanna: les Gens des Lieux: Histoire et Géosymboles d'une Société Enracinée: Tanna.* Vol. 2: *Les Fondements Géographiques d'une Identité: l'Archipel du Vanuatu.* Paris: Editions de l'ORSTOM.

———. 1994. *The Tree and the Canoe: History and Ethnogeography of Tanna.* Translated and adapted by Josée Pénot-Demetry. Honolulu: University of Hawai'i Press.

———. 1996. "Graded Societies and Societies Based On Title: Forms and Rites of Traditional Power in Vanuatu." In *Arts of Vanuatu,* ed. J. Bonnemaison et al., pp. 200–216. Bathurst: Crawford House Publishing.

Bonnemaison, J.; C. Kauffmann; K. Huffman; and D. Tryon, eds. 1996. *Arts of Vanuatu.* Bathurst: Crawford House Publishing.

Brunton, R. 1989. *The Abandoned Narcotic: Kava and Cultural Instability in Melanesia.* Cambridge: Cambridge University Press.

Bubandt, N. 1997. "Speaking of Places: Spatial Poesis and Localized Identity in Buli." In *The Poetic Power of Place,* ed. J. J. Fox, pp. 132–162. Canberra: Australian National University.

Buck, P. H. (Te Rangi Hiroa). 1926. *The Evolution of Maori Clothing.* Vol. 7 in *Memoirs of the Polynesian Society.* New Plymouth: Avey and Sons and the Board of Maori Ethnological Research.

Camden, B. 1977. *A Descriptive Dictionary: Bislama to English.* Port Vila: Maropa Bookshop.

Coates, I. 1999. "Lists and Letters: An Analysis of Some Exchanges between British Museums, Collectors, and Australian Aborigines (1895–1910)." Ph.D. thesis, Australian National University.

Codrington, R. H. 1891 (1981). *The Melanesians: Studies in Their Anthropology and Folk-lore.* Oxford: Clarendon Press.

Colomb, P. 1913. "Pigeon English ou Bichelamar." *Révue de Linguistique et de Philologie Comparée* 46:109–117, 184–198.

Crowe, P. N.d. (1977). Report to the Board of Management, New Hebrides Cultural Centre. Report in VCC files.

Crowley, T. 1990. *An Illustrated Bislama-English and English-Bislama Dictionary.* Vanuatu: Pacific Languages Unit and Vanuatu Extension Centre, University of the South Pacific.

Curtis, T. 1999. "Tom's *Tambu* House: Spacing, Status, and Sacredness in South Malekula, Vanuatu." *Oceania.* Special issue: *Fieldwork, Fieldworkers: Developments in Vanuatu Research* 70:56–71.

Danto, A. 1964. "The Artworld." *Journal of Philosophy* 61:571–584.

Deacon, A. B. 1934. *Malekula: A Vanishing People in the New Hebrides,* ed. C. H. Wedgwood. London: George Routledge and Sons.

Douglas, N., and N. Douglas. 1990. *Vanuatu—a Guide.* 2d ed. Alstonville, NSW: Pacific Profiles.

Edwards, R., and Stewart, J., eds. 1980. *Preserving Indigenous Cultures: A New Role for Museums.* Canberra: Australian National Commission for UNESCO.

Emery, I. 1980. *The Primary Structure of Fabrics: An Illustrated Classification.* Washington, D.C.: The Textile Museum.

Eoe, S. M. 1991. "The Role of Museums in the Pacific: Change or Die." In *Museums and Cultural Centres in the Pacific,* ed. S. M. Eoe and P. Swadling, pp. 1–4. Port Moresby: Papua New Guinea National Museum.

Eoe, S. M., and P. Swadling, eds. 1991. *Museums and Cultural Centres in the Pacific.* Port Moresby: Papua New Guinea National Museum.

Ewins, R. 1982. *Mat-weaving in Gau, Fiji.* Fiji Museum Special Publication, no. 3. Suva: Fiji Museum.

Flower, W. H. 1895. Presidential Address to Section H—Anthropology. *Report of the 1894 Oxford British Association for the Advancement of Science Meeting* 762–774.

Fox, J. J., ed. 1997. *The Poetic Power of Place: Comparative Perspectives on Austronesian Ideas of Locality.* Canberra: Australian National University.

Frater, A. 1991. *Chasing the Monsoon.* New York: Alfred A. Knopf.

Fusitu'a, E. 1991. "The Preservation of Cultural Property in Tonga." In *Museums and Cultural Centres in the Pacific,* ed. S. M. Eoe and P. Swadling, pp. 195–199. Port Moresby: Papua New Guinea National Museum.

Gardissat, P. Personal Archives, Port Vila.

Gell, A. 1998. *Art and Agency: An Anthropological Theory.* Oxford: Clarendon Press.

———. 1999. *The Art of Anthropology: Essays and Diagrams,* ed. E. Hirsch. London; New Brunswick, N.J.: Athlone Press.

Government of Vanuatu. 1980. *Constitution of the Republic of Vanuatu.* Port Vila: Government of Vanuatu.

Gregory, C. 1982. *Gifts and Commodities.* London: Academic Press.

Guiart, J. 1956a. *Grands et Petits Hommes de la Montagne, Espiritu Santo (Nouvelles-Hébrides).* Nouméa: ORSTOM.

———. 1956b. "Notes sur les Tambours d'Ambrym." *Journal de la Société des Océanistes* 12:334–336.

———. 1958a. *Espiritu Santo (Nouvelles-Hébrides).* Paris: Plon.

———. 1958b. *Un Siècle et Demi de Contacts Culturels a Tanna, Nouvelles-Hébrides . . . : Rapport General d'une Mission Effectuée au Cours de l'ete 1952–1953 sous les Auspices du Gouvernement du Condominium des Nouvelles-Hébrides.* Paris: Musée de l'Homme.

Guiart, J.; J. J. Espirat; M. S. Lagrange; and M. Renaud. 1973. *Système des Titres dans les Nouvelles-Hébrides Centrales d'Efate aux Iles Shepherd.* Paris: Institut d'Ethnologie, Musée de L'Homme.

Gupta, A., and J. Ferguson. 1997a. *Anthropological Locations: Boundaries and Grounds of a Field Science.* Berkeley: University of California Press.

———. 1997b. "Beyond 'Culture': Space, Identity, and the Politics of Difference." In *Culture, Power, Place: Explorations in Critical Anthropology,* ed. A. Gupta and J. Ferguson, pp. 33–51. Durham, N.C.: Duke University Press.

Gwero, J. N.d. (1981). Report blong Wok blong James Gwero. Manuscript in VCC files.

———. N.d. (1992). Woksop blong ol Woman Ambae: Minit. Manuscript in VCC files.

Harrisson, T. 1937. *Savage Civilisation.* London: Victor Gollancz.

Henningham, S. 1992. *France and the South Pacific: A Contemporary History.* Sydney: Allen and Unwin.

Herda, P. 1999. "The Changing Texture of Textiles in Tonga." *Journal of the Polynesian Society.* Special issue: *Kie Hingoa "Named Mats," 'Ie Tōga "Fine Mats" and Other Treasured Textiles of Samoa and Tonga* 108.2:148–167.

Hirsch, E. 1995. "Introduction." In *The Anthropology of Landscape: Perspectives on Place and Space,* ed. E. Hirsch and M. O'Hanlon, pp. 1–30. Oxford: Clarendon Press.

Hobsbawm, E., and T. Ranger, eds. 1983. *The Invention of Tradition.* Cambridge: Cambridge University Press.

Hoskins, J. 1989. "Why Do Ladies Sing the Blues? Indigo Dyeing, Cloth Production, and Gender Symbolism in Kodi." In *Cloth and Human Experience,* ed. A. B. Weiner and J. Schneider, pp. 142–173. Washington, D.C.: Smithsonian Institution Press.

Huffman, K. W. 1996a. "The Fieldworkers of the Vanuatu Cultural Centre and their Contributions to the Audiovisual Collections." In *Arts of Vanuatu,* ed. J. Bonnemaison et al., pp. 290–293. Bathurst: Crawford House Publishing.

———. 1996b. "'Su tuh netan 'monbwei: We Write on the Ground': Sand Drawings and Their Associations in Northern Vanuatu." In *Arts of Vanuatu,* ed. J. Bonnemaison et al., pp. 247–253. Bathurst: Crawford House Publishing.

———. 1996c. "Trading, Cultural Exchange, and Copyright: Important Aspects of Vanuatu Arts." In *Arts of Vanuatu,* ed. J. Bonnemaison et al., pp. 182–194. Bathurst: Crawford House Publishing.

Humphreys, C. B. 1926. *The Southern New Hebrides: An Anthropological Record.* Cambridge: Cambridge University Press.

Hunt, C. 1978. "Museums in the Pacific Islands, a Metaphysical Justification." *Museums* 30:2.

Hyslop, C. 1998. "The Lolovoli Dialect of the North-East Ambaean Language, Vanuatu." Ph.D. thesis, Australian National University.

————. 1999. "The Linguistics of Inhabiting Space: Spatial Reference in the North-East Ambae Language." *Oceania*. Special issue: *Fieldwork, Fieldworkers: Development in Vanuatu Research* 70:25–42.

Ingold, T. 1993. "The Temporality of the Landscape." *World Archaeology*. Special issue: *Conceptions of Time and Ancient Society* 25:152–174.

Jacomb, E. 1914. *France and England in the New Hebrides: The Anglo-French Condominium*. Melbourne: George Robertson.

Jolly, M. 1981. "People and Their Products in South Pentecost." In *Vanuatu: Politics, Economics, and Ritual in Island Melanesia*, ed. M. R. Allen, pp. 269–293. Sydney: Academic Press.

————. 1982. "Birds and Banyans of South Pentecost: Kastom in Anti-Colonial Struggle." *Mankind* 13:338–356.

————. 1989. "Sacred Spaces: Churches, Men's Houses, and Households in South Pentecost, Vanuatu." In *Family and Gender in the Pacific: Domestic Contradictions and the Colonial Impact*, ed. M. Jolly and M. Macintyre, pp. 213–235. Cambridge: Cambridge University Press.

————. 1991a. "The Politics of Difference: Femininism, Colonialism, and Decolonization in Vanuatu." In *Intersexions, Gender/Class/Culture/Ethnicity*, ed. G. Bottomley, M. d. Lepervanche, and J. Martin, pp. 52–74. Sydney: Allen and Unwin.

————. 1991b. "Soaring Hawks and Grounded Persons: The Politics of Rank and Gender in North Vanuatu." In *Big Men and Great Men: Personifications of Power in Melanesia*, ed. M. Strathern and M. Godelier. Cambridge: Cambridge University Press.

————. 1991c. "'To Save the Girls for Brighter and Better Lives': Presbyterian Missionaries and Women in the South of Vanuatu 1848–1870." *Journal of Pacific History* 26:27–48.

————. 1992. "Custom and the Way of the Land: Past and Present in Vanuatu and Fiji." *Oceania*. Special issue: *The Politics of Tradition in the Pacific* 62:330–354.

————. 1994a. "*Kastom* as Commodity: The Land Dive as Indigenous Rite and Tourist Spectacle in Vanuatu." In *Culture, Kastom, Tradition: Developing Cultural Policy in Melanesia*, ed. L. Lindstrom and G. White, pp. 131–144. Suva: Institute of Pacific Studies, University of the South Pacific.

————. 1994b. *Women of the Place: Kastom, Colonialism and Gender in Vanuatu*. Chur, Switzerland: Harwood Academic Publishers.

————. 1997. "Women-Nation-State in Vanuatu: Women as Signs and Subjects in the Discourse of *Kastom*, Modernity, and Christianity." In *Narratives of Nation in the South Pacific*, ed. T. Otto and N. Thomas, pp. 133–162. Amsterdam: Harwood Academic Publishers.

Jolly, M., and N. Thomas. 1992a. "Introduction." *Oceania*. Special issue: *The Politics of Tradition in the Pacific* 62:241–248.

———, eds. 1992b. *Oceania*. Special issue: *The Politics of Tradition in the Pacific* 62.

Kaeppler, A. 1994. "Paradise Regained: The Role of Pacific Museums in Forging National Identity." In *Museums and the Making of "Ourselves": The Role of Objects in National Identity,* ed. F. Kaplan, pp. 19–44. London; New York: Leicester University Press.

———. 1999. "*Kie Hingoa:* Mats of Power, Rank, Prestige and History." *Journal of the Polynesian Society*. Special issue: *Kie Hingoa "Named Mats," 'Ie Tōga "Fine Mats" and Other Treasured Textiles of Samoa and Tonga* 108.2:168–232.

Kalkoa, G. 1973. In *New Hebrides Viewpoints,* June / July, p. 10.

Kanegai, N. 1994. *Bure blong Ambae*. Port Vila: Vanuatu Cultural Centre.

Kasaherou, E. 1991. "The New Caledonia Museum." In *Museums and Cultural Centres in the Pacific,* ed. S. M. Eoe and P. Swadling, pp. 161–167. Port Moresby: Papua New Guinea National Museum.

Keesing, R. M. 1981. *Cultural Anthropology: A Contemporary Perspective.* 2d ed. New York: Holt, Rinehart and Winston.

———. 1982. "Introduction." *Mankind*. Special issue: *Reinventing Traditional Culture: The Politics of Kastom in Island Melanesia* 13:297–301.

———. 1989. "Creating the Past: Custom and Identity in the Contemporary Pacific." *Contemporary Pacific* 16–35.

———. 1993. "Kastom Re-examined." *Anthropological Forum*. Special issue: *Custom Today* 6.4:587–596.

Keesing, R. M., and R. Tonkinson, eds. 1982. *Mankind*. Special issue: *Reinventing Traditional Culture: The Politics of Kastom in Island Melanesia.*

Kele-Kele, K. M., et al. 1977. *New Hebrides: The Road to Independence.* Suva: Institute of South Pacific Studies and the South Pacific Social Sciences Association.

Kelly, S. 1999. "Unwrapping Mats: People, Land, and Material Culture in Tongoa, Central Vanuatu." Ph.D. thesis, University College, London.

Küchler, S. 1987. "Malangan: Art and Memory in a Melanesian society." *Man* (n.s.), 22:238–255.

Larcom, J. 1982. "The Invention of Convention." *Mankind*. Special issue: *Reinventing Traditional Culture: The Politics of Kastom in Island Melanesia* 13:330–337.

———. 1983. "Following Deacon: The Problem of Ethnographic Reanalysis, 1926–1981." In *Observers Observed: Essays on Ethnographic Fieldwork.* Vol.

1 of *History of Anthropology,* ed. J. G. W. Stocking. Wisconsin: University of Wisconsin Press.

―――. 1990. "Custom by Decree: Legitimation Crisis in Vanuatu." In *Cultural Identity and Ethnicity in the Pacific,* ed. J. Linnekin and L. Poyer, pp. 175–190. Honolulu: University of Hawai'i Press.

Layard, J. 1942. *Stone Men of Malekula: Vao.* London: Chatto and Windus.

Leggatt, T. 1910. "The Position of Heathen Women in the New Hebrides." *New Hebrides Magazine* 38:22–24.

Ligo, G. 1980. "Custom and Culture." In *Vanuatu: Twenti Wan Tingting long Taem blong Independens,* ed. W. Lini et al., pp. 54–65. Fiji: Institute of Pacific Studies, University of the South Pacific.

Lindstrom, L. 1980. "*Kastom* Leaves the Darkness: The Political Revaluation of Tradition in the New Hebrides." *Pacific Arts Newsletter* 11:24–27.

―――. 1982. "Leftamap Kastom: The Political History of Tradition on Tanna (Vanuatu)." *Mankind.* Special issue: *Reinventing Traditional Culture: The Politics of Kastom in Island Melanesia* 13:316–329.

―――. 1984. "Doctor, Lawyer, Wise Man, Priest: Big-Men and Knowledge in Melanesia." *Man* (n.s.) 19:291–309.

―――. 1990. *Knowledge and Power in a South Pacific Society.* Washington, D.C.: Smithsonian Institution Press.

―――. 1996. "Arts of Language and Space, South-East Tanna." In *Arts of Vanuatu,* ed. J. Bonnemaison et al., pp. 123-128. Bathurst: Crawford House Publishing.

―――. 1997. "Chiefs in Vanuatu Today." In *Chiefs Today: Traditional Pacific Leadership and the Postcolonial State,* ed. L. Lindstrom and G. White, pp. 211-228. Stanford, Calif.: Stanford University Press.

Lindstrom, L., and G. White, eds. 1993. "Introduction: Custom Today." *Anthropological Forum.* Special issue: *Custom Today* 6.4:467–474.

Lindstrom, L. and G. White eds. 1994. *Culture, Kastom, Tradition: Developing Cultural Policy in Melanesia.* Suva: Institute of Pacific Studies, University of the South Pacific.

Lindstrom, L., and J. Gwero, eds. 1998. *Big Wok: Storian blong Wol Wo Tu long Vanuatu.* Christchurch; Suva: Macmillan Brown Centre for Pacific Studies, Canterbury University; Institute of Pacific Studies, University of the South Pacific.

Lini, W. 1980. *Beyond Pandemonium: From the New Hebrides to Vanuatu.* Suva: University of the South Pacific.

Linnekin, J. 1991. "Fine Mats and Money: Contending Exchange Paradigms in Colonial Samoa." *Anthropological Quarterly* 64:1–13.

―――. 1992. "On the Theory and Politics of Cultural Construction in the

Pacific." *Oceania*. Special issue: *The Politics of Tradition in the Pacific* 62:249–263.

Linnekin, J., and L. Poyer eds. 1990. *Cultural Identity and Ethnicity in the Pacific*. Honolulu: University of Hawai'i Press.

Lovell, P. R. 1980. "Children of Blood, Children of Shame: Creation and Procreation in Longana, East Aoba, New Hebrides." Ph.D. thesis, McMaster University.

MacClancy, J. V. 1983. "Vanuatu and Kastom: A Study of Cultural Symbols in the Inception of a Nation State in the South Pacific." D. Phil., Oxford University.

MacKenzie, M. A. 1991. *Androgynous Objects: String Bags and Gender in Central New Guinea*. Chur: Harwood Academic Publishers.

Malinowski, B. 1922. *Argonauts of the Western Pacific: An Account of Native Enterprise and Adventure in the Archipelagoes of Melanesian New Guinea*. London: Routledge.

Malvatumauri. 1983. *Kastom Polisi blong Malvatumauri, Nasonal Kaonsel blong Kastom Chiefs long Ripablik blong Vanuatu*. Port Vila: Ripablik blong Vanuatu.

Mitchell, J. 1998. *Young People Speak: A Report on the Vanuatu Young People's Project, Vanuatu Cultural Centre, April 1997 to June 1998*. Port Vila: Vanuatu Cultural Centre.

———. 2002. "Roads, Recklessness, and Relationships: An Urban Settlement in Postcolonial Vanuatu." Ph.D. Thesis, York University, Ontario.

Molisa, G. 1980. "Women." In *Vanuatu: Twenti Wan Tingting long Taem blong Independens*, ed. W. Lini et al., pp. 256–269. Suva: Institute of Pacific Studies, University of the South Pacific.

———. 1983. *Black Stone: Poems*. Suva: Mana Publications.

———. 1987. *Colonised People*. Port Vila: Black Stone Publications.

———. 1990. *Kalja Buklet*. Port Vila: Vanuatu Nasonel Kaonsel Blong a Woman; Festivol Infomeson Mo Pablikesen Komiti.

———. 1991. "The Vanuatu National Council of Women." In *A Situational Analysis of Children and Women in Vanuatu*, ed. UNICEF, p. 68. Port Vila: Vanuatu Government.

Molisa, G. M., ed. 1990. *Rejistri blong ol Woman Lida blong Festivol Infomesen mo Pablikesen Komiti mo VNKW Eksekiutiv Komiti, Port Vila*. Port Vila: Vanuatu Nasonal Kaonsel blong ol Woman.

Moon, M., and B. Moon. 1998. *Ni-Vanuatu Memories of World War II*. Lyttleton: M. and B. Moon.

Moore, H. L. 1988. *Feminism and Anthropology*. Cambridge: Polity Press.

Morphy, H. 1998. *Aboriginal Art*. London: Phaidon Press.

———. 1992. "From Dull to Brilliant: The Aesthetics of Spiritual Power among the Yolgnu." In *Anthropology, Art, and Aesthetics,* ed. J. Coote and A. Shelton, pp. 181–208. Oxford; New York: Oxford University Press.

Myers, F. R. 1995. "Representing Culture: The Production of Discourse(s) for Aboriginal Acrylic Paintings." In *The Traffic in Culture: Refiguring Art and Anthropology,* ed. G. E. Marcus and F. R. Myers, pp. 55–95. Berkeley: University of California Press.

Munn, N. 1977. "The Spatiotemporal Transformation of Gawa Canoes." *Journal de Societé des Océanistes* 33.54–55:39–51.

O'Hanlon, M. 1999. "'Mostly Harmless'?: Missionaries, Administrators, and Material Culture on the Coast of British New Guinea." *Journal of the Royal Anthropological Society* 5:377–397.

National Audiovisual Collections. Vanuatu Cultural Centre (VCC), Port Vila.

Otto, T., and N. Thomas, eds. 1997. *Narratives of Nation in the South Pacific: Studies in Anthropology and History.* Amsterdam: Harwood Academic Publishers.

Page, G. 1993. *Coconuts and Coral.* Damgate, Norfolk: Geo. R. Reeve.

Patterson, M. 1976. "Kinship, Marriage, and Ritual in North Ambrym." Ph.D. thesis, University of Sydney.

Philibert, J.-M. 1986. "The Politics of Tradition: Towards a Generic Culture in Vanuatu." *Mankind* 16:1–12.

Ripablik blong Vanuatu. 1994. *Ripablik blong Vanuatu.* Port Vila: Imprimerie de Port Vila.

Rivers, W. H. R. 1914. *The History of Melanesian Society.* Cambridge: Cambridge University Press.

Rodman, M. 1981. "A Boundary and a Bridge: Women's Pig Killing as a Border-Crossing between Spheres of Exchange in East Aoba." In *Vanuatu: Politics, Economics, and Ritual in Island Melanesia,* ed. M. R. Allen, pp. 85–104. Sydney: Academic Press.

———. 1987a. *Masters of Tradition: Consequences of Customary Land Tenure in Longana, Vanuatu.* Vancouver: University of British Columbia Press.

———. 1987b. "Moving Houses: Residential Mobility and the Mobility of Residences in Longana, Vanuatu." *American Anthropologist* 87:56–72.

———. 1989. *Deep Water: Development and Change in Pacific Village Fisheries.* Boulder, Colo.: Westview Press.

———. 2001. *Houses Far from Home: British Colonial Space in the New Hebrides.* Honolulu: University of Hawai'i Press.

Rodman, W. L. 1973. "Men of Influence, Men of Rank." Ph.D. thesis, University of Chicago.

———. 1991. "When Questions Are Answers: The Message of Anthropology, According to the People of Ambae." *American Anthropologist* 93:431–434.

————. 2000. "Outlaw Memories: Biography and the Construction of Meaning in Postcolonial Vanuatu." In *Identity Work: Constructing Pacific Lives,* ed. P. J. Stewart, and A. Strathern, pp. 139–156. Pittsburgh: University of Pittsburgh Press.

Rodman, W. L., and M. Rodman. 1978. "Courts and Courtship in a New Hebridean Society." *Oceania* 49:35–45.

————. 1991. "Ambae." In *Encyclopedia of World Cultures.* Vol. 2: *Oceania.* Boston: G. K. Hall.

Rothwell, N. 1988. "Keeping the Language Alive: The Voices of Vanuatu Recorded for Posterity." *Pacific Islands Monthly,* May, pp. 14–15.

Rubinstein, R. L. 1978. "Placing the Self on Malo." Ph.D. thesis, Bryn Mawr College.

Sahlins, M. 1994. "Goodbye to Triste Tropes: Ethnography in the Context of Modern World History." In *Assessing Cultural Anthropology,* ed. R. Borofsky, pp. 377–394. New York: McGraw-Hill.

Sam, J.; L. Bolton; and J. Tarisesei. 1992. *Naoia olsem bifo. Fasin blong wokim ol mat Ambae.* Video. Vanuatu National Film Unit. 40 minutes.

Schmidt, H. 1956–1957. "Le Bichelamar." *Etudes Mélanesienne* (n.s.), 1011:119–136.

Schneider, J., and A. B. Weiner. 1989. "Introduction." In *Cloth and Human Experience,* ed. A. B. Weiner and J. Schneider, pp 1–29. Washington, D.C.: Smithsonian Institution Press.

Schoeffel, P. 1999. "Samoan Exchange and 'Fine Mats': An Historical Reconstruction." *Journal of the Polynesian Society.* Special issue: *Kie Hingoa "Named Mats," 'Ie Tōga "Fine Mats" and Other Treasured Textiles of Samoa and Tonga* 108.2:117–148.

Seiler-Baldinger, A. 1994 *Textiles: A Classification of Techniques.* Bathurst: Crawford House Press.

Specht, J., and C. MacLulich. 1996. "Changes and Challenges: The Australian Museum and Indigenous Communities." In *Archaeological Displays and the Public,* ed. P. McManus, pp. 7–49. London: Institute of Archaeology and University College, London.

Speiser, F. 1913. *Two Years with the Natives in the Western Pacific.* London: Mills and Boon.

Spriggs, M. 1997. *The Island Melanesians.* Oxford: Blackwell.

Statistics Office. 1991a. *Vanuatu National Population Census May 1989: Main Report.* Port Vila: Statistics Office.

————. 1991b. *Vanuatu National Population Census May 1989.* Population Atlas 3. *Ambae Maewo Pentecost.* Port Vila: Statistics Office.

Stephens, J. 1977. "Nagriamel." In *New Hebrides: The Road to Independence,* ed. K. M. Kele-Kele et al., pp. 35–41. Suva: Institute of Pacific Studies, University of the South Pacific.

Stocking, G. W. 1985. *Objects and Others: Essays on Museums and Material Culture.* University of the South Pacific. Vol. 3 in *History of Anthropology.* Wisconsin: University of Wisconsin Press.

Strathern, M. 1984. "Domesticity and the Denigration of Women." In *Rethinking Women's Roles: Perspectives from the Pacific,* ed. D. O'Brien and S. Tiffany, pp. 13–31. Berkeley: University of California Press.

———. 1988. *The Gender of the Gift: Problems with Women and Problems with Society in Melanesia.* Berkeley: University of California Press.

———. 1990. "Artefacts of History: Events and the Interpretation of Images." In *Culture and History in the Pacific,* ed. J. Siikala, pp. 25–44. Transactions of the Finnish Anthropological Society 27. Helsinki: Finnish Anthropological Society.

———. 1995. *Shifting Contexts: Transformations in Anthropological Knowledge.* ASA Decennial Conference Series. New York: Routledge .

———. 1999. *Property, Substance, and Effect: Anthropological Essays on Persons and Things.* London; New Brunswick, N.J.: Athlone Press.

———. N.d. *The Conference Theme: An Open Letter.* ASA IV Decennial Conference, July 1992: *The Uses of Knowledge: Global and Local Relations.* London: Association of Social Anthropologists of the Commonwealth.

Tarisesei, J. 1995. *Ol Mat blong Ambae: Ambae Mats May 1992.* Port Vila: Blackstone Publishing and Women's Unit of the Vanuatu Cultural Centre.

———. 2000. "Today Is Not the Same as Yesterday and Tomorrow It Will Be Different Again: Kastom on Ambae, Vanuatu." *Development Bulletin* (Canberra: Development Studies Network), 51:46–48.

Thomas, N. 1991. *Entangled Objects: Exchange, Material Culture, and Colonialism in the Pacific.* Cambridge: Harvard University Press.

———. 1997. *In Oceania: Visions, Artifacts, Histories.* Durham, N.C.: Duke University Press.

———. 1999. "The Case of the Misplaced Ponchoes: Speculations Concerning the History of Cloth in Polynesia." *Journal of Material Culture* 4.1:5–20.

Tonkinson, R. 1968. *Maat Village, Efate: A Relocated Community in the New Hebrides.* Eugene: University of Oregon.

———. 1981. "Church and Kastom in Southeast Ambrym." In *Vanuatu: Politics, Economics, and Ritual in Island Melanesia,* ed. M. R. Allen, pp. 237–268. Sydney: Academic Press.

———. 1982. "National Identity and the Problem of Kastom in Vanuatu." *Mankind* 13:306–315.

Tryon, D. 1972. "The Languages of the New Hebrides: A Checklist and General Survey." *Pacific Linguistics* (Canberra), series A, no. 35, pp. 43–85.

——. 1976. "New Hebrides Languages: An internal classification." Pacific Linguistics (Canberra), series C, no. 500.

——. 1996. "Dialect Training and the Use of Geographical Space." In *Arts of Vanuatu*, ed. J. Bonnemaison et al., pp. 170–173. Bathurst: Crawford House Publishing.

——. 1999. Ni-Vanuatu Research and Researchers. *Oceania*. Special issue: *Fieldwork, Fieldworkers: Development in Vanuatu Research* 70:9–15.

Tryon, D., ed. 1992. *Ples blong ol Pig long Kastom Laef long Vanuatu*. Vol. 1, buk 1 of *Presentations from the Vanuatu Kaljoral Senta Woksop blong Ol Filwoka, 20–29 Jun 1990)*. Port Vila: Vanuatu Kaljoral Senta.

Tutai, V. 1991. "The Cook Islands Museum." In *Museums and Cultural Centres in the Pacific*, ed. S. M. Eoe and P. Swadling, pp. 201–204. Port Moresby: Papua New Guinea National Museum.

Van Trease, H. 1987. *The Politics of Land in Vanuatu: From Colony to Independence*. Suva: Institute of Pacific Studies, University of the South Pacific.

Vanuatu Cultural Centre (VCC). 1984. *Samfala Kastom Storian blong Vanuatu Long Langwis mo Bislama*. Vanuatu Kaljoral Senta Woksop. Port Vila: Vanuatu Kaljoral Senta.

VCC files. N.d. (1978). New Hebrides Oral Traditions Project: Plans for 1978 to mid-1979. Report in VCC files.

Vienne, B. 1984. *Gens de Motlav: Idéologie et pratique sociale en Mélanésie*. Publication de la Société des océanistes, no. 42. Paris: Musée de l'Homme.

——. 1996. "Masked Faces from the Country of the Dead." In *Arts of Vanuatu*, ed. J. Bonnemaison et al., pp. 234–246. Bathurst: Crawford House Publishing.

Wagner, R. 1981 (1975). *The Invention of Culture*. Chicago: University of Chicago Press.

Walter, A. 1996. "The Feminine Art of Mat-Weaving on Pentecost." In *Arts of Vanuatu*, ed. J. Bonnemaison et al., pp. 100–109. Bathurst: Crawford House Publishing.

Webb, A. S. 1937. "The People of Aoba, New Hebrides." *Mankind* 2:73–80.

Weiner, A. B. 1977. *Women of Value, Men of Renown: New Perspectives in Trobriand Exchange*. St. Lucia, Queensland: University of Queensland Press.

——. 1989. "Why Cloth? Wealth, Gender, and Power in Oceania." In *Cloth and Human Experience*, ed. A. B. Weiner and J. Schneider, pp. 37–72. Washington, D.C.: Smithsonian Institution Press.

——. 1992. *Inalienable Possessions: The Paradox of Keeping-while-Giving*. Berkeley: University of California Press.

Weiner, A. B., and J. Schneider, eds. 1989. *Cloth and Human Experience*. Washington, D.C.: Smithsonian Institution Press.

West, M. K. C. 1981. "Keeping Place vs. Museum: The North Australian Example." *COMA Bulletin* (Australia) 7:9–14.

White, G., and L. Lindstrom. 1993. "Introduction: Custom Today." *Anthropological Forum* 6:467–473.

———. 1997. *Chiefs Today: Traditional Pacific Leadership and the Postcolonial State.* Stanford, Calif.: Stanford University Press.

Whyte, J., ed. 1990. *Vanuatu: Ten Years of Independence.* Australia: Other People Publications.

Wilson, M. 1999. "Bringing the Art Inside: A Preliminary Analysis of Black Linear Rock-art from Limestone Caves in Erromango, Vanuatu." *Oceania.* Special issue: *Fieldwork, Fieldworkers: Developments in Vanuatu Research* 70.1:87–97.

Woodward, K. N.d. (1978). "Historical Summary of Constitutional Advance in the New Hebrides, 1954–1977." Report prepared for the British Residency (manuscript). Vanuatu Collection, Vanuatu National Library, Port Vila.

Yorigmal, F., et al. 1992. *Wokabaot blong Olgeta blong V.C.H.S.S.* Port Vila: Vanuatu Cultural and Historical Site Survey.

Index

Numbers in **bold** type refer to illustrations.

Abbreviations: VCC   Vanuatu Cultural Centre
                VNCW Vanuatu National Council of Women
                WCP   Women's Culture Project

Allen, Michael, xxviii, xxix, 86, 87, 92, 101–102, 142, 163

Allen, Monica, 201

Ambae, 69, **79, 80,** 83, 154–155, 160; airstrips, 82, 83; districts, 81–82, 88, 106; geography, 78–80; hospital, 84, 89; households, 88; identity, 85, 131; kinship, 86–92; local government centre, 82–83, 84, 85; Manaro (volcano), 78, 80, 82, 110; map, **79;** myth of origin, 78; as *ples,* 78–105; population, 81; representation on VNCW, 90; village clubs, 90

Ambaebulu Primary School, 83

Ambae/Maewo: celebrations (1991), 154–155, 166; Island Council of Women, 65, 90, 169; Local Government Council (LGC), xiv, xxvi, 48, 65, 82–83, 84, 85

Ambae project. *See* Women's Culture Project (WCP)

Ambrym (island), *kastom* and churches, 16, 17–18

Anding, James, 65

Aneityum (island), 47

Anglicans, 81, 83, 90, 108. *See also* Christianity; churches; missionaries

art: anthropological understandings of, xxi–xxii; *Art and Agency* (Gell), 128; *Arts of Vanuatu,* xxix–xxx; distinguished from craft, xxii; and museums, xviii, xxi–xxii

Aru, Selwyn, 65, 66

Australian High Commission (Port Vila), xiv, 47; Australian aid, 27, 37, 45, 154

Banga, Chief John, 149, 170

baskets, xiii; small, 203; *tanga bunie,* 124–126, **125,** 127, 203, 207

Batik, Roman, 45, 47

Bislama, xxv, 3, 5, 6–7, 10–11, 53, 159

Boe, David, 162, 163

Boe, Miriam, **132**

Boeboe (Lovonda district) wedding, **XIV,** 97

Bongmatur Maldo, Chief Willie, 19–20, 43–44, 47, 193

Bonnemaison, Joel, xxviii–xxix, 16, 70

Bulekone, Vincent, 43

canoe as metaphor, xiv, 144, 202

Carlot, Maxime, 20, 34, 45

Catholics, 81. *See also* Christianity; churches; missionaries

ceremonies: and identity, 41; loss of knowledge of, 131; revival of, 41. *See also* funerals; *huhuru* (female status-alteration system); *huqe*

(male status-alteration system);
kastom; weddings

Charpentier, Jean-Michel, 37, 40

chief *(jif):* as category, 19, 43; hereditary, 3; and land ownership, 75

children, 94–95, 113, 127, 136, 161, 162,
176; announcement of birth, 109,
116, 180; illegitimate *(pikinini blong
rod),* 71; importance of daughters,
87, 94

Christianity: experiences of conversion, 10, 11, 20; good and bad
kastom, 12, 156–157; and *kastom,*
11, 13, 16, 17, 46, 51; *kastom* versus
skul, 10–12; translation of Bible
into Bislama, 53. *See also* churches;
missionaries

Church of Christ, 81. *See also* Christianity; churches; missionaries

churches, 81; and *kastom,* 16–18, 46,
108; and residence (Ambae),
88–90; schools, 83; support for
independence, 16; theological
training of Pacific Islanders, 83.
See also Christianity; missionaries

classificatory kinship, 69, 87, 91,
103–105. *See also* kinship

Cloth and Human Experience (Weiner
and Schneider), 112

clothing textiles *(sakole),* xiii, 111, 131,
138, 207

communications: telephones, 5–6, 83.
See also Radio Vanuatu (formerly
Radio Vila); travel

Condominium (Anglo-French), 7–8,
9, 26; Advisory Council, 198; alienation of land, 8, 12, 13–14, 188; British adviser, 19; British Information
Office, 27; education, 8; French
Residency Information Service, 28;
Joint Naval Agreement (1887), 7;
justice system, 7

*Contes et légendes des Nouvelles
Hébrides* (radio program), 30

Crowe, Peter, 36, 37, 39–40, 199

culture, 6, 20–21, 22–23; cultural construction, 23; defined by Gardissat,
30–31; derived from *ples,* 70;
disassociated from *ples,* 73; and
identity, 22, 40; "invention," 23–24;
and *kastom,* 22–23; meaning and
material culture, 127–129; Western
models, 40. *See also kalja; kastom*

Curtis, Tim, 69–70

dancing: by men, xxxiv–xxxv, 154–155;
by women, xxxiv–xxxv, 175–176,
180–181, 185, 203; disco, 6, 154;
lenga (type of dance), 29, 176; in
teams, 181–182, 193, 204

Deacon, Bernard, xxiii, 71

designs, xxiii, 142–145, 150–151

"Developing Cultural Policy in
Melanesia" conference (Honiara),
43–44

dictionary making. *See* languages

dyeing of textiles, xxxiii, 109, 130,
134–135; commercial dyes, 102, 109,
130, 131–133, 134, 189; dyeing log
(gai wesi), 131–133, **133,** 135, 138;
of *maraha,* 130, 131; of *qana,* 130,
131; red color, 102, 109, 115, 134, 135;
and sexual relationships, 135–136;
of *singo,* 130; and taboos, 130,
135–136; techniques, 131–135; traditional dyes *(laqe),* 130, 133–134, 135,
189, 205. *See also huhuru* (female
status-alteration system); stencil
patterns; textiles

education, 8, 158–159; Ambaebulu
Primary School, 83; theological
training of Pacific Islanders, 83;
Torgil Training Centre, 83, 84, 177;
Tunsissiro, 83; Vureas High School,
83, 177

Efate (island). *See* Erakor village; Port
Vila

Erakor village, 20, 21, 30, 34

Espiritu Santo (island): French

expelled, 21; land alienation, 13–14; naming, 7; protest in, 12, 75; Second National Arts Festival (1991), 154–155, 176; in Second World War, 10. *See also* Stephens, Jimmy

exchanges, 91, 99, 101–102, 142–143; of food, 95, 107; participation of men, 3, 96, 99, 107, 124, 126; of textiles, xiii, **XIV,** xxxiii, 3, 96, 99, **101,** 107, 114, 117, 121, 124–126

expatriates, 26, 83; perception of ni-Vanuatu women, 53–57, 188

explorers, 7, 32

fieldworkers, xvii–xviii, xxxiv, 41, 43, **48,** 74–77; men, 44–50; Oral Traditions Project, 41, 44; use of local language, 49; women, 61–66, 170, 193–194

food, 81, 95, 106–107; and *huhuru,* 146, 147, 149, 150; taboos, 98, 141, 142, 147, 149, 150

foreign aid, 4, 27, 32, 37, 45, 47, 154. *See also* Australian High Commission

funerals: feasts *(bongi),* 93, 205; pig killing, 104; textiles for body wrapping, 109, 111, 113, 114, 201

Garae, Roselyn, 102, 109, 155, **194,** 201

Garae, Ruth, **133**

Garae, Chief Simon, xxxiv, xxxv, 47, 154, 161, 172, 181–182, 185, 197; and loss of *kastom,* 156, 158

Gardissat, Paul, 28–32, 71–72, 198

gender (Ambae): analyses of gender relations, 53–57; and cooking, 106–107; equality of men and women, 58–61, 62, 64, 108–109, 142–143, 171–172; expatriate perception of, 53–57, 188; father's sisters, 107, 135, 143; and *kastom,* 51–66, 169–189, 191; relationships between wives and husbands, 100, 106, 107, 108, 145–146, 201; sister and brother relations, 107, 157; and

VCC, xxiv, 61–65. *See also* men; women

Gender of the Gift, The (Strathern), 54, 201–202

gigilugi, 130, 131, 138, 139; definition, 205; filming of technique, 173, 175; rights to produce, 137–138; stencil patterns, 117, 137, 138; technique of dyeing, 130, 131, 137

Godden, Charles, murder of, 9

government. *See* Condominium (Anglo-French); Vanuaaku Pati

graded societies, xxxi–xxxii, 92, 98–100, 104, 150. See also *huqe* (male status-alteration system); pigs

Guiart, Jean, xxviii–xxix, 33, 36, 40

Gwero, James, 37–49 *passim,* **48,** 65, 66, 152, 162, 169, 177

hamlets and households, 88–89, 97

Hango, Harrison, **120**

head covering, 100–102; *qana,* 113; *qana hunhune,* 100–102, **101,** 103–104, 115, 206

Huffman, Kirk, xvi–xviii, xxv, 12, 18, 36, 37, **38,** 40, 41–42, 46, 50, 62, 63, 74, 171, 187, 193, 203

huhuru (female status-alteration system), xxxii, 3, 102, 103–104, 130, 131, 142, 145–150, 205; compared with *huqe,* 103, 170, 175; and dyeing of textiles, 102–103, 130, 131, 145, 146, 147–148; filming of, 145, 154, 157, 162, 173, 175–177, 187; and food, 146, 147, 149, 150; loss of knowledge of, 131; regional differences, 145, 149; respect and status, 142, 143, 146–149; ritual specialists, 130, 142, 145, 146, 147–148; *singo maraha,* 138–140, 145, 146, 147, **147**. *See also* women; Women's Culture Project (WCP)

huqe (male status-alteration system), xxxii, 84, 92, 98–100, 113, 146, 199;

compared with *huhuru,* 170, 175; discussed as graded societies, xxxi–xxxii, 92, 98–100, 104; and exchanges, 98, 99, 122; and landscape, 99; rank and grade takers, 98–100, 139, 142, 145, 187; *ratahagi* (base for a leader), 99; and textiles, 99, 170; wearing of *singo tuvegi* by men, 139; women's participation in, 100, 104, 146, 202. *See also* pigs
Hyslop, Catriona, 68, 86

identity: and ceremonies, 41; and culture, 22, 40; defined, 22; inherited from mother, 87; and *kastom,* 22, 40–41, 51–52, 154, 159; and language, 159; of married women, 102, 146; national, 68, 72–73, 75, 189–191; and place, 68–72, 76–77, 81, 85, 89–92, 96, 131, 188, 190–191
independence, 14, 21; British support, 21; churches' support, 16; French opposition, 14, 21; and *kastom,* 17, 21–22, 26–27, 51–52, 183; and land, 71–72, 188; movements, 12–21; restoration of land, 21, 71, 72–73. *See also* Nagriamel
inheritance: heritable possessions, 92–93; of land, 87–88, 92–95, 96–97, 188; through matrilineal descent *(laen),* 91–92, 94, 96
invisible people *(vavi and mwai),* 96, 97, 107

Jasper, Lena, 147–148
John Frum movement, 10; affiliation with Nagriamel, 17; and *kastom,* 17, 51
Jolly, Margaret, 11, 23, 24, 69

kalja (culture), 29, 30, 46, 199
Kanegai, Nadia, xxiv, 62, 63, 143–144, 202
Kapere, Jacob Sam, xxiv, xxvii, xxxiv, xxxv, 74, 145, 157, 168, 172–173, **174,** 176, 177, 197, 203

kastom, 21–22, 23, 26–27, 40, 152–182, 185–186, 187, 189–190, 191; and Ambae, 154–160; analyzed as cultural construction, 23–24, 168; and Christianity, 11, 16, 17–18, 28, 51, 157; and culture, 6, 11, 22–25; and dancing *(see* dancing); definitions, xiii, 1, 6–7, 10–11, 24–25, 30–31, 51–53, 154, 159, 168–169, 170–171, 188–189, 199; development of, 10–22, 62, 183–186; and expatriate material technology, 15–16; idea of loss, 154, 156–158; and identity, 22, 40–41, 51–52, 154, 159; initially male dominated, 53, 57, 61, 64–65; moral evaluations of, 10–12, 17, 21, 25, 28–30, 51, 157–158, 183–184, 187; and national life, 26–50, 75, 154, 159–160, 183–184, 190, 191; as performance, xxxiv–xxxv, 16, 20–22, 30, 38–41, 44, 49–50, 52, 76, 154–156, 164–169, 172–182, 185–187, 190–191; *ples* and land, 71, 72–77, 162, 187, 188, 189; and politics, xxxiv–xxxv, 1, 12–22, 43–44, 46, 62, 65–66, 177–179, 181–182, 188; regional differences, 28, 30, 41, 44, 48, 75–77; and *skul,* 10–12, 18
Kastom, Kalja mo Tredisin (radio program), 29, 30–31
kava drinking, 22, 88, 106, 108, 121, 122, 200
Keesing, Roger, 23, 24
Keitadi, Jack, xxiii–xxiv, xxvi, 42, 63, 193
kinship, 55; on Ambae, 86–92, 94–95, 109, 171; clans, 87; *laen,* 87, 91–92, 94, 96; matriclans, 87, 109; moieties, 87, 91, 94; and place, 69–71, 92–95, 189. *See also* classificatory kinship
Koli, Aviu, 49, 64, 199, 203
Korman, Maxime Carlot. *See* Carlot, Maxime
Kwantangewele, 163–164

labor trade, 8–9, 68

land: agriculture, 4, 79–80; alienation, 8, 12, 13–14, 15, 71, 72, 188; cash cropping, 4, 74, 92, 95; cattle industry, 8, 80; disputes over ownership, 74, 188; expatriate freehold titles abolished, 21; inheritance, 87–88, 92–95, 96–97, 188; and *kastom,* 71, 76–77, 188; matrilineal descent *(laen),* 94; patrilineal transmission, 94–95; and *ples,* 72–77, 93, 188; restoration after independence, 21, 71, 72–73; rights and use, 92–97, 105. See also *ples* (place)

languages, 3, 49, 68–69; Ambaean languages, 68–69, 82, 200; Bislama, xxv, 3, 5, 6–7, 10–11, 53, 159; dialects and practices, 81–82; dictionary making, 46, 47; and *kastom,* 159; references to land, place, and space, 68–69, 86; sale of words, 161

Larcom, Joan, 69, 74, 75

Leona, Richard, 47, 49

Ligo, Godwin, 20–21, 27–28, 30, 42

Lindstrom, Lamont, 17, 24, 70

linguistics, xvii–xviii, 45–46, 47, 68–69, 193. See also languages

Lini, Hilda, and Vanuaaku Pati, 58

Lini, Walter (Vanuaaku Pati leader), 12, 13, 15, 68, 71, 181, 197

Lolokaro district, 82, 157

Lolovinue district, 81, 86, 110, 164

Lolovoli district, 82, 86, 161

Lolowai, 82–83, **83,** 84, 116

Lombaha district, 81, 82, 86, 96, 110, 162, 199–200

Loqirutaro hamlet, 90, 173, 174, 175

Lovonda village, 78, 156, 162, 201; Boeboe wedding, **xiv,** 97; filming of *huhuru,* 145, 154, 157, 162, 173, 175–177, 187; *kastom* cooking, 155

Luganville town, 10, 21; and Nagriamel, 10

Maasingyau, Longdal Nobel, 46

Malakula (island), 69–70, 71; arts festivals, 76; Huffman's work on, xvi–xvii

Malanga, Evelyn, 148, 150, 151, 175

Malvatumauri (National Council of Chiefs), 4; creation of, 19, 52; custodians of *kastom* at national level, 19, 42–44, 76; *kastom* and land, 76; as mediators, 44, 76; membership, 19–20; opposition to, 20; published policy on *kastom,* 43, 62; relationship with VCC, 42–44; representation in national assembly, 19

maraha, xiii, 111, 112, 113, 115, 116, 121, 124, 126, 127, 139, 150, 206; dyeing of, 130, 135; type *maraha vinvinu,* 110, 206; type *qiriqiri,* 115–116, 126, 206–207; type *vatu kule,* 207. See also *huhuru* (female status-alteration system)

marriage, 84, 86, 91, 99, 100, 102, 103, 146. *See also* weddings

material culture: anthropological approaches to, xviii–xxiii, 122–124, 127–129, 150–151; Pacific region attitudes to, 34–36

mats: discussion of term, xxx–xxxi, 111–113; in Polynesia, 120, 122. *See also* textiles

men: access to land, 92–95; attitudes to WCP, xxiv–xxv, 64–65, 161–164, 171–172; fieldworkers, 44–50; knowledge of textiles, 108–109, 117–118, 169–170; men's houses, 64, 88, 92; relationships between men and women, 106–109, 170–171, 177–179, 181–182; wearing textiles, 111–112. See also *huqe* (male status-alteration system); kava drinking

menstruation, 109; and dyeing of textiles, 135–136

missionaries, 8, 9, 10–12, 16, 56, 83. *See also* Christianity; churches

Molisa, Grace, 58–61, **59,** 155, 164, 167,

183–184; definition of *kastom,* 31,
60–61, 199; and Vanuaaku Pati, 42,
58, 60; and VCC, xxv, xxvi, 61–62,
63; and VNCW, 60–61, 184; and
WCP, 64, 65, 66, 177, 185
museums: and anthropology, xix–xxiii;
and art, xxi–xxii; development of
Australian museology, xviii–xxiii;
and indigenous Australians, xxi,
xxii–xxiii, 35; and material culture,
xviii–xxii; Pacific region, 34–36, 42.
See also Vanuatu Cultural Centre
(VCC)
music: recording *kastom,* 37–38, 176;
string bands, 154, 202
Mwera, Jennifer, 1, 155, 161, 163, 167,
176, 180, 186, 189, **194**

Nagriamel, 10, 12, 14, 21; and John
Frum movement, 17; and *kastom,*
12, 15, 18, 51, 157, 198, 202; radio, 15
names, creative use of, 85–86, 113–114
National Arts Festival: First (1979),
20–21, 30, 52, 72, 76; Second (1991),
154–155, 176
National Conference of Native
Women, First, 60
National Council of Chiefs. *See* Malvatumauri (National Council of
Chiefs)
National Women's Festival (1990),
60–61, 175–176, 179
Nduindui district, 81, 82, 110, 152, 160
"New Hebrides," 7, 67
New Hebrides Cultural Association,
12–13
New Hebrides National Party, 13–17;
and *kastom,* 15–17, 18; and land
alienation, 13–14, 15, 188; renamed
Vanuaaku Pati, 20. *See also*
Vanuaaku Pati
ngava hangavalu, 114, 115, 124–126, **125**
ngava hangavalu tavalu, 109, 148, 206
ngava hangavalu vinvinu and *singo,*
149, 206

nokwiari, reintroduction in Tanna, 16,
41

Office of Women's Affairs (Port Vila),
58, 63
Oral Traditions Project, 36–50, 187;
fieldworkers, 44–50; knowledge as
possession, 161–162; music, 36–38
passim; objectives, 38–39; radio
programs, 40, 41; recordings,
37–40, 161, 193; training, 37, 39–40,
41. *See also* fieldworkers
ORSTOM, xxviii–xxix, 160; ethnobotanical survey, 48

Pacific Arts Festival (Noumea 2000),
193
pandanus *(veveo),* 110–111, 118, 207;
grown by women, 110, 118; origin
story, 110; preparation, 109–110,
118–119; varieties and uses, 118
Pentecost (island), 11, 69, 70, 76;
Sa, 53, 56, 70, 165–167
Philibert, Jean-Marc, on culture, 9–10,
21, 24
photographs as research tool, xx, 163,
165–167
pigs, 126; classification and ranking,
98–99, 142, 143; in exchanges, 126;
and *huqe* (Ambae), 98–100, 104,
107, 122, 139, 146, 147; and status-
alteration systems, 3; and tattooing
rituals, 143; tusks, 99–100, 143, 155
place: Ambean terms for, 86. *See also*
identity; *ples* (place)
plaiting, xxxiii, 116–124; by women
only, 109, 117, 121–122; cooperative,
121–123, 130; designs, 114, 138–141;
learning, 116–117; methods, xxxiii,
118–120, **119, 120,** 139, 166, 205
ples (place), 55, 67–77, 88, 97, 106, 200;
and concept of roads, 71; and hamlets, 88–89, 94, 97, 100–102, 106;
and identity, 67–77, 81, 89–92, 96,
131, 188, 190–191; and *kastom,* 71,

72–77, 162, 187, 188, 189; and kinship, 69–70, 94, 189; and knowledge, 69, 70, 72, 161–162; as land, 72–77, 93–94, 188, 189; as landscape, 68–69, 73–74, 99; and marriage, 91–95, 100–102, 104–105; perceptions of (Ambae), 81–105, 200; public and private, 55, 88, 106; terms (Ambae), 86, 207

politics: and *kastom,* xxxiv–xxxv, 1, 12–22, 43–44, 46, 62, 65–66, 177–179, 181–182, 188; and women, 58–60. *See also* Condominium (Anglo-French); *kastom;* New Hebrides National Party; Vanuaaku Pati; Vanuatu

population profile (Vanuatu), 3, 4, 26, 73, 74, 81, 194

Port Vila, 4, 26, **27**

Presbyterians, 16, 17–18. *See also* Christianity; churches

qana (textile type), xiii, 111, 112, 113, 114, 115, 116, 126, 127, 138, 206; as *buresi,* 111, 127, 205; dyeing of, 130, 131; exchanges, 113; *qana hunhune* (textile placed on head), 100–102, **101,** 103–104, 115, 206; *qana mavute,* 102–103, 114, 135, 146, 206; *qana memea,* 114, 134, 206; *qana mwaho,* **xxxii,** 115, 116, 206; *qana vivi,* xiii, **xxxii,** xxxiii, 115, 116, 206; *qana vulvulu,* 114, 115, 127, 206; uses of, 111, 113; *vule* (the moon) stencil pattern, xiii, **xxxii,** xxxiii, 144, 207

qegavi stencil patterns, 110, 117, 131, **133,** 136, 137, 138, 206

qiriqiri (type of *maraha*), 115–116, 126, 206

Radio Vanafo, 15

Radio Vanuatu (formerly Radio Vila), xiv, 5, 26–32, 52, 74–75, 165; radio programs (VCC), 5, 27, 29, 30–31, 32, 42, 44, 45, 49, 50, 52, 76, 162, 172, 176, 186–187; recordings from Oral Traditions Project, 40, 41; use of Bislama, 27, 53; and VCC, 32, 52; and WCP, 172

rank and status. *See* status-alteration systems

Regenvanu, Ralph, 193

Regenvanu, Minister Sethy, xxxiv–xxxv, 47, 178–179, 181

research moratorium, xvii–xxx *passim*

residence patterns (Ambae), 85–86, 88–89, 91, 99

respect *(rispek),* 3–4, 10, 100, 131, 143, 148–150, 187, 191

Rodman, Margaret, 7, 81, 85–95 *passim,* 107

Rodman, W., 81, 85, 98

Rubenstein, Robert, 18

Rueben, Alben, **48**

sakole (clothing textile), xiii, 111, 131, 138, 207

Sam, Jacob. *See* Kapere, Jacob Sam

sara (dancing ground), 56, 57, 64, 70, 82, 84–85, 88, 92, 124, 207

sawea. See ngava hangavalu

Second World War, 10

secret societies. *See* status-alteration systems

Seventh-Day Adventists, 81. *See also* Christianity; churches; missionaries

sexual relations, 135–136, 144

singo maraha, 138–140, 150, 151, 207; *golo vudolue* (one hundred tails), 148; *mimi rawe* (urethra of a hermaphrodite pig), 148, 206; restricted rights to, 142–148 *passim;* type *bebe* (moth, butterfly), 140, 141; type *bugu* (triggerfish), 140, 141; type *gingini* (to pinch with fingers), 140–141; type *singo tau marino* (*singo* from Malo), 140, 148, 151; type *vatu tawaga* (broken stone), 148, 207

singo (textile type), 111, 112, 113, 114, 116, 117, 128; designs, 140; dyeing of, 137–142; and *ngava hangavalu,* 148; power of, 141–142, 150; and rank, 111, 130–131, 139, 140, 142–143, 145, 207, 250; restricted rights to, 130, 137–141 *passim; walivetu* technique of plaiting, 138–139
singo tuvegi, **104,** 138–139, 151, 207; and rank, 139, 140; type *buto vudoloe,* 140; type *matai talai,* 110, 140, 141, **178,** 206; type *vovaho,* **104,** 139, 140, **141,** 151; worn by women and men, 139
skul, 10–12, 18
sorcery, xxvi, 49, 55, 64, 158, 199, 203
spirits, 96, 99
sport, 154
status-alteration systems, xxxi–xxxiii, 3; male and female different, 142–143; pigs, xxxi, 3, 98–99, 100, 104; rank and designs (Ambae), 142–145. *See also* graded societies; *huhuru* (female status-alteration system); *huqe* (male status-alteration system)
stencil patterns, 110, 115, 117–118, 131, **132,** 138, 139, 140, 141; *gigilugi* (technique), 117, 130, 131, 137–138, 139, 173, 175, 205; log-wrap, 131–132; *qegavi* (technique), 110, 117, 131–132, **132, 133,** 135–138 *passim,* 206; sand-drawing designs, 118, 201; for *singo,* 110, 139–141, **140,** 148; and tattooing of women, 143–145; *vule* (the moon), xiii, **xxxii,** xxxiii, 115, 144, 207
Stephens, Jimmy, 12, 14, 15, 17, 157
stories: origin of Lombaha *vola walugiri,* 202; origin of textiles, 110; related to landscape, 78, 79, 98, 103; and sand drawings, 201; Tagaro (culture hero), 78, 79, 109; Tahigogona (culture hero), 110; Tariboeaga (culture hero), 99; told to children, 98

Strathern, Marilyn, xvi, 22, 54, 56–57, 128
string bands, 167, 202

taboos: associated with *singo,* 141–142; on discussion of sexual relations, 135–136; and dyeing of textiles, 130, 135, 136; and food, 98, 141, 142, 146, 147, 150; and knowledge, 70, 161–162, 180; and textile production, 117, 137–138, 168, 169
Taga, Emma, **178**
Tagaro, culture hero (Ambae), 78, 79, 109, 144
Taki, Jerry, 47
Talei, Philip, **48**
Tanna (island), 3, 10, 16, 41, 70, 75
Tari, Chief Marcel, 96, 149, 150, 170
Tarileo, Gloria, 65
Tarisesei, Jean, **xxvi,** xxxiii, **125,** 163; as WCP coordinator, xxvi–xxviii, xxxiv, 66, 74, 78, 102, 103, 106, 112, 117, **125,** 126, 134, 153–200 *passim*
tattooing of women, 62, 130–131, 143–144, 170; and designs in textiles, 143–145
Tephahae, Phillip, 47
textiles, 100–103, 104, 106–129, 130–151, 164–182, 185, 191; as art or craft, xxii; classification and ranking, xxxi, 111–113, 114–116, 127, 143, 205; as context of interaction, 121–123, 130, 150–151; exchanges, xiii, **xiv,** xxxiii, 3, 96, 99, **101,** 107, 113, 117, 121, 122, 123, 124–126, **125;** exclusive to women, 108–109; filming of, 145, 154, 162, 172–173, 175; and fines, 97, 127; innovation, 167–168; men's knowledge of, 108–109, 117–118, 135, 169–170; regional differences, 110, 166–167, 179, 202; response to museum collections, 163, 165–167; rights to produce, 137–138, 168, 169; sequence in presentation, xiii, 124, 126; story of origin, 110; terminology, xxx–xxxi, 110–112, 168–169;

trade between districts, 170, 185; unfolding, xiii, **xiv**, xxxiii–xxiv, 124–126. *See also* clothing textiles; dyeing of textiles; *huhuru; maraha;* plaiting; *qana; singo;* stencil patterns; *wasmahanga*

Thompson, Chief, 156, 158, 186

tok haed (hidden speech), 20, 198

Tonkinson, Robert, 15–16, 17–18, 23

Totali, Kolambas, **48**

trade networks, 3, 8, 52, 67, 84, 99, 170, 185, 190

travel: air services, 6; airstrips, 82, 83; inter-island, 6, 81, 99; within Ambae, 80–81, 84, 99

tredisin (tradition), 29, 40, 46; definitions, 30–31, 199

Tryon, Darrell, xvii–xviii, xxv, 10–11, 45–46, 74, 193

Ture Leo, Leah, xxv–xxvi, 64, 66, 78, 106, 152, 156, 158, 166, 173

tuvegi, 112, 116, 207. See also *singo tuvegi*

Uliboe, Jeffrey, 37, **48**

UNESCO, xxii, 36–37

Vanuaaku Pati, 20; as government, 21–22; and *kastom,* 21–22, 42–43, 51–52, 57, 75; women's wing, 58; youth members, 58. *See also* New Hebrides National Party

Vanuatu: Constitution, 19, 21, 71; and "development," 4–5; first elections for national assembly, 18–19; geography, 1–3; history, 1–25; Joint Naval Agreement (1887), 7; local recognition of national boundaries, 67–68, 190; map, **2;** mobility of population, 26, 89, 90, 91–92; named New Hebrides, 7; national anthem, 73, 199; national flag, 73; national identity, 68; political instability, 194; politics and *kastom,* xxxiv–xxxv, 1, 12–22, 43–44, 46, 62,

65–66, 177–179, 181–182, 188; prehistory, 3, 13; research moratorium, xvii–xxx *passim*

Vanuatu Cultural Centre (VCC), xii–xvii *passim,* 26–27, 32–36, **32,** 40, 194–195; audio recording of *kastom,* xxvii, 36–40, 41, 45, 49–50, 52, 74, 76, 161–162, 163, 164, 172, 193; documentation and confidentiality, 49, 74, 98, 162; films and videos, 48, 145, 154, 162, 172–173, 193; government support, 42–43, 46–47, 160, 162; history, xvi–xvii, 32–39, 41–42, 193–195; and land disputes, 74–76; museum, xvi–xviii, xxiii–xxiv, 33–34; new building, 198–199; and *ples,* 76–77; radio programs, 5, 32, 42, 44, 45, 49, 50, 52, 76, 162, 172, 176, 186–187; relationship with Malvatumauri, 42–44; workshops, 45–50, 153, 172, 177–182, 193. *See also* fieldworkers; Oral Traditions Project; Women's Culture Project (WCP); Woodward, Keith

Vanuatu Historical and Cultural Sites Survey, 47–48, 160, 199

Vanuatu National Council of Women (VNCW), xiv, 60, 63, 179, 184; Ambae/Maewo Island Council of Women 65, 90, 178; National Women's Festival (1990), 60–61, 155, 175–176, 179; radio program, 5; and status of women, 108; women's rights, 65, 90, 178, 194

Vanuatu Television and Broadcasting Corporation (VTBC), 5. *See also* Radio Vanuatu (formerly Radio Vila)

Vanuatu Young People's Project, 193

veveo. See pandanus

video, xxiv, xxxiv–xxxv, 48, 145, 154, 163, 172–176, 177, 180, 181–182, 193

Vila Cultural Centre (1956–1980). *See* Vanuatu Cultural Centre (VCC)

villages (Ambae): church-based, 89;

councils, 89, 90, 106; and hamlets, 88–89, 96; as local government units, 89; village court, 97, 106

Walter, Annie, xxx
Walurigi district, 110, 166, 200; textile types, 110, 166, 202, 207
wasmahanga (textile worn by men), 111–112
weddings, **xiv,** 90–91, 97, 100–102, **101,** 103–105; at Boeboe (Lovonda district), **xiv,** 97; exchanges, **xiv,** 97, 101–103, 113, 135; film of, **101,** 173, 181; payment for bride, 126, 144; and status-alteration system *(huhuru),* 102–103, 135, 145–146; and status-alteration system *(huqe),* 100, 146, 202; and textiles, **xiv,** 97, 100–102, 135, 139–140, 144, 145–146; and women's *ples,* 102
Wesley, Amy, **104,** 151
Woivire, Susan, **101**
women: access to land in Longana, 93–96; Ambae/Maewo Island Council of Women, 65, 90, 178; and childbearing, 103, 109; cooperatives and social groups, 57–58, 106, 121–123, 130; discussion of sexual issues, 135–136; importance of daughters, 87, 94; and *kastom,* xiii–xiv, xxxiv, xxxv, 61–62, 66, 109, 152–154, 160, 168–171, 183–184; matrilineal descent (Ambae), 87, 91–92, 94, 131; naming (Ambae), 113, 127; National Women's Festival (1990), 60–61, 155, 175–176, 179; Office of Women's Affairs (Port Vila), 58, 63; participation in *huqe,* 100, 104; and *ples,* 100–105, 188–191; and politics, 58–60; status enhancement, xxxi–xxxii, 3, 93, 108, 143;

tattoos (Ambae), 62, 130–131, 143–144, 170; unmarried, 102; weddings and textiles, **xiv,** 97, 100–102, 135; work and employment, 53, 108. *See also* gender (Ambae); *huhuru* (female status-alteration system); *kastom;* textiles; Vanuatu National Council of Women (VNCW); weddings; Women's Culture Project (WCP)
Women's Culture Project (WCP), xiv–xxxv *passim,* 47, 63–66, 78; agent of change, 153; and Christianity, 157–158; documentation and revival as objectives, 160–168; effect on men, xxxiv, 64–65, 169–172, 181–182, 183, 185; equality of women and men, 171–172; foundation of, xxiv–xxviii, 61–66; opposition to, xxxiv, 160–164, 186, 202–203; outcomes, 160–169, 176, 180–182, 191, 193–195; Saramata workshop, xxiv–xxv, 172, 177–182; support from men, xiv–xv, xxv, xxxiv–xxxv, 64–66, 152, 157, 158, 163–164, 177–179, 181–182, 185, 186; training officer, xiv, xxiv–xxviii, 63–64, **104,** 152, 180; transmission of knowledge, xxxiv–xxxv, 47, 145, 154, 157, 162, 172, 173, 175–182, 186–187; use of photographs, 163, 165–167; and video documentation, xxxiv–xxxv, 145, 154, 163, 172–176, 177, 180, 181–182, 193; women honoured by national attention, 160, 176–177. *See also* fieldworkers; Vanuatu Cultural Centre (VCC)
Woodward, Keith, 19, 33, 39, 40, 42, 187, 198
World War Two. *See* Second World War

About the Author

Lissant Bolton is curator of the Pacific and Australian Collections at the British Museum. She has undertaken long-term collaborative research with the Vanuatu Cultural Centre and has been advisor to the Women's Culture Project there since 1991. She is the editor of the volume *Fieldwork, Fieldworkers: Developments in Vanuatu Research* (*Oceania* Special Issue, September 1999) and, with colleagues from London University, has worked on the major research project "Clothing the Pacific" (2001–2003), investigating the introduction of European cloth into indigenous textile systems in the Pacific.

Production Notes for Bolton / *Unfolding the Moon: Enacting Women's* Kastom *in Vanuatu*

Cover and interior designed by Josie Herr;
text and display type in Minion and Goudy.

Composed in QuarkXPress.

Printing and binding by The Maple-Vail Book
Manufacturing Group.

Printed on 60 lb. Text White Opaque.